SKEPTICISM
and Political
Participation

SKEPTICISM
and Political Participation

ARYEH BOTWINICK

Temple University Press
Philadelphia

Temple University Press, Philadelphia 19122
Copyright © 1990 by Temple University. All rights reserved
Published 1990
Printed in the United States of America

The paper used in this publication meets the minimum
requirements of American National Standard for Information
Sciences—Permanence of Paper for Printed Library Materials,
ANSI Z39.48-1984

Library of Congress Cataloging-in-Publication Data
Botwinick, Aryeh.
    Skepticism and political participation / Aryeh Botwinick.
        p. cm.
    Bibliography: p.
    Includes index.
    ISBN 0-87722-657-1 (alk. paper)
    1. Political participation. 2. Social participation.
3. Equality. I. Title.
JF2051.B67 1990
323'.042—dc20   89-32964
                                                   CIP

For Imma

רב יוסף כי הוה שמע קל כרעא דאמיה אמר איקום מקמי שכינה דאתיא.
(קידושין לא:)

Knowledge must turn its sting against itself.

Friedrich Nietzsche

Supporting an argument means looking for a "paradox" and legitimating it with new rules in the game of reasoning.

Jean-François Lyotard

Contents

Preface

Can philosophical reflection about the limits of knowledge generate insight concerning the proper social and political ordering of human beings? This book argues that an intuitively and historically acceptable reconstruction of liberal principles that is attentive to their linkage with skepticism yields a rhetorically compelling argument in favor of political participation. Skepticism cannot be formulated consistently without also undermining itself. A recoil into some version of a mitigated skeptical position seems to be necessitated by the very drive to formulate skepticism. The only way that skepticism can be articulated thus appears to be in action—through vastly increasing forums of collective decision making in human social life.

This book is structured as a discursive analogue to a Platonic dialogue. Just as Socrates often exchanges argumentative roles with the people he is arguing against, so too in this book I come to inhabit some of the points of view I had previously attacked. I try to encircle the limits of argument of both positions, pursuing antagonistic conceptions until each trails off into unintelligibility.

The book centers on the possibility of formulating a philosophically coherent version of extreme skepticism—and the possible political implications of such an enterprise. In appropriate dialogic fashion, each of its chapters radiates off the same central theme concerning the radical political implications of skepticism. Each contributes to illuminating in different and often contrasting ways the same master conceptions.

In the eight-year course of writing this book, I have incurred many debts. My Temple colleague and friend Peter Bachrach has enabled me to appreciate the centrality of participation as a theme in Western political philosophy and has been a constant source of stimulation and encouragement. I have benefited tremendously from the many critical discussions I have had with him concerning political participation. My friend Bruce Jennings of the Hastings Center, through his critical acumen and broad scholarship, has helped to heighten my sensitivity to the proper role and limits of political participation as a topic in contemporary political philosophy. Although they might take issue with me on particular points, my teachers Michael Oakeshott and Sheldon Wolin have served as my strongest models of what it means to tackle the issue of participation theoretically. Fred Dallmayr has been, by his prodigious example and in face-to-face encounters, a continuing guide and source of encouragement. Michael Shapiro's brilliant avant-garde extensions and applications of political philosophy and stimulating personal conversations have also provided unfailing inspiration, instruction, and encouragement. Portions of the book were read at various national and regional political science association meetings, and at faculty–graduate student seminars at Princeton University and Catholic University of America. I am grateful to the audiences present on each of these occasions for their questions and comments.

Jane Cullen of Temple University Press has been an exemplary editor, patient, prodding, and persevering. I hope that this book will repay her confidence. The expertise and acuity of Richard Gilbertie and Frank Austin—my production editor at Temple University Press and my copyeditor respectively—have been invaluable in preparing the manuscript for publication. Linda Scherr and Gloria Basmajian lent their expert assistance in typing the final version of the manuscript. I am also grateful to Dan DiLeo, Kathy Lambert, and Susan Wallace for their assistance in proofreading and to Kathy Lambert for compiling the index.

Sections of the text have appeared or will appear in a number of different journals. "A Neo-Pragmatist Defense of Democratic Participation" was published in the Summer 1988 issue of the *Journal of Social Philosophy*, and "Wittgenstein and Skepticism" was included in volume 12 of *Philosophy Research Archives*. "Tacit Knowledge in Plato" appeared in the second issue of *Commonwealth*, vol. 2 (1988). "The Argument of Federalist Number Ten" was printed in the *Proceedings of the Twenty-Second Conference on Value Inquiry* held at the State University of New York at Geneseo in 1988 and edited by James Wilbur; a shortened version of the chapter appears in *The U.S. Constitution and Its American Philosophers: Into Their Third Century*, edited by Christopher Gray (Lewiston, N.Y.: Edwin Mellen, 1989). A version of "Nietzsche, Foucault, and the Prospects of Postmodern Political Philosophy" will be presented in the October 1989 issue of *Manuscrito*. I am grateful to the editors of these periodicals and books for permission to reprint material that appeared or will appear in them.

As I reflect upon what I have written, I recognize that my father, Abraham Isaiah Botwinick (who died suddenly in 1980), has served as an implicit model for many of the political virtues that are extolled, directly or indirectly, here. I realize that I have sought to emulate his unique combination of compassion and criticalness and openness—a permanent simultaneous commitment to the insider and the outsider perspectives—in my delineation of philosophical and political possibilities in contemporary political philosophy.

Needless to say, I alone am responsible for all errors and shortcomings that remain.

SKEPTICISM
and Political
Participation

CHAPTER 1

Introduction

And if the one is absolutely without participation in time, it never had become, or was becoming, or was at any time, or is now become or is becoming, or is, or will become, or will have become, or will be, hereafter.

Most true.

But are there any modes of partaking of being other than these?

There are none.

Then the one cannot possibly partake of being?

That is the inference.

Then the one is not at all?

Clearly not.

Then the one does not exist in such way as to be one; for if it were and partook of being, it would already be; but if the argument is to be trusted, the one neither is nor is one?

True.

But that which is not admits of no attribute or relation?

Of course not.

Then there is no name, nor expression, nor perception, nor opinion, nor knowledge of it?

Clearly not.

Then it is neither named, nor expressed, nor opined, nor known, nor does anything that is perceive it.

So we must infer.

But can all this be true about the one?

I think not.

Plato, Parmenides[1]

Introduction

The Inescapability of Skepticism and Its Consequences

The issue of elitism versus broad political participation has classically hinged in political theory on the implications of certain epistemological positions. Plato's denial of direct political participation to the masses was largely motivated by a hierarchical conception of knowledge, from whose upper reaches the masses were excluded.

In taking up the thread of this ancient argument, I contend that the legacy of modern epistemology in both its empiricist and idealist forms is to emphasize the inescapability of skepticism. From Descartes, for example, we have learned to question the reliability of our everyday judgments. If a penny looks round from one perspective and elliptical from another, which shape constitutes the true penny? If a stick looks straight in air and bent in water, how do we determine the true nature of the stick? If in dreams we sometimes have tremendously vivid impressions of being in particular places and observing particular things, only to wake and discover to our great consternation that we had been dreaming, what guarantee do we have that we will not experience a comparably disillusioning anticlimax to our so-called waking states, disclosing them to be as unreal as our dream states?

Philosophers have not only questioned the existence of material objects and an external world, but have sought to undermine the defensibility of a concept of personal identity and of other minds. Hume, for example, is famous in the history of philosophy for regarding the self as a bundle of perceptions. In trying to move beyond this bundle to delineate and justify a stable substratum of personal identity, he felt himself approaching philosophical incoherence and muddle. If, from Hume's perspective, we lack an empirical warrant for personal identity, we are on even shakier philosophical ground when we project the reality of other people's minds, to whose immediate perceptions we are not even directly privy.

Historical and cultural relativists have sought to exhibit the local rootedness of some of even our most basic categories of perception and understanding. In the writings of such cultural anthropologists as E. E. Evans-Pritchard, a process of historical relativization occurs, which strips some of our most basic moral and epistemological judgments of their universal aspirations.

4

Introduction

Some linguists and idealist philosophers have emphasized the mind, language, and concept dependence of our most basic construals of reality. Here, for example, is a capsule summary of the Sapir–Whorf hypothesis:

> We dissect nature along lines laid down by our native languages. The categories and types that we isolate from the world of phenomena we do not find there because they stare every observer in the face; on the contrary, the world is presented in a kaleidoscopic flux of impressions that has to be organized by our minds—and this means largely by the linguistic system in our minds.

The later Wittgenstein argued that the world was a "fifth wheel" on the wagon of philosophy. The focus of the philosopher should be language. Traditional metaphysical puzzles concerning the reality of the external world and of other minds could be resolved by excavating the implicit rules of particular language regions and language games, which would reveal the metaphysical philosopher as illegitimately extending those rules in order to generate the traditional puzzles. For example, the language games where the word "know" is typically employed usually invoke the word relative to particular contexts. One knows or fails to know specific things about particular contexts—one knows that a book is on the table. One does not question whether the context is real or even exists. Wittgenstein claims that by failing to pay attention to the linguistic environment in which a word like "know" has its being, epistemologists are guilty of illegitimately extrapolating the vocabulary of knowledge from those internal spheres (particular contexts) where they make sense to external spheres (entire contexts or the world as a whole) where they lose intelligibility.

Wittgenstein thus seeks to dissolve the dilemmas of such skeptical metaphysicians as Hume and Descartes, whose presupposition of the existence of an external world lent the formulation of their philosophical problems their special poignancy, by postulating a more sweeping skepticism of his own. If philosophical inquiry focuses exclusively on language—and the disparate sets of rules governing individual language games—and thus dispenses with the concept of the world, traditional metaphysical puzzles are simply banished from the scene.

Thomas Kuhn's philosophy of science, by pointing to the centrality of paradigms (master theoretical conceptions and models) in the way particular scientific disciplines are structured, highlights the disjunction between science and truth. The reason individual scientific disciplines often seem cumulative, progressive, and productive does not lie in the privileged contact that their dominant concepts and categories make with reality. Their apparent success has to do, rather, with the great rigor with which the implications and interconnections of these concepts and categories are investigated and explored. In an astounding reversal of our commonsense assumptions, Kuhn argues that method defines the character of scientific knowledge and sets its standards of truth, rather than truth independently determining the nature of the appropriate method to be employed in scientific work. Kuhn says that there is no transparadigmatic perspective from which to assess comparatively the rational merits of Einsteinian physics versus Newtonian physics versus Aristotelian physics. In fact, Kuhn points to a cyclical pattern of development in the history of theoretical formulation in physics, with Einstein being in many ways closer to Aristotle than either of them is to Newton.

W. V. Quine advances a pragmatic understanding of how our theories relate to reality. It is never the case, he says, that particular theoretical statements are hauled before the bar of experience individually. The most cogent way to conceive of the relationship between theory and reality is to envisage the totality of statements that we regard as true at any given historical moment—from statements of fact to scientific theories to laws of logic and truths by definition—as constituting the holistic subject for revision in the face of any recalcitrant experience. Confronted by an adverse experience, we can revise a factual statement that is close to the periphery of the field of statements that we regard as correct or a more abstract statement that lies in the interior of the field. For example, I make the statement that I left my pencil on the desk. I look five minutes later and discover that the pencil is not on the desk. Assuming that no factual explanation such as my having removed the pencil from the desk is available, I am not immediately compelled to abandon my earlier factual statement that the pencil is on the desk. My experience of not finding the pencil on the desk could still be accommodated in relation to the totality of statements that I regard as true by revising in the interior of the field. I could revise the laws concerning physical objects and attribute mobile properties to physical objects, or—moving further into the interior of the field of statements—I could revise the laws of logic so as to accommodate suspension of the law of excluded middle. The pencil could thus both be and not be on the desk at the same time. Quine emphasizes that the so-called facts of the case are not intrinsically coercive. When a particular experience diverges from my expectations, pragmatic considerations of economy, manipulability, and elegance intervene to influence and shape my choice of which class of statement to revise in the face of the adverse experience.

In the history of political thought, skepticism has served to justify conflicting varieties of political philosophy. Plato's skepticism concerning the validity of sense experience (he considers it less real than the nonsensuous ideas intuited by a philosophical intelligence) leads him to confine political leadership to a philosophical elite that can organize and govern society in accordance with its greater cultivation of reason. Hume's skepticism prompts him toward political conservatism, where the nonrational mechanisms of habit, custom, and usage rightfully cement the allegiances and dictate the glacial pace of change of civil society.

The political implications that I seek to draw from skepticism lie in the direction of a radical egalitarianism. If skepticism in some of its different guises states that none of us is in a position to affirm the rational superiority of his views or values over those of his fellows, then the appropriate political response is to have as many members of society as possible participate in the numerous collective decisions affecting our lives. Skepticism delegitimizes the formation of any permanent hierarchies in society and provides a continually renewing impetus for the expansion of political participation.

A crucial stumbling block in the way of the recognition of the radical political implications of skepticism is the difficulty of formulating a consistently skeptical position. Consistent skepticism seems to engulf itself reflexively, so that the consistent skeptic has to be skeptical of his own skepticism as well as of all other competing philosophical approaches. The model established by Hume in response to this dilemma has been followed by conservative as well as by liberal political philosophers in the twentieth century. In the famous backgammon passage in *A Treatise of Human Nature*, Hume retreats from the extreme skepticism voiced elsewhere in the *Treatise* to a more mitigated version that tolerates, indeed requires, skepticism of itself. Philosophy in this passage is situated on the same ontological plane as backgammon: They are both portrayed as self-contained intellectual exercises that can lay no claims to any privileged contact with reality. Twentieth-century political philosophers have by and large followed Hume's lead in opting for some version of mitigated skepticism (without sufficiently considering the possibility of unraveling other, more extreme forms of skepticism), which has blinded them to the radical political implications of skepticism.

A Fundamental Difficulty and Strategies for Resolution

The logical form of the problem of expressing a consistent version of skepticism is a special case of the broader conundrum known as the Liar paradox. This paradox stems from Epimenides the Cretan, who said that all Cretans were liars. "If he spoke the truth, he was a liar."[2] Benson Mates cites a later formulation attributed to the Aristotelian commentator Alexander of Aphrodisias, who said, "The man who says 'I am lying' is both lying and telling the truth."[3] Similarly, the argument of the consistent skeptic founders on the paradox that if skepticism is correct (that it is justifiable to doubt everything) then skepticism too becomes a valid subject of doubt, so that skepticism gets aborted even before it can get formulated. The reduction to language of a consistently skeptical position seems to self-destruct before the targets of skepticism can be negotiated.

I deploy several strategies for grappling with this paradox. The approach developed in Chapter Two consists in drawing an explicit connection between skepticism and political participation. If people intuitively feel or act as if skepticism were correct, but it cannot even get consistently formulated, then the appropriate move is to acknowledge that skepticism cannot be coherently stated: It can only be enacted. By multiplying participatory networks across society—from informal social settings to the workplace to official governmental contexts of decision making—we enact skepticism by affording people an equal opportunity to participate in decisions that shape their lives, without having to shoulder the burden of stating skepticism.

This approach is problematic because the enactment of skepticism through participation is not the only recourse available to us in the face of the unstatability of skepticism. If we are locked into a doubly solipsistic universe, where we not only feel skepticism to be the most defensible philosophical position but feel that the resources of language defeat the very possibility of coherently stating this, then self-destructive, suicidal withdrawal seems as inherently plausible an option as fashioning expanding networks for political participation. There appear to be intervening layers of decision and argument between the recognition of the paradox attending formulations of skepticism and attaching primacy to participation.

The preference for participation, therefore, can only be defended rhetorically, not rigorously established by logic.[4] In Chapter Three, I try to show how Wittgenstein's persistent attempts to formulate a consistent version of skepticism cannot be accommodated even within the confines of his celebrated distinction between "showing" and "saying." One needs to envisage such rhetorical translations of skepticism as the establishment of widespread political participation in order for the issue of consistency to be more satisfactorily resolved.

My second approach to grappling with the problem of formulating a consistent version of skepticism invokes, in Chapter Four, Michael Polanyi's concept of tacit knowledge. "Tacit knowledge" suggests that all of our knowledge statements are more "knowing" than what they can state or justify. Skepticism is qualitatively no different in this regard from the experience highlighted by Gestalt psychologists of being able to recognize a face without being able to set forth the indicators that enable us to discern it. Skeptical statements can most judiciously be construed as suppressed action statements that, while registering a limit of thought, covertly point to the transcendence of that limit through leaps into action that cannot be justified rationally. From the perspective of "tacit knowledge," statements of skepticism constitute a more heightened expression of the "justification gap" affecting even our ordinary statements in the world.

Chapter Five argues that the peculiarly modern stress on "right method" as the chief clue for resolving theoretical as well as practical problems is to some extent inspired by a philosophy of tacit knowledge. A classic modern proclamation of the triumph of method over a vexatious subject matter, Madison's Federalist Number Ten, is chosen to illustrate the subterranean connection between "method" and "tacit knowledge."

A third approach that I take in trying to formulate a consistent version of skepticism (in Chapter Six) employs Gramsci's "dialectically historical" notion of hegemony. "Hegemony" calls attention to the interrelatedness of the cultural products of an age and to the utter historical rootedness of even the most abstract philosophical speculations of a historical epoch. From this perspective, skepticism, with its attendant paradoxes, becomes a "self-consuming artifact"[5]—a mode of discourse, a style of self-understanding, whose very ground rules of intelligibility will be transformed as the proliferation of "organic intellectuals," an "intellectualized proletariat,"[6] articulates new rational canons more in conformity with its ethos of continual deconstruction of class-biased concentrations of power.

A fourth approach that I consider in formulating a consistent version of skepticism focuses on an intuitionistic logic, which maps the suspension of the law of excluded middle, combined with a concept of reverse causation. With its rejection of realism, this approach, elaborated in Chapter Seven, constitutes an alternative to the one developed in Chapter Two.

Finally, in the concluding Chapter Eight, I pursue a fifth approach toward the problem of consistency by arguing in defense of postmodernism that the requirement of "metanarrativity", the fashioning of justificatory background narratives, is metaphysically dispensable, and that this dispensability constitutes the most effective purchase on the problem of stating skepticism consistently.

Reflexivity and Skepticism

There are three dimensions to the problem of reflexivity that one might want to say affect the five philosophical strategies I have summarized for grappling with the problem of formulating a consistent version of extreme skepticism.[7] I will summarize these three dimensions of reflexivity first in relation to a "tacit knowledge" approach for dealing with skepticism and then show how versions of these three dimensions are present in relation to the four other philosophical strategies adopted for coping with skepticism.

One might argue against my position in Chapter Four that "tacit knowledge" leaves the problem of reflexivity unresolved. To theorize tacit knowledge is already to be behaving inconsistently with the tenets of tacit knowledge. If tacit knowledge predicates that some dimensions of knowledge must remain implicit and suppressed, then to theorize what those dimensions are—to render them explicit—is already to be violating the tenets of tacit knowledge. The theorist of tacit knowledge is thus engulfed in a position where he needs to affirm that our knowledge statements have a preponderantly tacit character, except for the reflexive formulation of the tenets of "tacit knowledge" themselves. These, given the nature of theorizing, have an inexpugnably explicit character.

In response one might say that this criticism conflates "tacit knowledge" as an epistemological doctrine with the linguistic apparatus through which the doctrine gets expressed. As an abstract, disembodied, linguistically denuded epistemological doctrine, "tacit knowledge" *appears* to be inconsistent with its own premises. (If our knowledge statements harbor elements that remain partially tacit, contextual, and submerged, how can the theorist of tacit knowledge hope to disclose the content of whatever it is that remains tacit, contextual, and submerged?) However, from the perspective of the linguistic mechanics whereby the content of "tacit knowledge" is expressed, the theorist of tacit knowledge can validly and consistently say that in conformity with its premises the tenets of "tacit knowledge" too can only be incompletely stated—that they are not susceptible of receiving a fully explicit treatment. In this way, the formulation of the tenets of "tacit knowledge" can remain faithful to the protocols of statability enshrined in its theory.

A second dimension to the problem of reflexivity in relation to the theory of tacit knowledge is that the theorist of tacit knowledge has to concede intellectual space to what we might call a countervailing theory of explicit knowledge—that all of our knowledge statements and claims can be thoroughly, explicitly rationalized and justified—in order for the theory of tacit knowledge to have explanatory force. If all human utterance and written expression is conceptualized as communicable only through the machinery of "tacit knowledge," then "tacit knowledge" constitutes a gigantic tautology. In order for "tacit knowledge" to retain its explanatory force and for invocations of the concept to constitute more than tautologies, the theoretical approaches to utterance and writing that the theory of tacit knowledge rejects must somehow continue to exist even after the theorist of tacit knowledge has postulated that no statement that we make can ever be fully rationalized. The explanatory force of "tacit knowledge" is parasitic upon the continued existence of contrasting theoretical understandings concerning the ever-expanding character of explicit knowledge that the theory of tacit knowledge was designed to displace.

There is a third dimension to the problem of reflexivity that one might claim haunts a tacit-knowledge approach to the issue of formulating a consistent version of extreme skepticism and recapturing its participatory political implications. This problem is patterned after Fred Dallmayr's identification of an analogous question in the work of Jürgen Habermas.[8] With regard to the broad distinction between instrumental and communicative rationality in Habermas, Dallmayr writes, "As in the previous distinction between form and content, one can ask what mode of reasoning or rationality informs this differentiation itself—since it is clearly not covered by either the instrumental or the purely communicative type."[9] From Habermas's particular perspective, instrumental and communicative rationality, as well as the distinction between form and content, are supposed to be two mutually exclusive, exhaustive categories. Yet the *distinction* between instrumental and communicative rationality is neither instrumental nor communicative, and the *distinction* between form and substance is neither formal nor substantive. Analogously, one might want to say that the *distinction* between tacit knowledge and explicit knowledge is neither tacit nor explicit, and therefore encounters difficulties in being reflexively sustained.

I do not believe that Richard Bernstein's defense of Habermas against Dallmayr's criticism works.[10] Bernstein says that Dallmayr, in pushing the argument concerning reflexivity, is still a captive of a foundationalist paradigm for doing philosophy, whereas Habermas is doing philosophy nonfoundationalistically. "Philosophy does not rest," Bernstein says, "on any ultimate foundations. It always begins in medias res, in response to problems, crises and conflicts. It is a hermeneutical enterprise that seeks to enlarge our critical understanding. This is the procedure that Habermas has followed in seeking to clarify the character and interrelations between cognitive-instrumental and communicative reason. It is Dallmayr (not Habermas) who still seems to harbor a nostalgia for foundational projects when he constantly pursues self-referential arguments—asking what is the mode of reasoning that is presupposed when we differentiate instrumental and communicative rationality. . . . Of course when Habermas makes these distinctions he is advancing claims that are themselves subject to modification and revision by further argumentative inquiry."[11]

The argument that Bernstein makes in defense of Habermas can be converted into an argument against Bernstein himself. Does not Bernstein's rejection of self-referential arguments constitute a lingering foundationalism? Is not Bernstein, in rejecting these sorts of arguments, to some extent presupposing them—or at least giving them enough intellectual space so that his rejection has a conceptual target to latch on to? Bernstein's argument fails to meet the test of self-referentialism—of reflexivity—and he cannot prejudge whether this test has to be met at all without his argument becoming viciously circular, assuming the very thing it is trying to prove. Bernstein is presupposing precisely that which he is supposed to be establishing argumentatively.

On the basis of logic, one can neither affirm nor reject the role of self-referential arguments in philosophy. To invoke the requirement of reflexivity—to stress the need that arguments be self-referentially sound—is an extension of the requirement of consistency in the formulation of arguments generally. There is no higher order of justification of consistency beyond saying that this is the way we (certain cultures or certain groups within cultures) do things. This is the way we make our case in support of particular positions.

Introduction

The all-important question therefore becomes the use(s) to which rejecting—or affirming—self-referential arguments can be put. In order for this overarching perspective of pragmatism to emerge as virtuously rather than as viciously circular—to itself conform to the requirements of consistency—any kind of ultimate linkage between pragmatism and reality would have to be denied because otherwise pragmatism as an explanatory philosophical theory would fail the test of reflexivity: It would be privileging itself in relation to the theories that it criticizes. *They* all lack a realistic foundation and are merely pragmatically grounded, whereas pragmatism itself is responsive to the order of reality. In order for pragmatism to emerge as consistent, the concepts of "use" and of "reality" have to be dissociated to such an extent that pragmatism can be viewed as one possible ordering principle among many. That is to say, the so-called reality that pragmatism captures and whose exigencies constitute the ultimate determinative factors in our theoretical and practical constructions and construals is itself one of many possible realities, whose particular configurations of exigencies (or some other alternative, or counterpart, notational term) could have been registered by sets of notational principles aside from pragmatism.

A consistent pragmatism offers us the opportunity to formulate a more global response to the first dimension of the problem of reflexivity in relation to "tacit knowledge" than the one sketched out above. The linguistic response elaborated earlier is more local to the tenets of tacit knowledge, which is, after all, at least partially a theory about language and its radical incompleteness. From a more global perspective, however, one might say that the statement, "You can't theorize the tenets of tacit knowledge without violating the tenets of tacit knowledge," is true only if one holds that linguistic utterances make an unreserved claim concerning what the world is like. But if linguistic utterances are construed in a consistently pragmatic way, then they harbor no commitments concerning the nature of the world; it could be that a multivalued logic which maps the suspension of the law of excluded middle accurately reflects what the world is like.[12] In that case, knowledge both is and is not (in the requisite senses) tacit, so that the *theorizing* of tacit knowledge does not emerge as inconsistent with the tenets of tacit knowledge.

Introduction

A consistent pragmatism that recoils before linkage with any particular version of reality also enables us to resolve the second dimension of the problem of reflexivity in relation to the theory of tacit knowledge. Such a pragmatism can accommodate a theory of tacit knowledge that is parasitic upon the persistence of theories of explicit knowledge because a pragmatic construal of tacit knowledge betrays no commitment concerning what the structure of the world is like. The world's actual structure might be appropriately mapped by multivalued logics that accommodate the suspension of the law of excluded middle so that knowledge both is and is not in the appropriate senses tacit.

A multivalued logic also helps us resolve the third dimension of the problem of reflexivity in relation to tacit knowledge. A consistently pragmatic construal of the *distinction* between tacit knowledge and explicit knowledge enables us to circumvent the issue of reflexivity because knowledge of the world might be both tacit and not tacit, explicit and not explicit at the same time, so that the distinction between "tacit" and "explicit" has validity in our notational universe but has no counterpart in the "real" universe. Another factor contributing to resolving the third dimension of the problem of reflexivity in relation to tacit knowledge is that the world itself might facilitate the construction of analytical grids that would enable us to trace possibilities intermediate between "explicit" and "tacit" that our current conceptual schemata are incapable of elucidating.

Versions of all three dimensions of the problem of reflexivity are present in relation to the other four approaches adopted in the book for achieving a consistent formulation of extreme skepticism. In addition, versions of the strategies for overcoming these three dimensions of the problem of reflexivity are also available for the remaining four approaches.

1a. With regard to the first approach—extreme skepticism cannot be stated; it can only be enacted through massive participation—a version of the first dimension of the problem of reflexivity is present because "enactment" cannot take place outside a linguistically ordaining interpretive context that establishes the link with participation. Therefore, the relationship between enactment and participation that this approach underscores is being begged rather than proved. "En-

15

actment" cannot be the only appropriate translation of skepticism without transcending its character as mere enactment.

1b. The translation of skepticism as enactment through participation is parasitic upon an understanding of skepticism as not requiring a participatory translation in order for the first delineation of skepticism to have explanatory force. Otherwise, it constitutes a mere tautology.

1c. The *distinction* between the conceptualization of skepticism as crucially predicated upon enactment through participation and as not so predicated is neither participatory nor nonparticipatory. How can the distinction itself be reflexively justified?

A pragmatic construal of the first thesis—the only way to formulate skepticism is through enactment by collective participation in decision making—would emphasize that this statement harbors no commitments as to the nature of the world. In terms of what the world itself is like,[13] it might be such that experiences can only be linguistically mediated. This would give rise to the first dimension of the problem of reflexivity in relation to my first thesis concerning skepticism. Then again the world might be such that experiences and their import can be perceived and grasped nonmediationally, and it is only our various cultural traditions that generate the illusions of the linguistically mediated nature of experience. Since a consistently pragmatic construal of the first thesis requires one to be unremittingly agnostic concerning the nature of the world, the first inconsistency attendant to my first thesis concerning skepticism falls by the wayside.

The second dimension of the problem of reflexivity with regard to my first thesis can also be resolved by acknowledging that the world might be most accurately mapped by a multivalued logic that accommodates the suspension of the law of excluded middle. The appropriate translation of skepticism could thus both be and not be enactment through collective participation.

The third dimension of the problem of reflexivity in relation to my first thesis can be resolved by the recognition that the distinction between skepticism as crucially predicated upon enactment through collective participation and as not so predicated when translated into the notational terms of a multivalued logic recoils upon itself, and each possibility can both be and not be at the same time. The distinction that has validity in our notational universe might thus have no counterpart in the "real" universe. In addition, the world itself might facilitate the construction of analytical grids that would enable us to trace possibilities intermediate between the two extremes of "enactment" and "non-enactment" that our current conceptual schemata are incapable of elucidating.

To proceed now more schematically with my remaining three theses concerning how extreme skepticism might be philosophically accommodated:

3a. To theorize dialectical historicism is already to be behaving inconsistently with its tenets. If the break between current and future hegemonically mutually reinforcing paradigms of thought and action is as total as dialectical historicism predicates, then how would we have access to the intellectual tools to plot and theorize the nature of this very break itself? To theorize cultural development as a movement of artifacts in a process of mutual self-consumption has to allow, inconsistently, for the persistence of one artifact that remains unconsumed—namely, the cultural artifact of self-reflection that enables the otherwise global cultural movement toward self-consumption to get recorded.

3b. "Dialectical historicism" is contingent upon a "nondialectical historicism" in order not to constitute a tautology and to wield explanatory force.

3c. The *distinction* between dialectical historicism and nondialectical historicism is neither dialectically nor nondialectically historicist.

4a. As I indicate more fully in Chapter Seven, the tenets of intuitionism cannot be theorized without violating those same tenets. When one regresses the tenets of intuitionism into a background theoretical framework in order to gauge their sense and reference more reliably, it emerges that intuitionism is formulated as an alternative to realism. This means that intuitionism's suspension of the law of excluded middle is not something that can itself be suspended. A doctrine of reverse causation constitutes a local resolution to this problem because, if we can conceptualize the arrow of time moving from future to past (from effect to cause), then we can circumvent the movement of regression that discloses the inconsistency between intuitionism applied to other theoretical statements and intuitionism applied in relation to its own tenets.

4b. With regard to the concept of reverse causation, a version of my second dimension of the problem of reflexivity remains. The explanatory force of reverse causation is parasitic upon the continued existence of "regular causation"—moving from cause to effect. Otherwise, "reverse causation" emerges as a tautology. How then can "reverse causation" work to resolve the first dimension of the problem of reflexivity manifest in the formulation of the tenets of an intuitionist logic when "reverse causation" itself is reflexively unsustainable?

4c. The *distinction* between intuitionism and realism is neither intuitionistic nor realistic.

5a. The theorist of postmodernism is already behaving in ways inconsistent with its tenets by metatheoretically demarcating the ways in which postmodernism differs from modernism. Such a theorist presents us with a justificatory metanarrative regarding the cogency and legitimacy of dispensing with justificatory metanarratives.

5b. In order for postmodernism to be an adequate metaphilosophical theory it must presuppose the existence of modernism. Otherwise, postmodernism emerges as a tautology possessing zero explanatory power.

5c. The *distinction* between modernism and postmodernism is neither modernistic nor postmodernistic.

With regard to 3a above, a consistently pragmatic construal of the third thesis would preclude any linkage between one's statements and the world, so that a multivalued logic might provide the most accurate mapping of what the world is truly like. In that case, one could say that the movement of historical change both was and was not, in the appropriate senses, dialectically historical. The same strategy would apply with regard to 4a. A local response to this conundrum (as we have seen) is reverse causation. A more global response would be to say that the structure of the world might be such that the law of excluded middle fails to hold, so that the tenets of intuitionism can be construed both intuitionistically (in relation to all other statements) and nonintuitionistically (in relation to themselves). Concerning 5a, the tenets of postmodernism can be construed so that postmodernism both is and is not, in the requisite senses, true.

Regarding 3b, 4b, and 5b, all can be resolved from the perspective of a multivalued logic, which consistent pragmatism affords, so that dialectical historicism, reverse causation, and postmodernism, respectively, can conceptually recede to make room for their theoretical opposite numbers.

The issues in 3c, 4c, and 5c become intelligible if one reflects that in each case, when the dichotomies between dialectical historicism and nondialectical historicism, intuitionism and realism, and modernism and postmodernism are translated into the notational terms of a multivalued logic, each side of the respective dichotomies recoils upon itself and each possibility can both be and not be at the same time. This signifies that the respective distinctions that have validity in our notational universe might have no counterpart in the "real" universe. In addition, a consistent pragmatism underscores for us the possibility that the world itself might facilitate the construction of analytical grids that would enable us to trace possibilities intermediate between the extremes of dialectical and nondialectical historicism, intuitionism and realism, and modernism and postmodernism that our current intellectual schemata are incapable of elucidating.

My five approaches for accommodating extreme skepticism philosophically have contradictory implications concerning the nominalism–realism dispute. In Chapter Two, I try to derive from my first approach of enactment of skepticism through collective participation indirect support for the doctrine of realism in philosophy. Also, a tacit knowledge approach, by calling attention to certain permanently unrationalizable elements in discourse, might be appropriately linked with realism, in contrast to nominalism, in philosophy. Dialectical historicism, intuitionism, and postmodernism, on the other hand, clearly point in the direction of antirealism—of nominalism. In the light of our previous discussion, we can discern the three dimensions of the problem of reflexivity haunting the nominalism–realism debate.

First, one might argue that nominalism cannot be theorized without violating its own tenets. If only discrete particulars exist, then ascending to a theoretical level to be able to designate and justify those particulars in contrast to universal essences or general terms is already to be exceeding the warrant of nominalism. The demarcated, conceptualized, named particular is not in experience, but is constructed out of our experience. In this sense, to be a nominalist is already to be committed to more than nominalism.

Second, in order for nominalism to have explanatory force as a philosophical theory, it is parasitic upon the continued granting of philosophical space to realism. It is the effect yielded by contrast with its opposite number that confers upon nominalism or realism whatever explanatory power each concept might possess. Reflexively considered, therefore, the theorist of nominalism is committed to the continued "existence" of realism in order for his elucidation of nominalist theory to work—and not to constitute a tautology.

Finally, is the *distinction* between nominalism and realism itself nominalist or realist? How can it be reflexively justified?

All three dimensions of the problem of reflexivity in relation to the nominalism–realism distinction can again, I think, be most satisfactorily resolved from the perspective of a consistent pragmatism that entails no commitments concerning the structure of the world. The world itself, therefore, might be most accurately mapped by a multivalued logic that accommodates the suspension of the law of excluded middle. If nominalism both is and is not true, then the overlapping with realism that the first dimension of the problem of reflexivity calls attention to can be rendered intelligible. By the same token, the theoretically simultaneous existence of both nominalism and realism—a further specification of the sense in which nominalism both is and is not true—can begin to make sense.

With regard to the third dimension of the problem of reflexivity: When the dichotomy between nominalism and realism is translated into the notational terms of a multivalued logic, each side of the dichotomy recoils upon itself and each possibility can both be and not be at the same time. This signifies that the distinction between nominalism and realism, which has validity in our notational universe, might not have any counterpart in the "real" universe. Another factor contributing to resolving the third dimension of the problem of reflexivity in relation to the nominalism-versus-realism issue is that the world itself might facilitate the construction of analytical grids that would enable us to trace possibilities intermediate between nominalism and realism that our current conceptual schemata are incapable of elucidating.

The general approach pursued by Thomas Nagel in his book, *The View from Nowhere* (published in 1986), for reconciling conflicts between subjectivity and objectivity can be extended to encompass the problem of formulating a consistent version of skepticism and overlaps with the strategy I have adopted here. I will illustrate Nagel's approach in one region of ethical theory—the role of reason in ethics—and indicate what I think the implications are for the issue of formulating a consistent version of skepticism.

According to Nagel, linguistic formulations of an agent expressive of his subjective value allegiances and preferences have to be regarded as part of an enlarged concept of objectivity: Our everyday descriptions of our experiences—of what we think we are doing—are as much a part of what is in the world as a physicist's or neurophysiologist's account of people's actions. Nagel calls this approach a version of realism. "Physicalism," he says, "is based ultimately on a form of idealism: an idealism of restricted objectivity. Objectivity of whatever kind is not the test of reality. It is just one way of understanding reality."

Nagel's rezoning of subjectivity, so that it becomes as constitutive of reality as more officially objective indicators of reality are, is suggestive of a philosophical position that we might term "generalized agnosticism in relation to the world"—or "generalized agnosticism" for short. Nagel appears to be telling us that as long as human experience—including scientific experience—of the world continues, no definitive, exhaustive account of objective reality exists. All kinds of subjective ramifications of our experience belong as data in the objective account. From this perspective, skepticism and relativism are ultimately salvageable as historical emergences that have managed to carve out theoretical and social space for themselves. Justification in both cases is *a posteriori* and *ex post facto*—with commitment endlessly deferred as to what the nature of the world is like.

A strategic philosophical advantage of my two-tier approach toward skepticism (I introduce what amounts to a generalized agnosticism at the second level of argument) over Nagel's one-tier approach

(Nagel introduces a generalized agnosticism at the first level of argument) is that it enables me to make the point that skepticism is only sustainable as a generalized agnosticism. The only way that I can do this is by pursuing the circuitous route that I follow with my five theses. These five theses try to keep skepticism afloat. Then I try to show that these theses themselves work only if they are agnostically interpreted. To follow the more direct route that Nagel does and introduce a generalized agnosticism at the outset of argument appears like a mere substitution—stipulatively substituting a generalized agnosticism for skepticism—rather than showing that the latter is only expressible through (as) the former.

The upshot of my argument, therefore, is that all five theses accommodating extreme skepticism—in their nominalist and realist varieties—can be reflexively sustained in the senses I have summarized. The consistent skepticism that I am advocating links up with the world through the medium of political participation. Political participation enables us to fashion modes of living in the world that are congruent with our uncertainties because they are dependent upon mutual agreement rather than being in harmony with something transcendent.

Toward Collective Rationality

A skeptical approach to political participation calls attention to the incompleteness of thought in order to be able to make sense of and justify what we do. Thought, the conceptualization of what is involved in thinking, needs to be supplemented by action, a recognition of the centrality of an action context, in order to emerge more coherently as thought. More specifically, participation in diverse forms of collective doing and decision making needs to be invoked in order to make sense of the process of thinking itself. A consistently pragmatic approach to political participation seeks to provide an epistemological backdrop in terms of which the naturalness and inevitableness of participation seem especially persuasive and compelling.

There is a central difference between a tacit-knowledge approach and a postmodernist approach to grasping the nature and limits of democratic theory and practice. Some postmodernists[14] at least argue that the abandonment of background justificatory narratives means that all tenets and categories of thought and action are subject to continuing revision by ever-shifting majorities in democratic society. The very ground rules in terms of which personal and social identity are articulated can validly be redrawn in a democratic society attuned to a postmodernist sensibility. Theorists of tacit knowledge would argue by contrast that certain background structures (of a largely tacit character) that facilitate human communication and mutual understanding, a democratic coming together, are not susceptible to complete rationalization and unraveling. Their presence and their boundaries—even if they are only registered in our notational universes and have no counterpart in the "real world"—can only be acknowledged and faithfully affirmed in the way we conduct our lives. These tacit background conditions to communication and knowledge cannot themselves be dismantled and democratically reassembled. They make democracy, as well as all other forms of social life and human interaction, possible.

The political implications of skepticism cannot be tightly, logically drawn. The connection between extreme skepticism and participation is explicated in this book as being largely rhetorical. There is no tight logical compulsion between the two theses. Under whatever theoretical auspices the validity of skepticism is achieved, the stage is merely set for drawing informal connections between skepticism and political participation. The most significant of these connections is that if secure knowledge is unattainable concerning life's most fundamental questions, then the most justifiable course to take is the evolution of a collective rationality through the active participation of democratic citizens in networks of decision making affecting as many areas of their lives as possible. Natural-rights claims that have historically been advanced in liberal-democratic society can most fruitfully be seen as an outgrowth of skepticism. In the absence of secure knowledge about the central questions of life, we convert respect for persons in all of its manifold dimensions into a central organizing principle of democratic political life. In the absence of substantive certainty, skepticism yields the procedural norm of participation.

Introduction

Since the transition between skepticism and widespread political participation can only be informally, pragmatically negotiated, within a political ontology assigning highest priority to participation there is also room for accommodating the countervailing political principles of majority rule, representation, protection of minority rights, and leadership. The impulse concerning this accommodation should always be toward maximum possible integration of participation in the delineation and justification of these alternative concepts. Preliminary attempts at such integration are suggested in Chapters Two and Six. For example, from a Gramscian perspective I try to sketch in Chapter Six a theory of democratic leadership suffused with a recognition of the imperatives of equality. Gramsci wants leadership to emerge from within a participatory political setting so that the identities of leaders and led remain fluid and porous. He theorizes this relationship on analogy with the relationship between teacher and pupil, which "is active and reciprocal so that every teacher is always a pupil and every pupil is a teacher." In order for a political movement to achieve greater equalization in the distribution of power, the way the movement itself is structured must already reflect the preeminence assigned to the value of equality. Therefore, leadership has to be delineated and actualized as temporarily crystallizing moments in the extension of democratic equality as shocks of recognition are registered between those less in the know and those more in the know concerning configurations of power. Moreover, such moments should set the stage for later reversals of roles between the two groups, enabling the formerly less knowledgeable to exercise leadership roles of their own in relation to previously marginalized or excluded groups within society.

This book helps to underscore a pattern of convergence between Anglo–American and Continental philosophy. "Philosophy calling itself into question" might serve as an appropriate title for the philosophical projects of such thinkers as Richard Rorty and Wittgenstein, as well as Nietzsche and such a postmodernist as Jean-François Lyotard. The extent to which such a project can be sustained without undermining itself—a variation on the problem of reflexivity with regard to skepticism—forms a constant preoccupation of the book.

CHAPTER 2

A Neopragmatist Defense of Democratic Participation

A number of democratic theorists have argued that given the precise ways in which democratic institutions and values are articulated in late-capitalist societies, the best way to preserve equality is through a participatory translation of those institutions and values.[1] This chapter addresses questions that fall outside current radical defenses of participation. Is it possible to transcend pragmatism? Can one provide a secure, objectivist foundation for the doctrine of equality and its institutional translation as participation? In order to answer these questions I shall have to explore the epistemological ramifications of liberal-democratic theory.

My conclusion will be that an objectivist foundation for equality and participation is impossible. Nevertheless, in straining logical resources to formulate such a position, I will be moving beyond current expressions of pragmatism by defending a pragmatic position that gestures toward objectivism by presupposing the philosophical validity of realism in contrast to nominalism.

Epistemological Ramifications of
Liberal-Democratic Theory

Liberalism was cradled in Hobbes's insight that there is "nothing in the world universal but names; for the things named are every one of them individual and singular. . . . Truth consisteth in the right ordering of names in our affirmations."[2] The agenda of problems of modern epistemology—proof of the existence of an external world, of other minds, of a nonfictitious substratum for the notion of personal identity—is coeval with the rise of liberal political theory. Liberalism begins in Hobbes and flourishes throughout most of its development in Great Britain and the United States in a philosophical context where most supraindividual supports for knowledge and belief have been knocked out and where most cultural products, from philosophy, science, and art to politics and religion, are ultimately validated out of the empirically certifiable resources and needs of individuals. The basic concepts in the liberal political vocabulary—rights, representation, and consent, for example—have historically been persuasive in an Anglo–American political setting precisely to the extent that the negative arguments concerning the denial of supraindividual supports for knowledge and belief were regarded as true.

A major paradox concerning liberal political theory thus emerges. I believe it has inhibited the clear recognition and articulation of the implications of the liberal system of ideas. Liberal political ideas appear most convincing if the claims of skepticism and relativism are regarded as true.[3] Yet inherent in the notions of skepticism and relativism is the incoherence attached to formulating their tenets as independent philosophical theses. As Barry Barnes and David Bloor formulate the problem, "It is said . . . that the relativist has undermined his own right to use words like true and false."[4] Or as Hilary Putnam states even more pointedly, "No relativist wants to be a relativist about everything." According to Putnam, extreme skepticism and relativism cannot possibly be true because they are in a certain way self-refuting. "A self-refuting supposition is one whose truth implies its own falsity."[5]

Because the extreme skepticism and relativism upon which classical liberalism is predicated can only (in a Wittgensteinian sense) be shown but not coherently stated, it is my contention that liberalism from its inception has been insufficiently aware of the magnitude and radicalness of its own premises. If from an absolutist epistemological perspective the furthest reaches of a genius's thinking are to be accorded an equal epistemological weight with the daily ruminations of a more ordinary person, then the mobilization of political power in furtherance of the genius's scheme to the detriment of other members of the community would be *as* illegitimate. And so would the mobilization of power to advance the ordinary person's preferences to the detriment of the genius's vision. The epistemological foundations of classical liberalism carry momentous *political* implications that undermine the legitimacy of the mobilization of power in support of any political program that cannot claim the sanction of strict equality. If even one person is against a particular proposal, liberalism's epistemology disbars it in principle from enforcing its overwhelming majority view against that person. The only scheme of political arrangements that makes sense under the epistemology of classical liberalism is one stressing the importance of a participatory ethos that nurtures the formation of provisional consensus among a group (or groups) of epistemological equals.[6]

In the world of everyday democracy, if the participatory consensual requirement were strictly enforced, governmental machinery would grind to a standstill and nothing would ever get done. Most members of a democratic society, on a pragmatic basis, would probably endorse the principle of majority rule as the most rational procedure to follow in transacting governmental business and in meeting basic citizen needs. Similar pragmatic considerations would probably impel citizens in a country as large and diverse as the United States to favor a scheme of representative political institutions to supplement purely participatory ones. However, the establishment of representative institutions and submission to majority rule does not mean that the principle of democratic participation is not primary. Participatory networks (spread across industrial, social, and political focal points of society where power was being mobilized and distributed) could serve as a first tier of decision making,[7] which would then on pragmatic grounds be channeled through more traditional representative, majoritarian routes. The principles of political participation that follow from the skeptical epistemological premises of liberalism would not just serve as a hypothetical, idealized touchstone for assessing the validity of representative, majoritarian political decisions. Instead, these principles would find institutional embodiment and legitimacy in far-reaching participatory structures nurtured at the grass roots, to which the system of majority rule and the scheme of political representation would be continually accountable.

Is a Consistent Formulation of Skepticism Possible?

If the inability to state coherently the skeptical epistemological premises underlying classical liberalism has been to an important extent responsible for the failure to elicit and elaborate upon the participationist implications inherent in classical liberalism, what philosophic strategies have been evolved from the seventeenth to the twentieth centuries to enable liberalism to reclaim this important link in its philosophic argument? Are these strategies successful? If not, what philosophical alternatives are available to us?

Kant's "Copernican revolution" in philosophy, with its focus from an anthropocentric perspective on what the conditions of true knowledge and right action are, was a milestone in the philosophic quest to both adhere to skepticism and to be able to state it intelligibly. Two outstanding contemporary political philosophers who have appropriated Kantian methodology to state contemporary, if contrasting, versions of liberalism are John Rawls and Robert Nozick. Comparatively assessing their varying deployment of a Kantian approach will sensitize us to the limitations of Kantianism in resolving the original philosophical conundrum bequeathed by classical liberalism.

"In order to find an Archimedean point," Rawls says, "it is not necessary to appeal to a priori or perfectionist principles. By assuming certain general desires, such as the desire for primary social goods, and by taking as a basis the agreements that would be made in a suitably defined situation, we can achieve the requisite independence from existing circumstances."[8]

Partially because of the difficulties encountered in formulating a skeptical position in philosophy that does not become self-refuting, Rawls (following Kant) wants to arrive at a "transcendental deduction" of his theory of justice as fairness by invoking a veil of ignorance and projecting what the most rational decision-making procedure would be in such a hypothetical situation. According to Rawls this social-contractarian context would yield allegiance to his two principles of justice—that of equal liberty for all and that of competition for resources and offices being open to all (with only those sorts of inequalities being acceptable that would benefit the least-well-off members of society). The justificatory procedure assumes the priority of the right over the good—the inviolability of the principle of the separateness of persons over any individual's conception of what the good life requires. Both Nozick and Rawls accept the Kantian reformulation of skepticism in the ethical sphere—that each person is to be regarded as an end rather than as a means, that the plurality of persons inhabiting a particular political unit, with their conflicting views of the good life, constitute the rock-bottom layer of justification in ethical argument— and differ largely over the issue of how far a denatured conception of the right might go and still be rendered philosophically plausible.[9] Rawls argues that "the two principles are equivalent . . . to an undertaking to regard the distribution of natural abilities as a collective asset so that the more fortunate are to benefit only in ways that help those who have lost out."[10] In contrast, Nozick argues that this sort of construal of natural abilities constitutes an illegitimate extension of the Kantian notion of the priority of the right over the good.

> People will differ in how they view regarding natural talents as a common asset. Some will complain, echoing Rawls against utilitarianism, that this does not take seriously the distinction between persons; and they will wonder whether any reconstruction of Kant that treats people's abilities and talents as resources for others can be adequate. "The two principles of justice . . . rule out even the tendency to regard men as means to one

another's welfare." Only if one presses *very* hard on the distinction between men and their talents, assets, abilities and special traits.[11]

The dispute between Rawls and Nozick concerning the moral
defensibility and desirability of society engaging in redistributive
schemes thus hinges upon their respective interpretations of the Kantian transcendental approach, which posits the inviolability of persons
and asks us to consider how persons affirming their separateness and
bereft of any particular conceptions of the good might justify a scheme
of reciprocal rights and obligations between themselves. The theoretical disagreements between Rawls and Nozick depend upon the limits
to state action that such parties to the original contract might impose.
However, a significant distortion is introduced into the argument by
Rawls's and Nozick's Kantianism. The skepticism concerning political
knowledge that leads both Rawls and Nozick to opt for varieties of
Kantian transcendentalism is misleading. The Kantian skepticism (the
justifying of political judgments by reference to what distinct individuals proclaiming the gospel of their separateness would sanction) has
been made to look like a form of assurance—that a secure source can
after all be fashioned for anchoring political judgments. In order for
the full political implications of skepticism to become evident—that
we are all, as it were, epistemological equals, and industrial and
governmental power cannot be invoked legitimately in furtherance of
any particular individual's conception of the good unless that conception has managed to attract what we might call a participatory consensus—skepticism needs to be stated in and for itself in a raw, un-
blinkered idiom. The paradox underlying modern political thought,
particularly the history of liberalism, is that from its inception skepticism could only be suggested but never formulated as an independent
philosophical thesis. In Kant's political thought, as its strategies of
argumentation are refracted in the writings of Rawls and Nozick, the
intractability of the problem of certainty is deflected into a particular
mode of justification: At least the separate individuals composing the
political unit constitute, as bearers of the right of their separateness
and ultimately as bearers of a plurality of rights stemming from this
more basic right, a set of incarnated limits to what the state might

legitimately do. The unstatability of extreme skepticism, having forced liberal political theorists into adoption of a vocabulary of rights, has led them to jettison the original, albeit implicit, link between skepticism, equality, and participation.

If I am correct in contending that the philosophical difficulty of stating skepticism consistently has obscured, at least in part, the radical participatory implications of classical liberalism from even some of its foremost spokesmen, then we should expect this problem to bedevil the founder of liberalism, Hobbes. Hobbes's grappling with this concern is evidenced by his resorting to the hypothetical construct of a social contract to justify the establishment of civil society. Instead of openly confronting the problem of stating a non-self-refuting version of skepticism, Hobbes shows us in proto-Kantian fashion how atomized and equalized individuals can generate the degree of legitimacy for political authority that ensures their own survival and well-being. Because the issue of skepticism has been sidetracked by the demonstration that it is possible to fashion out of its homely materials a sufficient basis for political certainty, Hobbes is able to avoid the participationist implications inherent in his skeptical epistemology. One might say that these implications guide Hobbes in selecting the social contract as the supreme justificatory myth of civil society. This suggests that conformable to the egalitarian horizons of his time at least all male members of society have to be shown as agreeing in the establishment of civil society. However, one might also say that by circumventing the nonstatability of the skepticism premise and by having the plurality of individuals (as bearers of abstract right) composing civil society serve as the limiting factor concerning what governments may and may not do, Hobbes has evaded the participationist implications inherent in his powerfully intimated skeptical premises to the extent of favoring a static representative scheme as the enduring institutional form for civil society.

Michael Sandel's recent attempt to overcome the "epistemic deficit" in Rawls's theory of justice is again predicated on a misreading of the liberal tradition.[12] According to Sandel, Rawls's theory, by assigning priority to a sparse and denatured conception of the right over the good, prevents us from having "cognitive access to others."[13] In order to correct this deficiency, we need to rehabilitate the notion of community as a constitutive element in the formation of the self. My criticism of Sandel is limited to the textual, historical ground that one does not need to step outside of the defining texts of classical liberalism to arrive at a notion of the participatory community as a shaper and validator of norms.[14] Implicit in the skepticism underlying the foundation of classical liberalism is a doctrine of equality that leads directly to primacy being attached to political participation. The inability of skepticism to get straightforwardly and self-consciously articulated in the classic liberal texts has led to a blindness in those texts to the centrality of political participation as the political consequence of the doctrines of skepticism and equality.

Bruce Ackerman's philosophical justification of at least one version of the liberal state in *Social Justice in the Liberal State* is much more attentive than is Rawls's to the conceptual links between skepticism, equality, and participatory consensus.[15] Ackerman wants to show that the most cogent way to legitimize the establishment of the liberal state is from the perspective of neutral dialogue. By "neutral dialogue" he means conversation organized according to ground rules that disallow justification of particular policies made by individual participants in terms of the intrinsic superiority of their conception of the good over others' or the unconditional superiority of the speakers themselves based upon historical, genetic, religious, or other factors. If the concept of neutral dialogue is taken seriously, Ackerman believes, the ideal of undominated equality follows, which introduces specific constraints in a whole range of policy areas, from state compensation for genetic defects to the proper design of an educational system to the laws of inheritance. Thus on an abstract, utopian level, Ackerman is willing to accommodate the skeptical challenge of liberalism and to confront the political implications of skepticism by emphasizing the ideal of "undominated equality."[16] Unfortunately, a sizable portion of his book is taken up with adapting his ideal of neutral dialogue to the everyday world of contemporary liberalism, with its rampant inequalities and flagrant violations of the principles of political participation. Instead of the denuding of content occurring on the theoretical level, with the assigning of priority to the concept of the right over the good as in Rawls, in Ackerman the draining of content occurs at the level of application as soon as he begins to juxtapose "neutral dialogue" to the daily exigencies of liberal politics.

In contrast to the ideal of participation that I would like to see embodied institutionally in participatory networks established in all areas of significant societal decision making, in Ackerman there is only a tenuous connection between what the ideal of neutral dialogue imposes and what he is prepared to justify in the actual working arrangements of liberal society. Whereas I envisage participation serving as an ongoing theoretical and institutional check on majoritarian and representative political arrangements, Ackerman relegates the requirements of strict participation—his notion of neutral dialogue— to the realm of an ideal technology of justice, and leaves current standards and practices largely removed from what the ideal situation would dictate.

Hans-Georg Gadamer's hermeneutics attempts to deal with the problem of the self-refuting nature of skepticism by generalizing un- statability into the normative condition of all texts, of all utterance.[17] According to Gadamer, "understanding must be conceived as a part of the process of the coming into being of meaning, in which the signifi- cance of all statements—those of art and those of everything else that has been transmitted—is formed and made complete."[18] "Meaning," in Bernstein's paraphrase of Gadamer's argument, "comes to realiza- tion only in and through the 'happening' of understanding."[19] That is to say, meaning and interpretation are historically rooted and con- tinual processes, which constantly belie the finality or fixity of any particular text or utterance. This suggests that the phenomenon of unstatability is not a unique logical feature of skeptical positions in philosophy, but inheres in all texts and utterance as such. Since their meaning is quite literally inexhaustible—depending on all past, pres- ent, and future historical contexts and horizons in reference to which acts of interpretation proceed—their full content can never be ex- hausted in one concerted linguistic statement. The nonstatability of skepticism thus constitutes merely a heightened manifestation of a pervasive linguistic phenomenon—the radical incompleteness of all texts and utterances, growing out of the inextricable connection between a thoroughly historicized conception of understanding and the concept of meaning.

If the Hobbesian, Kantian, Rawlsian way of dealing with the problem of the self-refuting nature of skepticism constitutes a strategy of evasion (by providing a transcendental deduction for a set of familiar arrangements and obligations that show how a suitably emasculated notion of the individual, one who is preeminently a bearer of abstract right, can ground and justify those arrangements and obligations), Gadamer's approach constitutes a more sophisticated and *aufgehöben* strategy of evasion. Nonstatability is declared to be a universal phenomenon which suggests that we collectively inhabit a universe impervious to third-person translation and summary. Quine's thesis of the indeterminacy of radical translation is now located in the heart of ordinary discourse itself as we seek to make paraphrases into a spectator mode of our first-person transactions with the world. Gadamer's world is hopelessly split down the middle—with third-person spectator statements shown to be translatable into first-person agency statements, but with agency statements exhibiting no comparable translatability into third-person spectator statements.

This pointing to an asymmetrical relationship between first-person and third-person modes of discourse constitutes a strategy of evasion because it leads Gadamer to believe that he has purchased a new and subtler form of objectivity with his strategy of argument, whereas in fact he hasn't. What you get in Gadamer—his innovative twist on the objectivity–subjectivity debate—amounts to a kind of eternalizing of subjectivity. Gadamer believes that the philosophic impossibility of transcending a theoretically endless series of interpretive statements revolving around a first-person utterance is tantamount to discerning a new mode of objectivity. This, I think, is fallacious because the most Gadamer can salvage from a series of first-person statements is a universe of subjectivity, not something that can be reasonably labeled as objectivity. Therefore, Gadamer has not dissolved the problem of the self-refuting nature of extreme skepticism by providing it with an appropriate niche in a more "sophisticated" version of objectivity. Had Gadamer fully appreciated the limits and significance of his own argument, he would have realized that the most plausible solution to the problem of a universe of subjectivity remains the political one—which leads to the establishment of participatory networks across society where "epistemological equals" can reach decisions on the spectrum of issues that affect their lives.

Putnam's way of dealing with the extreme skeptic—the sort who adheres to the radical nominalist positions cited from Hobbes at the beginning of this chapter—carries uncomfortable implications that he does not confront. Putnam says that "a self-refuting supposition" is one whose truth implies its own falsity. Sometimes a thesis is called self-refuting "if it is the supposition that the thesis is entertained or enunciated that implies its falsity. For example, 'I do not exist' is self-refuting if thought by me (for any 'me'). So one can be certain that oneself exists, if one thinks about it (as Descartes argued)."[20] According to Putnam, extreme skepticism and relativism exhibit the same logical vulnerability as statements that purport to doubt a person's existence: "Like Sextus Empiricus, who eventually concluded that his own skepticism could not be expressed by a statement (because even the statement 'I do not know' could not be one he knew), the modern relativist, were he consistent (and how could one consistently hold a doctrine which makes nonsense of the notion of consistency?) should end by regarding his own utterances as mere expression of feeling."[21]

In arguing against Putnam, one could say that the self-refuting nature of unmitigated skepticism, instead of inducing a recoil to a more moderate version of skepticism, as Putnam argues, actually helps to underscore the lack of symmetry between language and reality—so that when one wants to make a statement denying the possibility of attaining objective knowledge, one appears to be violating basic logical protocols in even attempting to formulate such a statement—which in a sense serves as a clinching argument in favor of skepticism. It is the lack of symmetry between language and reality, and the skepticism to which it leads, that forms the philosophical case for an equal distribution of power within society—to ensure that no one person's or group's conception of the good should be allowed to prevail over others simply because they happen to enjoy a preponderance of power. Equality in the enjoyment and exercise of power becomes from this perspective the social-ontological analogue to skepticism and does not represent a solution to it. Equal participation, in an important sense, becomes the only "formulation" of skepticism possible. Since no one individual's or group's claims to knowledge or authority can be better intellectually grounded (from an absolutist philosophical perspective) than any other, an equality between citizens' power positions should be preserved throughout the life span of a particular society. Extreme skepticism thus remains invulnerable to Putnam's philosophical sallies, and the appropriate response to the philosophical conundrum to which it gives rise—the arguments in favor of extreme skepticism appear convincing; yet one cannot both believe in the doctrine and state it at the same time—again is the establishment of participatory networks of decision making across the whole sweep of society. Rather than pull back from extreme skepticism and embrace more mitigated versions of it as Putnam does, the proper response is to accept the logical implications of skepticism: to assign paramount importance to equality and participation.

There is no way to get around the conclusion that no one in society is in an epistemologically favored position vis-à-vis anyone else. Political participation therefore makes sense because, given the lack of symmetry between language and reality, it seems plausible to forge the goals of collective action in a shared, participatory setting rather than in an atomistic one that merely duplicates the epistemological problem: We are alone with our thoughts in a world in which no secure foundation exists to demarcate between language and reality.

Donald Davidson takes an approach to issues of skepticism that is antithetical to Putnam's. Instead of having us revise and scale down our philosophical claims concerning skepticism so that they would not be vulnerable to charges of self-refutation, Davidson advises us to get rid of what might be regarded as the irreducible distinction between conceptual scheme and reality, or what I have been calling language and reality, that renders the philosophical enterprise possible.

> In giving up dependence on the concept of an uninterpreted reality, something outside all schemes and science, we do not relinquish the notion of objective truth—quite the contrary. Given the dogma of a dualism of scheme and reality, we get conceptual relativity, and truth

relative to a scheme. Without the dogma, this sort of relativity goes by the board. Of course truth of sentences remains relative to language, but that is as objective as can be. In giving up the dualism of scheme and world, we do not give up the world, but reestablish unmediated touch with the familiar objects whose antics make our sentences and opinions true or false.[22]

The antinomies and resolutions that have historically been the stock-in-trade of philosophers—including primarily the central antinomy between objectivity and subjectivity—cannot withstand the barrage of reflexive philosophical criticism. Formulating the antinomy between objectivity and subjectivity presupposes a rigid demarcation between conceptual scheme and an uninterpreted reality that cannot be philosophically sustained.

I do not think that Davidson has successfully undermined the inescapability of the dilemma surrounding philosophical skepticism—that philosophical argument incessantly drives one in this direction and yet one cannot state the position formally without its becoming self-refuting. Davidson cannot opt out of this dilemma by disparaging the terms in which it is formulated. To say that the distinction between intellectual scheme and uninterpreted reality cannot be philosophically sustained is already to presuppose the conceptual elements that are constitutive of the philosophical dilemma concerning skepticism if only for the sake of denying them. This too represents an inconsistency that a sufficiently rigorous philosophical approach must reject. What emerges in the end is that the most persuasive resolution for the epistemological dilemma is political—the institutionalization of participatory networks of decision making throughout society.

The strategy that Richard Rorty follows to absolve pragmatism of the charge of relativism also will not work. Rorty claims that those who accuse pragmatists of being relativists have failed to draw the appropriate distinction between philosophical theories and real theories. "Relativism only seems to refer to a disturbing view, worthy of being refuted," he says, "if it concerns real theories, not just philosophical theories. Nobody really cares if there are incompatible alternative formulations of a categorical imperative, or incompatible sets of categories of the pure understanding. We *do* care about alternative concrete, detailed cosmologies, or alternative concrete, detailed proposals for political change. When such an alternative is proposed, we debate it, not in terms of categories or principles but in terms of the various concrete advantages and disadvantages it has."[23] The pragmatist's relativism about philosophical theories that Rorty regards as wheels "that play no part in the mechanism"[24] is entirely compatible with (indeed, in the history of pragmatism has been used to support) focusing on the real-world differences of real theories—theories that plug into the actual management of life in human communities. With regard to these sorts of theories, the antirelativist nonpragmatist can come up with no better, more "objective" sets of considerations than the type the pragmatist typically adduces in defending one particular this-worldly theory against its rivals.

Rorty's response to the relativist assumes that there is a safe preserve of "real theories" whose criteria of acceptability are sufficiently objective to render harmless the relativist consequences that follow from the compatability of these "real theories" with a multiplicity of contradictory "philosophical theories." There is, however, no such preserve. There is no neutral, noncircular, non-question-begging way of identifying theories as real or philosophical in character. As Quine classically formulated the point in "Two Dogmas of Empiricism,"[25] the terms "real theory" and "philosophical theory" are basically honorific, depending upon which statements in the body of statements collectively regarded as true by a particular community at a particular moment in its history have been placed at the periphery of its encounters with experience—and therefore are most immediately subject to revision—and which statements are regarded as remote from the periphery and therefore are less likely to be changed in the light of recalcitrant experience. Those statements coming under the first category, or standing right behind them, as it were, certifying to their validity, correspond to Rorty's "real theories"; those more general statements remote from the periphery of experience—whether laws of logic, truths by definition, or traditional metaphysical theories—correspond to Rorty's "philosophical theories." Quine's point is that the line separating real from philosophical theories is shifting and pragmatically determined. "But the total field is so underdetermined by its boundary conditions, experience, that there is much latitude of choice as to what statements to reevaluate in the light of any single contrary experience. No single experiences are linked with any particular statements in the interior of the field, except indirectly through considerations of equilibrium affecting the field as a whole."[26]

Given the magnitude of certain conceivable adverse experiences, what in all likelihood would get revised would be philosophical theories remote from the periphery. This strategy would be resorted to if it would enable us to preserve greater economy, elegance, and manipulability with regard to the totality of statements that we accept as true than more ad hoc strategies of revision would. There is thus no noncircular, nonpragmatically motivated way of being able to distinguish real theories from philosophical theories. Therefore, the same relativism—comparable historically and empirically exigent factors—that leads us to revise real theories would under other circumstances lead us to revise philosophical theories. From a strictly pragmatic perspective, there is no way to qualitatively distinguish real theories from philosophical theories nor to establish fixed categories among the circumstances that lead us to revise one group of theories rather than the other. Given the holistic approach recommended by pragmatism—the merging of real theories into philosophical theories and the modulation of the totality of both by the body of experience considered as a whole—how can the relativist be held at bay? Does not the very holism of a pragmatic approach commit it to relativism, and is not relativism a self-refuting philosophical thesis?

The only way out of this dilemma, it seems to me, is again the political one. Relativism seems philosophically inescapable, yet one cannot state a non-self-refuting version of it. The resolution does not seem to be intellectual but existential—to encourage the establishment of participatory structures throughout society. The case for participation (and the link with pragmatism) is stated very well by Rorty himself in another part of his essay:

> To accept the contingency of starting-points is to accept our inheritance from, and our conversation with, our fellow-humans as our only source

of guidance. To attempt to evade this contingency is to hope to become a properly-programmed machine. This was the hope which Plato thought might be fulfilled at the top of the divided line, when we passed beyond hypotheses. Christians have hoped it might be attained by becoming attuned to the voice of God in the heart, and Cartesians that it might be fulfilled by emptying the mind and seeking the indubitable. Since Kant, philosophers have hoped that it might be fulfilled by finding the a priori structure of any possible inquiry, or language, or form of social life. If we give up this hope, we shall lose what Nietzsche called "metaphysical comfort," but we may gain a renewed sense of community. Our identi-fication with our community—our society, our political tradition, our intellectual heritage—is heightened when we see this community as ours rather than nature's, shaped rather than found, one among many which men have made. In the end, the pragmatists tell us, what matters is our loyalty to other human beings clinging together against the dark, not our hope of getting things right. James, in arguing against realists and ideal-ists that "the trail of the human serpent is over all," was reminding us that our glory is in our participation in fallible and transitory human projects, not in our obedience to permanent nonhuman constraints.[27]

A Neopragmatist Defense of Democratic Participation

After this whole litany of inconsistent philosophical positions has been recited, the objection might be raised—"Doesn't the leap into a participatory social praxis which I recommend as a way out of the di-lemmas posed by a thoroughgoing skepticism itself violate the tenets of a consistent skepticism? How can the dogma of action itself be defended?" The epistemological and the ethical question coincide: Why should a leap take place into constructive action rather than into suicidal, destructive action?

In order to avoid the dilemma of having to state a belief that skepticism is correct and that the only way that such a statement can be made is in action—through the institutionalization of a participa-tory praxis in society—I should perhaps more consistently say that this very move itself, to transfer my statement into the arena of action, is the result of a rhetorical argument that appeals to the judgment rather than being a demonstrative argument whose sanction is the rational intellect. Therefore, this argument itself in favor of a pragmatic, participatory response to the limitations of human reason has a pragmatic, rather than a more purely rational, sanction. The argument exhibits a virtuous circularity.

The position I am defending could thus most fittingly be described as one of pragmatic equality. I am arguing in favor of equality because of the implications of skepticism. My position, however, remains pragmatic because of the logical protocols and constraints I confront in stating those implications. (How can the leap into action be justified?)

Once my position is reformulated in this way, a crucial question becomes how to distinguish my view from that of Rorty and Davidson, the two pragmatic philosophers criticized earlier in this chapter. Have I not attacked them only to end up in a position similar to theirs?

As a first approximation to a solution, I might say that what is at stake between Rorty and Davidson and myself is a principle of parsimony: Does pragmatism offer a third, middle way between radical skepticism and positivism (or some other version of certainty), or does pragmatism merely constitute the response to the dilemma of both believing radical skepticism to be inescapable and being able to state it coherently? Pragmatism then would not be a third alternative, but the appropriate continuation and resolution for one of the two major protagonists, skepticism. Radical skepticism from this perspective would thus be the shadow, inarticulable, unacceptable doctrine in relation to which a pragmatic position gets formulated. Radical skepticism constitutes the ideal philosophical limit against which more manageable forms of skepticism, such as the virtuously circular type I mentioned earlier, get articulated.

At first blush, therefore, it would appear that what is at stake between Rorty and Davidson and myself is how the philosophical terrain should be landscaped: Are there three positions—positivism or some other version of certainty, radical skepticism, and some mitigated version of skepticism such as pragmatism? Or are there only two positions—because the formulation of radical skepticism encounters conceptual problems so dense that this position must be (immediately) reformulated into some version of mitigated skepticism such as pragmatism?

41

Upon deeper reflection, however, it appears that much more hangs in the balance. A radical skeptical position in philosophy, as we have seen, is in the highly anomalous situation that it cannot be refuted and cannot be stated. The relationship between these two factors, however, is asymmetrical. Radical skepticism's irrefutability is not attributable to the fact that it cannot be stated. The causal relationship is almost the other way around. Radical skepticism's unstatability is a consequence of its being irrefutable. Since skepticism cannot be refuted—there is no way to limit its scope or its implications—it cannot be stated either. Skepticism thus emerges as a position that seems airtight that cannot be meaningfully formulated.

The philosophical paradigm and support for realism as opposed to nominalism in philosophy comes from this—that when the limits of thought are reached in skepticism, the unstatability of skepticism is grounded in its irrefutability and not the other way around. It is not some arbitrary designation of meaning but a substantive argument that signals at once a limit of thought and the beginnings of its release from that limit.

Realism versus nominalism might therefore be at stake in the question of whether one adopts a two-position or a three-position landscaping of the philosophical terrain. The three-position theorist, by regarding radical skepticism as an autonomous philosophical position, is committed to the view that philosophic fiat—philosophic stipulation—is all. The two-position theorist, by recognizing that the radical skeptical position is compromised from the start as a result of certain rational considerations over which the distinguishing and naming fecundity of man can exercise no veto, is in effect committed to realism in philosophy.

CHAPTER 3

The Political Implications of Wittgenstein's Skepticism

A unifying perspective to bring to bear on Wittgenstein's thought is that it represents a continual grappling with the problem of formulating a consistent version of skepticism—one that would not succumb to the charge of being self-refuting. His ultimate resolution of this problem hinges upon the precise content to be invested in his famous philosophical doctrine of the priority of *Gezeigt* (showing) over *Gezagt* (saying). I will argue for a democratic participatory gloss of this doctrine as offering the most satisfactory resolution to the skeptical dilemmas haunting Wittgenstein.

Wittgenstein and Skepticism I

Recent commentators have argued that a dominant animating impulse behind Wittgenstein's philosophy is the desire to effectively end philosophy.[1] How to end philosophy without leaving any loose ends—without being entrapped in a philosophical strategy oneself—forms one of the major motives of his thought. This is the way Wittgenstein expresses the goal in the *Philosophical Investigations*: "For the clarity that

43

we are aiming at is indeed complete clarity. But this simply means that the philosophical problems should completely disappear. . . . The real discovery is the one that makes me capable of stopping doing philosophy when I want to.—The one that gives philosophy peace, so that it is no longer tormented by questions which bring itself in question. . . . Instead, we now demonstrate a method by examples; and the series of examples can be broken off.—Problems are solved (difficulties eliminated), not a single problem. . . . There is not a single philosophical method, though there are indeed methods, like different therapies."[2]

Wittgenstein in the first and only philosophical book he published during his lifetime—the *Tractatus Logico-Philosophicus*—adopts a rigorous skepticism with regard to the question of what can be acknowledged as meaningful discourse. Wittgenstein believed that it was possible to analyze our ordinary uses of language and to break down our heterogeneous and abstract expressions of thought in such a way that they would yield a class of elementary propositions. He further believed that the two crucial features of elementary propositions— that the names they contained named objects and that their configurations of names depicted possible configurations of objects (the so-called picture theory of the proposition)—constituted the essence of language itself. Since elementary propositions are configurations of names (and thus possible pictures of states of affairs), and since all propositions are either elementary propositions or truth-functions of elementary propositions, and the totality of propositions is language, one now possesses criteria for demarcating the limits of language and of thought. We are thus able to distinguish sense from nonsense. "Is the specimen either (a) an elementary proposition, consisting of an immediate concatenation of names for objects and functioning as asserting the existence of a determinate state of affairs, or (b) a truth-function of such elementary propositions? If so, it is a genuine piece of language and is the expression of a genuine (even if false) thought. If not, then the utterance is shown to be a piece of nonsense and thus not a thought at all."[3]

It is important to note, as David Pears has argued by way of underscoring a latent continuity between Wittgenstein's earlier and later work, "the aloofness of this theory of meaning and its detachment from any particular theory of knowledge."[4] Although Wittgenstein's theory of meaning fixes its outer limit in relation to elementary propositions, a central question remains unformulated and unanswered. Wittgenstein tells us that the *meaning* of elementary propositions can be reliably ascertained by relating the components of elementary propositions to the facts they picture, but he crucially omits to tell us how the configuration of facts in the external world can be *known* so that the task of squaring elementary propositions with them can proceed. In particular, Wittgenstein remains silent concerning the question of whether what is appropriated through the senses has epistemological priority over what is generated from internal imaginative resources or other possible sources of knowledge.[5]

A philosophically illuminating way for conceiving the relationship between the *Tractatus* and Wittgenstein's later philosophy that is steeped in intimate knowledge of Wittgenstein's biography has been advanced by Peter Winch. Winch quotes Rush Rhees (a disciple, and editor and translator of Wittgenstein's works) as having said in discussion that Wittgenstein once remarked that what was wrong with his conception of elementary propositions in the *Tractatus*—his notion that there must be propositions of which no further analysis is possible: They just consist of names in immediate mutual concatenation; these names are immediately correlated with objects, which are again in immediate mutual concatenation—was that it confused the "method of projection" with the "lines of projection."[6] Winch tries to clarify this distinction by juxtaposing to it Wittgenstein's discussion of the hidden complexities of the notion of "ostensive definition" in sections 26 to 37 of the *Philosophical Investigations*. "Suppose," Winch says, "we say that an ostensive definition establishes a correlation between a name and an object. Perhaps we think that as it were a string has been attached to the name at one end and to the object at the other end, or that, as it were, a label has been attached to an object. But what has this by itself achieved? Suppose I have a desk and attach various labels to it, as follows: 'medium brown,' 'oval,' 'desk,' 'item of furniture,' 'late Victorian,' etc. Any of these labels could be called 'naming an object,' but the mere fact that I have carried out this operation, considered in isolation, says nothing. I have got to understand how the label is being used; its grammar; otherwise I just don't know what has been labelled. In other words, the lines of projection don't do what is required of them; they only function in the context of a method of projection. If I do suppose that the lines of projection carry all the weight in establishing the correlation between name and object, then it will appear to me that I have got to have the object clearly in view before I can draw the lines. But once I see that it is the method of projection which is important, then, as Wittgenstein says, 'the object drops out of consideration as irrelevant.' That is, the Tractarian objects are quite unnecessary, an idle wheel, the intrusion of which is masking the true workings of the mechanism."[7]

The upshot of this argument is that reference to physical objects— to what Elizabeth Anscombe has labeled "brute facts"[8]—is metaphysically (ontologically) otiose. What matters in the way we live our lives, and communicate with others and with ourselves about them, is what Anscombe has called "institutional facts," the multiplicity of man-made contexts (methods of projection) in which we link up the raw furniture of the universe with our ways of talking about them.

Expanding upon the organizing perspective introduced by Winch, I think that the most fruitful way to conceptualize the pattern of unity linking the *Tractatus* with the intervening works of the thirties[9] and the *Investigations* is in terms of a broadening and deepening skepticism. The doctrine of logical atomism that is integral to Wittgenstein's argument in the *Tractatus* leads to the exclusion of certain regions of experience (the ethical, the esthetic, the religious, and the philosophical) as falling outside the scope of rational resolution within language. These areas of experience have been completely "privatized," being confined to inner states of feeling and having no objective translation in the shared resources of language. One might say that the *Investigations* completes the project begun in the *Tractatus*. In the *Tractatus* a good deal of ordinary language can still be salvaged as a vehicle of knowledge and of truth. In the *Investigations*, ordinary discourse itself emerges as problematic in character. There are no external points of reference by which to verify even our typical, everyday assertions, so that with regard to the brute facts of any given situation the agent's institutional description enjoys no logical priority over that of any other observer. The "privatization" of our experience begun in the *Tractatus* is extended in the *Investigations* from the more specialized realms of esthetics, religion, ethics, and philosophy to encompass our everyday transactions with the world, staked out and captured by language.[10]

An element of complexity that needs to be restored to this perhaps overly flattened picture of the unity of Wittgenstein's thought is that while the metaphysics of logical atomism is abandoned in the later work elements of the picture theory of the proposition remain. In support of this view, Anthony Kenny cites the following passage from the *Investigations*:

> The agreement, the harmony, of thought and reality consists in this: If I say falsely that something is red, then, for all that, it isn't red. And when I want to explain the word "red" to someone, in the sentence, 'that is not red,' I do it by pointing to something red.[11]

However, as Wittgenstein's thought progressed, the picture theory came to be seen as needing to be supplemented by a perspective which emphasized that "the meaning of a word is its use in the language"—or, to use the vocabulary introduced earlier, that lines of projection from objects to words were inert outside of a prior, tacitly ordained context of a method of projection. The fusing of the two perspectives of the picture theory of the proposition and the stress on meaning as a function of use is neatly conveyed in a passage such as the following from the *Investigations*:

> Imagine a picture representing a boxer in a particular stance. Now, the picture can be used to tell someone how he should stand, should hold himself; or how he should not hold himself; or how a particular man did stand in such and such a place; and so on. One might (using the language of chemistry) call this picture a proposition-radical.[12]

Saul Kripke in his book on Wittgenstein[13] also regards the later Wittgenstein as manifesting a more thoroughgoing skepticism than that present in the *Tractatus*. Kripke tries to show how a characteristic and influential argument in the *Investigations* (that against the notion of a private language) constitutes a skeptical response to the challenge articulated in Section 201 of the *Investigations*: "This was our paradox: no course of action could be determined by a rule, because every course of action can be made out to accord with the rule." Kripke illustrates this paradox by a mathematical example. He refers to the word "plus" and the symbol "+" to denote the familiar mathematical function of addition. Kripke, explicating Wittgenstein, says that "one point is crucial to my 'grasp' of this rule. Although I myself have computed only finitely many sums in the past, the rule determines my answer for infinitely many new sums that I have never previously considered. This is the whole point of the notion that in learning to add I grasp a rule; my past intentions regarding addition determine a unique answer for indefinitely many new cases in the future."[14]

Suppose now that the wielder of this simple arithmetical rule concerning the plus sign is confronted by a "bizarre" skeptic. All of us in our previous instances of learning and applying the rule have dealt only with finite examples. Surely, for each of us there exist problems in addition both of whose arguments exceed numbers we have previously worked with. For the sake of argument, Kripke assumes that 68 + 57 constitutes a problem in addition that a particular person has not worked with in the past, and also that these numbers represent magnitudes greater than the person has dealt with before. It is now open to the skeptic to argue against the person performing the addition problem that the sum of 68 + 57 is not 125 but 5. The counterargument would go as follows: Since the numbers the person doing the addition had previously been involved with were all less than 57, perhaps when the person was saying "plus" what he meant was "quus." "Quus" could be defined as requiring that when dealing with integers less than 57 addition should be performed in the normal way; with integers greater than 57, the quus sign would always yield a result of 5.

How could such a skeptic who questioned whether any course of action could be determined by a rule be refuted? According to Kripke, the private-language argument found in the *Investigations* constitutes Wittgenstein's answer to this imaginary skeptic. "The impossibility of private language," according to Kripke, "emerges as a corollary of his skeptical solution of his own paradox, as does the impossibility of 'private causation' in Hume. It turns out that the skeptical solution does not allow us to speak of a single individual, considered by himself and in isolation, as ever meaning anything."[15] Wittgenstein accepts the skeptic's challenge concerning the possibility of communicating in accordance with a rule to the extent of acknowledging that meaning is never individual in character. In the course of jettisoning the concept of individual meaning, Wittgenstein is also deflating our traditional conception of truth. Normally, we take the utterance of truth to be the result of a particular action conforming to the intention(s), principles, judgments, and so on present to the mind of the individual actor as he goes about performing a particular action. But if meaning is not appropriated or validated individualistically, neither can truth be what is at stake in the discourse individuals employ to communicate and describe their intentions and achievements. Assertability and utility must take the place of truth. "Wittgenstein replaces the question, 'What must be the case for this sentence to be true?' by two others: first, 'Under what conditions may this form of words be appropriately asserted (or denied)?'; second, given an answer to the first question, 'What is the role, and the utility, in our lives of our practice of asserting (or denying) the form of words under these conditions?' "[16]

In contrast to Winch's historical approach for achieving a purchase on the unity of Wittgenstein's thought (which seeks to employ Wittgenstein's own terms, such as "lines of projection" and "method of projection," to account for the transition from the *Tractatus* to the *Investigations*), Kripke uses a more abstract, philosophically motivated vocabulary—which bears an internal relation to Wittgenstein's argument rather than being externally related to certain autobiographical statements that he made—to arrive at similar conclusions. For both Winch and Kripke, the movement from the *Tractatus* to the *Investigations* can be most reliably characterized as a movement from a more limited to a more extreme skepticism, from a philosophy that left a safe preserve of statements that were securely anchored in reality to a philosophy that eroded even that preserve. Given that the modifications in Wittgenstein's philosophy all take place within the purview of skepticism, a compelling question to raise involves how he deals with the self-refuting nature of extreme skepticism. Even the *Tractatus*, which does allow for a privileged class of statements (the elementary propositions), evokes the question of how one can sustain in the metalanguage of philosophy the destructive arguments that invalidate all save elementary propositions and truth-functions of them without having that destructive force turn inward and undermine the philosophical language itself for failure to consist of elementary propositions or truth-functions of them. Grappling with the problem of being able both to adhere to skepticism and to state it coherently forms one of the major motive forces of Wittgenstein's philosophy from beginning to end and serves as the point of entry for our discussion of the political dimension of Wittgenstein's thought. We must now address the question of how Wittgenstein dealt with the problem of formulating a consistent version of skepticism.

Wittgenstein and Skepticism II

Wittgenstein's approach to the nonstatability of a consistent version of skepticism is put very succinctly in a letter to Russell written in 1919: "Now I'm afraid you haven't really got hold of my main contention to which the whole business of logical propositions is only corollary. The main point is the theory of what can be expressed (*gesagt*) by propositions, i.e., by language (and, which comes to the same thing, what can be thought) and what cannot be expressed by propositions, but only shown (*gezeigt*); which I believe is the cardinal problem of philosophy."[17] Since the philosophical statements that speak about elementary propositions and the picture theory of the proposition cannot themselves be analyzed into elementary propositions and shown to link up with reality in the direct way required by the picture theory, Wittgenstein takes these philosophical statements to be nonsense. Other types of discourse coming under the category of nonsense for failing to meet the rigorous criteria of meaning established by the

Tractatus include truths of logic and mathematics, ethics, esthetics, and religion.

The *Tractatus* is replete with many statements testifying to Wittgenstein's awareness that his philosophical enterprise is in many ways ironic and self-defeating. Since Wittgenstein believed that "the limits of my language mean the limits of my world,"[18] then those types of understandings such as the notion of elementary propositions and the picture theory of the proposition that point beyond language toward the way language hooks up with reality cannot, strictly speaking, be stated in language. This insight is voiced even more forcefully earlier in the *Tractatus*: "What expresses itself *in* language, *we* cannot express by means of language."[19] "What can be shown, cannot be said."[20]

With regard to philosophy conceived as a whole, Wittgenstein tries to sidestep the unstatability issue by invoking the image of philosophy as activity. "Philosophy aims at the logical clarification of thoughts. . . . Philosophy is not a body of doctrine but an activity. . . . A philosophical work consists essentially of elucidations. . . . Philosophy does not result in 'philosophical propositions,' but rather in the clarification of propositions. . . . Without philosophy thoughts are, as it were, cloudy and indistinct: its task is to make them clear and to give them sharp boundaries."[21]

In this passage, Wittgenstein tries to play down the fact that philosophy involves the formulation of arguments in language. By calling philosophy an activity and pointing to its critical, parasitic role with regard to other, more primary realms of discourse, Wittgenstein hopes to reconcile the skeptical teaching of the *Tractatus* with the skeptical philosophical statements contained in that work. However, as Wittgenstein's friend the Cambridge mathematician and philosopher F. P. Ramsey is reported to have said, "What you cannot say, you cannot say; and you cannot whistle it either."[22] Calling philosophy an activity and denigrating its character as formulated statement is a form of "whistling" that seems at odds with the philosophical implications of Wittgenstein's own skepticism.

Apparently Wittgenstein himself was dissatisfied with this strategy of reconciliation, because at the end of the *Tractatus* he invokes a different set of metaphors to elucidate the relationship between the substantive skeptical doctrine of the *Tractatus* and the steps he has traversed in formulating it.

> There are, indeed, things that cannot be put into words. They make themselves manifest. They are what is mystical.[23]

> My propositions serve as elucidations in the following way: anyone who understands me eventually recognizes them as nonsensical, when he has used them—as steps—to climb up beyond them. (He must, so to speak, throw away the ladder after he has climbed up it.)
>
> He must transcend these propositions, and then he will see the world aright.[24]

> What we cannot speak about we must pass over in silence.[25]

This strategy of divestiture of the philosophical statement in the light of the outcome of the substantive philosophical argument will again, I think, not work. Wittgenstein is not whistling anymore, because he forthrightly says that one must throw away the ladder after one has climbed up it. Nevertheless, the philosophical work of disenchantment—forcing us to shed our innocence with regard to the plethora of statements that are made in the world, and recognizing only narrowly circumscribed ranges of statement as making the privileged contact with reality—has already been accomplished by that philosophical ladder which Wittgenstein bids us throw away. The words—Wittgenstein's philosophical words—have already achieved their special effect. The impasse Wittgenstein has reached in his argument is reminiscent of the situation of the narrator in Proust's *A la recherche du temps perdu*: "I summoned up all my courage and said to him: 'Tell me, sir, do you, by any chance, know the lady—the ladies of Guermantes?'; and I felt glad because, in pronouncing the name, I had secured a sort of power over it, by the mere act of drawing it up out of my dreams and giving it an objective existence in the world of spoken things."[26]

It seems to me that confronted with the problem of rendering his version of skepticism consistent, Wittgenstein is faced with a choice. Since the philosophical statements that compose the metaphysics of logical atomism and articulate the picture theory of the proposition cannot themselves be validated in accordance with that metaphysics and that theory, one can attempt to slough off these philosophical statements after one's philosophical theory has been fully laid out by relegating these statements to a realm of what might be called the "higher nonsense." The "lower nonsense" consists of those statements rendered invalid by logical atomism and the picture theory that are truly to be discarded, and the "higher nonsense" consists of what Wittgenstein at 6.522 calls *das Mystiche*—the statements that emerge as problematic because of his philosophical theory but which one remains committed to, or are otherwise indispensable (as the philosophical statements are), on other grounds.

However, given that a good deal of the "higher nonsense" contains words and sentences of a tranformational sort that can be cherished (as we saw from Proust's narrator) because of their power-enhancing effects, one could perhaps equally plausibly engage in an act of rezoning on the other side of the great divide that separates intelligible discourse from nonsense. What I am suggesting is that it is possible to trace the transition from the early to the later Wittgenstein in relation to a set of internal factors—namely, the unresolved problematics surrounding the issue of showing versus saying that needs to be invoked in order to render Wittgenstein's skepticism consistent. In the *Tractatus*, Wittgenstein opts for a rezoning to take place on the nonsense side of the great divide between a higher and a lower nonsense. With the work commencing in the 1930s and culminating in the *Philosophical Investigations*, Wittgenstein deploys the resources of rezoning on the side of intelligible discourse, consigning the category of what amounts to the "higher nonsense" to oblivion. In the new terrain mapped by the *Investigations*, everything can be said as long as the different rules governing different language regions are observed. There are no sanctions higher than, and no court to appeal to beyond, the disparate sets of rules governing different language games.

The thesis that I am advancing therefore is that it was Wittgenstein's dissatisfaction with working out a consistent version of skepticism, evidenced by his successive attempts in the *Tractatus* to carve out an appropriate conceptual niche for his philosophical statements, that led him from the 1930s onward to relegitimize the realm of ordinary discourse and to make its boundaries coextensive with the philosophically acceptable. In order to make this thesis as convincing as possible, I would like to briefly restate my case for regarding the *Investigations* as expressing a broader and deeper skepticism than that present in the *Tractatus*. I will argue, however, that the dilemma concerning showing versus saying resurfaces in the *Investigations* and is again not satisfactorily resolved, thus making plausible a political resolution to Wittgenstein's epistemological dilemma.

The Problem of Formulating a Consistent Version of Skepticism in the *Investigations*

The *Philosophical Investigations* exemplifies an implicit form of radical skepticism, implicit in the sense that a deceptive tolerance pervades the surface of Wittgenstein's argument which leads one to think that epistemologically "anything goes." But epistemologically "anything goes" only because metaphysically—ontologically—nothing matters. Whether the topic is the laws of logic or the foundations of mathematics, religion or esthetics, the moves that we make in these disparate regions of discourse are ultimately grounded in "the linguistic practices which embody them"[27]—and nothing else.

Wittgenstein is finally able to establish a charmed circle of secure knowledge invulnerable to logical attack—the original project of empiricism inaugurated in Britain by Hobbes and elaborated in a more sophisticated fashion by Hume—simply because for Wittgenstein this charmed circle is coextensive with the realm of ordinary language itself. The "outside" has been turned "inside." (There is no longer any "outside.") There is no level of certainty beyond what is secured by linguistic convention within particular regions of discourse. Wittgenstein emasculates all special philosophical concepts and makes all forms of activity, all forms of life (including the philosophical) metaphysically equal, uniformly leveled by the irremediable opacity of language.

Wittgenstein needs to invoke a doctrine of showing versus saying in the *Investigations* in order to render his philosophical case more coherent. He argues that the notion of language game yields the appropriate sanction for correct linguistic usage in each sphere of discourse.

> Our mistake is to look for an explanation where we look at what happens as a "proto-phenomenon." That is, where we ought to have said: This language-game is played.
>
> The question is not one of explaining a language-game by means of our experiences, but of noting a language-game.[28]

Wittgenstein also says that "we may not advance any kind of theory. . . . We must do away with all explanation, and description alone must take its place."[29] "Philosophy may in no way interfere with the actual use of language; it can in the end only describe it. For it cannot give it any foundation either. It leaves everything as it is."[30]

Given the pivotal role assigned to the concept of a language game in guiding the philosopher in performing his therapeutic task, a crucial question becomes what status to assign to those statements I have just marshaled out of Wittgenstein (and others like them I could have cited) that stake out the central philosophical role assigned to "language-games." If these statements are merely illustrative ("descriptive," in Wittgenstein's word) of how the philosophical language game is played, then why should they be normative—why should they provide the controlling model—for analyzing and restoring coherence to nonphilosophical regions of discourse? In what sense can Wittgenstein's many statements in the *Investigations* about how philosophy should be practiced legitimately obtrude upon other regions of discourse and set them in order when incoherencies of various sorts threaten?

Wittgenstein's response to questions of this sort—his invocation of the doctrine of "showing" in the *Investigations*—is I think suggested by such statements as the following: "Meaning it is not a process which accompanies a word. For no process could have the consequences of meaning."[31] "This was our paradox: no course of action could be determined by a rule, because every course of action can be made out to accord with the rule. The answer was: if everything can be made out to accord with the rule, then it can also be made out to conflict with it. And so there would be neither accord nor conflict here."[32]

The first statement I have cited points to the deep grammar of the family of language games in which the word "mean" is ordinarily employed, which shows that meaning is inseparable from the process of grouping certain words into sentences or into any other type of articulable cluster and pronouncing them either internally to oneself or publicly to others. If the depth grammar of the word "meaning" is examined in the multiple, related language games in which it is typically used, we notice that meaning is communicated almost as a by-product of the actions of speaking, writing, and so on; it is not a separable, isolable component of the process, but something established through such actions.

Similarly, with regard to the second example cited above: Wittgenstein wants to dissolve the paradox pertaining to following a rule that is a variation on Hume's problem of induction (and which, as we have seen, Kripke made central to his interpretation of the *Investigations*) by scrutinizing the depth grammar of the phrases "to accord with a rule" and "to conflict with a rule" in the language games where these phrases are most frequently employed. The paradox surrounding following a rule where every course of action can be made to accord with it after the manner summarized from Kripke earlier in this chapter can be dissolved when we recall that the phrase "to accord with a rule" normally forms part of a contrasting pair whose opposite number is "to conflict with a rule." But if everything can be made out to accord with a rule, the same kind of skeptical attack can also lead to everything being made out to conflict with a rule. The point is that the contrastive force of this pair of terms will have been destroyed by the skeptical argument mentioned by Wittgenstein. Since the skeptical argument violates how the phrases "to accord with a rule" and "to conflict with a rule" function in their original language settings, the philosophical argument is discredited and the skeptic is refuted.

Similar strategies of argument are deployed by Wittgenstein in the notebooks that he was working on in the last few months of his life, since published as *On Certainty*. "Moore's mistake lies in this—countering the assertion that one cannot know that, by saying 'I know it.' "[33] "A doubt that doubted everything would not be a doubt."[34] "Doubt itself rests only on what is beyond doubt."[35] "Do I want to say then that certainty resides in the nature of the language-game?"[36]

In these passages, Wittgenstein criticizes Moore for the approach he adopts in refuting the Cartesian skeptic and points the way to his own method for unraveling the Cartesian doubts. Moore is wrong in attempting to answer the skeptic's mistrust of his senses by a display of a commonsense-inspired confidence in the evidence of his own senses. His resorting to the opposite extreme from the skeptic suggests that he accepts the frame of reference established by the skeptic: To extreme doubt, Moore counterposes extreme confidence. But according to Wittgenstein, the very formulation of the skeptic's doubt concerning the evidence of his senses is misplaced. It involves an illegitimate extension of the term "doubt" from the original language games in which it is at home to alien contexts and uses. In the typical language games in which the term "doubt" is employed, it forms part of a contrastive pair of terms, together with "certainty." In everyday situations, for example, I typically doubt if I left my shoes in a certain place—not whether material objects exist. In the familiar language games in which the terms "certainty" and "doubt" are employed, they are correlative. Certainty is usually not so sweeping in an everyday context that it rules out the possibility of doubt. Neither is doubt so total that it excludes the possibility of attaining knowledge or assurance about a particular state of affairs. Both the skeptical philosophers who raise doubts about central features of our ordinary experience and Moore's extravagantly affirmative rejoinder have illegitimately extended the vocabulary of certainty and doubt that is very useful and makes a good deal of sense when employed internally in relation to particular language games (such as locating a pair of shoes) to an external use, in relation to whole language games themselves, and it is this characteristic that generates the traditional epistemological puzzles.

All of the examples I have cited from Wittgenstein's later work manifest his doctrine of showing versus saying and also suggest why he thinks the doctrine is more successfully embodied in these cases than it is in his earlier work. By analyzing how the language game works in each particular case, Wittgenstein thinks that he has shown rather than stated what has gone wrong to generate the philosophical puzzle and the therapy that needs to be applied to restore language to a condition of health.

But it appears that Wittgenstein has succumbed to the myth of the given. Now all regions of discourse are officially declared to be within the semantic pale—no region is consigned at the outset to the realm of nonsense—and the depth grammar of troublesome words, phrases, and sentences is also a given that is disclosed by minute examination of the language games in which these words, phrases, and sentences are typically employed. Because there is a double given here—the different regions that periodically give rise to perplexities and the depth grammar revealed by close scrutiny of the language games deployed within particular language regions[37]—Wittgenstein believes that he has successfully evaded the necessity of stating and generalizing his skeptical principles. Through the proliferation of examples culled from diverse regions of discourse and disparate language games, he has dramatized skepticism, as it were, without having to confront the necessity of stating it.

It is precisely here, however, that I believe Wittgenstein has committed a blunder that is reminiscent of his earlier self-acknowledged error of confusing the "lines of projection" with the "method of projection." The double structure of the given that Wittgenstein discerns still does not license him to extrapolate from the practice of one language region, philosophy, to all other language games.[38] The concepts of language regions and language games, after all, are originally at home in a philosophical setting. They were fashioned to help resolve some of the perplexity growing out of Wittgenstein's first formulation of his skepticism. Their extension to spheres of discourse outside philosophy is not a function of natural necessity, but a deliberate act. What is suggested by Wittgenstein's initial image of separate regions of discourse governed by their disparate language games are self-contained, Foucauldian mini-epistemes. There is nothing inevitable about their all being orchestrated through the extension of the philosophical technique of unraveling the implicit rules of language games to their separate domains. This imperialistic takeover did not have to take place. Its occurrence is neither vouchsafed nor legitimized by the double structure of necessity Wittgenstein points to in the linguistic landscape around him.

If the notions of language regions and language games are extended from philosophy to other regions of discourse, so that they are remade in philosophy's image (if this move is not self-evidently justifiable in terms of the double-barreled structure of necessity Wittgenstein discerns), then he cannot resort to the vocabulary of showing in contrast to saying to ward off the dilemmas associated with formulating a consistent version of skepticism. He must be able to justify in an explicit idiom why the vocabulary appropriate to philosophy is licensed to establish an imperium over other regions of language and thought. If Wittgenstein is cutting other language regions and language games down to size through the application of his linguistic therapy—if this is skepticism in action—why are the philosophic language games allowed to loom larger than the rest? Wittgenstein cannot say that philosophy is merely being deployed in action—that there is no doctrine that is being advanced here—because, as we have seen, the extension of the imperium of philosophy to encompass other areas of language and thought takes him beyond what is strictly validated by his double-barreled structure of necessity. The skepticism at this point is being directed toward all other language regions except philosophy.

Wittgenstein thus appears to be trapped in a dilemma. In order to avoid the problem of having to formulate a non-self-refuting version of skepticism, he dramatizes skepticism by eliciting through the proliferation of examples the informal rules that govern usage in disparate language regions and language games. But in dramatizing skepticism, Wittgenstein has also dramatized the dilemmas of skepticism, because the concepts of language regions and language games are, after all, philosophical tools that are being extended beyond the hope of reasoned justification to encompass other regions of discourse. If the skeptical insights of philosophy are true but cannot be unraveled into a reasoned idiom of discourse—if philosophical reflection genuinely contributes toward catapulting its devotees out of philosophy into a sphere of action—then perhaps what is salvageable in negotiating the transition from thought to action is the structuring of whatever field of action one chooses to engage in along egalitarian, participatory lines, according (at least initially) equal epistemological weight to each participant in the common enterprise. One could not tease out from this removal to a practical sphere of a central motif of philosophy anything resembling a philosophical principle. But if Wittgenstein is right in his critique of philosophical activity, this is as it should be. Philosophy offers a false hope of transcendence, which can only be redeemed by the integration of philosophically inclined individuals into more traditional forms of social life. If such individuals try to structure those forms in the skeptical image of philosophical reflection by organizing them in a participatory manner, then their aspirations and their practice conform to what propels ordinary men and women to do what they do in fashioning their separate life-styles. What emerges, at best, is a pragmatic sort of justification that moves in a virtuous circle—continually relating idea to act and using each as a touchstone for the other.

CHAPTER 4

Participation and Tacit Knowledge in Plato, Machiavelli, and Hobbes

The concept of tacit knowledge helps to disclose a remarkable continuity between Plato, Machiavelli, and Hobbes. In several key areas in their respective political theories, the concept of tacit knowledge illuminates obscurities and mitigates incoherencies in their thought.[1] Moreover—independently of the role that "tacit knowledge" plays in their work—it provides a promising avenue for resolving a central epistemological problem that has occupied Western philosophy from its inception, and that has received, as we have seen, renewed urgency and prominence in the writings of Davidson, Putnam, and Rorty, among others. The problem has to do with formulating a consistent version of skepticism, one that would not be self-refuting. Finally, "tacit knowledge" reveals the extent to which theorists who have traditionally been regarded as antagonistic or largely indifferent to democratic values can be seen as harboring a democratic political aspect— with a keen appreciation, at any rate, of the role of participation.

Tacit Knowledge

What is tacit knowledge? In the writings of Michael Polanyi, the physical chemist turned philosopher who has done more than anyone else to popularize and justify the notion in the twentieth century, it originates as a solution to a problem. The problem is very succinctly stated at the beginning of Polanyi's 1962 Terry Lectures, *The Tacit Dimension*:

> It seemed to me then that our whole civilization was pervaded by the dissonance of an extreme critical lucidity and an intense moral conscience, and that this combination had generated both our tight-lipped modern revolutions and the tormented self-doubt of modern man outside revolutionary movements. So I resolved to inquire into the roots of this condition.[2]

The cultural schizophrenia of modernity (which nurtures a "critical lucidity" that cannot justify action, and evokes periodic mobilizations of moral passion that are not rationally informed or tempered) needs to be healed by a more adequate, post-Kantian conception of knowledge. Tacit knowledge, at its simplest level, means that "we can know more than we can tell."[3] We can all adduce homely examples in support of this thesis. For instance, we recognize people's faces, but cannot tell how we know. The scientific evidence that Polanyi invokes in defense of tacit knowledge comes from the field of psychology and is mainly of two sorts, the discernings of integrated wholes studied by Gestalt psychologists and the process called "subception." Gestalt psychology has shown how we may know a physiognomy by "synthesizing" our awareness of its particulars without being able to identify those particulars. The phenomenon of "subception" refers to experiments in which psychologists presented subjects with a large number of nonsense syllables and, after showing some of the syllables, administered an electric shock. Very soon, the subjects were able to anticipate the "shock syllables" without being able to identify what they were. An analogous experiment designed almost a decade later confirmed the phenomenon of "subception."

Polanyi distinguishes between four aspects of the structure of tacit knowing, the functional, the phenomenal, the semantic, and the ontological. The functional structure of tacit knowing consists in our knowing the first term (the nonsense syllables) only by our relying on our awareness of it for attending to the second term (the electric shock). Borrowing from the language of anatomy, Polanyi calls the first term "proximal" and the second term "distal." With regard to a human physiognomy, "we are attending from the features to the face, and thus may be unable to specify the features."[4] The features, the proximal term of our knowledge, remain tacit in relation to the face, the distal, the more explicit focus of our knowledge.

We are aware of the proximal term in an act of tacit knowing (the nonsense syllables, the facial features) only in the *appearance* of the distal term (the electric shock, the face). Polanyi calls this the phenomenal structure of tacit knowing.

By the semantic aspect of tacit knowing, Polanyi is referring to the fact that "all meaning tends to be displaced away from ourselves."[5] The point of the analytic separation into the proximal and the distal terms of tacit knowing is to call attention to how the undifferentiated former term cues us onto the more distinct latter term, so that, semantically speaking, the meaning of the proximal term of tacit knowing in each case is its use in alerting us to the presence of something else.

The ontological aspect of tacit knowing emphasizes what tacit knowing is a knowledge of. There are whole units of knowledge going to compose the world that are constituted by their proximal and distal phases or moments. Both terms, by their functional, phenomenal, and semantic patterns of interrelationship, inform us of the actual furniture of the world by a qualitative delineation of a significant segment of experience we encounter within it.[6]

The paradigm for this construal of tacit knowing—and the central importance attached to it—is our body. "Our body is the ultimate instrument of all our external knowledge, whether intellectual or practical. In all our waking moments we are relying on our awareness of contacts of our body with things outside for attending to these things. Our own body is the only thing in the world which we normally never experience as an object, but experience always in terms of the world to which we are attending from our body. It is by making this intelligent use of our body that we feel it to be our body, and not a thing outside."[7]

By way of extension of this insight, Polanyi says that when we make something function as the proximal term of tacit knowing "we incorporate it in our body—or extend our body to include it—so that we come to dwell in it." It is in this manner that Polanyi comes to assimilate the teaching of one of the foremost theorists of German historical method as it applies to intellectual history, Wilhelm Dilthey,[8] to his own doctrine of tacit knowledge. Dilthey believed that the mind of a person could be understood only through a process of reenactment, "by reliving its workings." Polanyi regards the vocation of the intellectual historian as delineated by Dilthey—the "indwelling" of the historian in the mind of the thinker he seeks to study—as merely a special case of the larger phenomenon of tacit knowing, which requires a proximal term as the basis for an "indwelling" that can generate knowledge.

The same process of "indwelling" is at work in both moral knowledge and scientific understanding. Acceptance of moral teachings is sometimes described as their "interiorization." To interiorize is to identify with a particular moral teaching to such an extent that it functions as the proximal term of a tacit moral knowledge, by which we structure and evaluate action. An analogous pattern of relating to phenomena is present in the case of science. To adhere to a scientific theory means a large-scale investment in a particular proximal term of tacit knowing—in relation to which a certain segment of reality will now be organized, investigated, and evaluated. Thus, in both morality and science it is only through the "indwelling" that the presence or cultivation of the proximal term of tacit knowing affords that knowledge and action become possible.

The concept of "indwelling," the role of the proximal term of tacit knowing, suggests that knowledge is exploratory not only in terms of its ground (of how it gets initiated and organized) but also in terms of its end (in relation to more ultimate patterns of coherence). If we are able to know only through "indwelling" in the proximal term of tacit knowing, then what we learn on any one occasion can have only a limited, provisional character, dependent upon what the particular tacit background is to our act of knowing and which intimation we pursue from within that background. The acquisition of knowledge therefore presupposes commitment—to a particular proximal term and to the "mining" of its "vein" over a sustained period. "You cannot formalize the act of commitment," Polanyi writes, "for you cannot express your commitment non-commitally. To attempt this is to exercise the kind of lucidity which destroys its subject matter. Hence the failure of the positivist movement in the philosophy of science."[9]

Polanyi's arguments in defense of a tacit dimension to knowledge can be supplemented by arguments found in Plato of a distinctively philosophical character. These arguments are present mainly in the *Phaedrus*, with the *Meno* and the *Republic* serving as two important additional sources. A built-in limitation of written discourse (which extends to spoken discourse as well, except that which exhibits a special character, to be discussed shortly) is its giving rise to an infinite regress of interpretation.

> *Socr.* They must be really ignorant of Zeus Ammon's method of delivering prophetic truth if they believe that words put in writing are something more than what they are in fact: a reminder to a man, already conversant with the subject, of the material with which the writing is concerned.
>
> *Phaedr.* Quite right.
>
> *Socr.* Writing, you know, Phaedrus, has this strange quality about it, which makes it really like a painting: the painter's products stand before us quite as though they were alive; but if you question them, they maintain a solemn silence. So, too, written words: you might think they spoke as though they made sense, but if you ask them anything about what they are saying, if you wish an explanation, they go on telling you the same thing, over and over forever. Once a thing is put in writing, it rolls about all over the place, falling into the hands of those who have no concern with it just as easily as under the notice of those who comprehend; it has no notion of whom to address or to avoid. And when it is ill-treated or abused as illegitimate, it always needs its father to help it, being quite unable to protect or help itself.
>
> *Phaedr.* You're right about that, too.
>
> *Socr.* Well then, are we able to imagine another sort of discourse, a legitimate brother of our bastard? How does it originate? How far is it better and more powerful in nature?
>
> *Phaedr.* What sort of discourse? What do you mean about its origin?
>
> *Socr.* A discourse which is inscribed with genuine knowledge in the soul of the learner; a discourse that can defend itself and knows to whom it should speak and before whom to remain silent.

65

Phaedr. Do you mean the living, animate discourse of a man who really knows? Would it be fair to call the written discourse only a kind of ghost of it?

Socr. Precisely.[10]

Given the unavoidable ambiguities of discourse—the open texture of language giving rise to multiple possibilities of meaning—how is meaning to be pinned down? How is one person to ascertain reliably what another is trying to communicate to him? If one were to say that alongside each text there should be formulated another accompanying interpretive text, to clarify the ambiguities present in the primary text, the same problem would emerge to affect the interpretive text as undermined the original text. The interpretive text would also of necessity be couched in language, with its attendant ambiguity and multivalence. To the extent that the primary text defied precise translation, so would the interpretive text. The same logical formalistic problem would reappear no matter how frequently the interpretive texts were multiplied and how precise and detailed they were made to appear.

Following Polanyi, one might say that the solution to this problem of an infinite regress of interpretation is to postulate an additional dimension to discourse beyond the explicitly formulated. It is only by acknowledging a tacit dimension that we are able to resolve the problem of an infinite regress of interpretation. Our philosophy of discourse has to make allowances for processes of comprehension that transcend the purely verbal (to use Polanyi's idiom, the presence of a proximal term to knowing that facilitates the distal term coming into focus) in order for us to make sense out of the communication of information and ideas and the transmission of knowledge.

In the passage quoted, Plato refers to a "living, animate discourse" that is to be contrasted with the ordinary discourse whose naive presuppositions he is criticizing. What I think he has in mind here (and what he develops more fully in the *Republic*) is the notion of dialectic—or dialectical discourse—as the appropriate corrective to the inherent limitations of ordinary discourse. The engagement in dialectical discourse refers to the attempt to purge ordinary discourse of its usually suppressed presuppositions and implications in order to reach the humanly approachable limit of totally self-aware discourse. "The method of dialectic is the only one which takes this course, doing away with assumptions and traveling up to the first principle of all, so as to make sure of confirmation there."[11] Plato in the passage I have cited from the *Phaedrus* offers us the infinite-regress argument by way of undermining the legitimacy of ordinary discourse naively understood as a medium for communicating knowledge and truth. Dialectic becomes a rationalistic surrogate for tacit knowing, but the arguments in its defense are precisely those needed to render plausible the concept of tacit knowing.

Another argument in favor of tacit knowing is suggested by the following discussion in the *Phaedrus*:

> *Socr.* Tell me now: suppose someone were to go to your friend Eryximachus or his father Acumenus and say to them, "I know how to apply such and such to bodies so as to induce a fever or, if I wish, to lower a temperature. If the fancy takes me, I can make them vomit or, again, move their bowels, and so forth and so on. Since I have this knowledge I claim that I am a physician and can make the same of any other man to whom I communicate this knowledge." What do you think they would reply?
>
> *Phaedr.* Surely they would ask if the fellow also knew who it was that ought to be treated and the proper occasion for each treatment and how far it should proceed.
>
> *Socr.* And what if the man replied, "Not at all. Yet I expect anyone who has studied these questions under my tutelage to be able by himself to do what you are asking about."
>
> *Phaedr.* I imagine they would say that the fellow was crazy, that because he had read something in a book or came across some old nostrums, he fancied himself a physician, though he knew nothing of the art of healing.[12]

When we try to account philosophically for how a translation between theory and practice becomes possible, we encounter a variation of the infinite-regress problem present when we try to make sense of our understanding of discourse generally. How is a translation between theory and practice effected? The proliferation of theoretical texts, each attempting to be more comprehensive than its predecessors in the detail and specificity of its practical applications, will not solve the problem. No event in practical life presents itself to us in a sufficiently prepackaged, predelineated fashion so as to facilitate a translation of textbook precepts into immediate recipes for action. The theoretical gap between theory and practice can never be closed from the side of theory. It can only be bridged from the side of practice, by philosophically postulating a tacit dimension to knowledge that enables the individual actor to draw inferences and make judgments whose epistemological warrant cannot be fully theoretically certified.

An additional aspect of tacit knowledge is suggested by the following passage in the *Phaedrus*:

> *Socr.* Every great art must be supplemented by leisurely discussion, by stargazing, if you will, about the nature of things. This kind of discussion seems somehow or other to be the source of the characteristic we are looking for: that loftiness of mind that by all means and at all times strives to attain perfection. It was this that Pericles acquired to supplement his great natural talents. I fancy that he happened to meet in Anaxagoras a man already endowed with such a trait; that when he had had his fill of stargazing and had reached a concept of the nature of intelligence and conscious design—topics that Anaxagoras used to discuss constantly— he was able to derive from this discussion and to apply to his own rhetorical art what was applicable to it. [13]

Plato seems to be suggesting in this paragraph that there was a whole tacit dimension that nurtured Pericles' mastery of the practical arts of rhetoric and statesmanship, and that in Pericles' case this tacit dimension received support from his relationship with the metaphysician Anaxagoras. Mastery of an art or a craft can be viewed as a concentrated distal moment that derives part of its sustenance from contact with the proximal moments, the tacit framework of understanding, that lends point and relevance to the enterprise one is engaged in. Expertise in a particular field of activity should be viewed as an abstraction that in order to be rendered concrete needs to be connected with a never fully articulated appreciation of where the particular activity fits in one's sense of life as a whole.

Tacit knowing is again evinced in the following passage:

> *Socr.* Since it is in fact the function of speech to influence souls, a man who is going to be a speaker must know how many types of souls there are. Let us, then, state that they are of this or that number and of this or that sort, so that individuals also will be of this or that type. Again, the distinctions that apply here apply as well in the case of speeches: they are of this or that number in type, and each type is of one particular sort. So men of a special sort under the influence of speeches of a particular kind are readily persuaded to take action of a definite sort because of the qualitative correlation that obtains between speech and soul; while men of a different sort are hard to persuade because, in their case, this qualitative correlation does not obtain. Very well. When a student has attained an adequate grasp of these facts intellectually, he must next go on to see with his own eyes that they occur in the world of affairs and are operative in practice; he must acquire the capacity to confirm their existence through the sharp use of his senses. If he does not do this, no part of the theoretical knowledge he acquired as a student is as yet of any help to him. But it is only when he can state adequately what sort of man is persuaded by what sort of speech; when he has the capacity to declare himself with complete perception, in the presence of another, that there is the man and here the nature that was discussed theoretically at school— here, now, present to him in actuality—to which he must apply this kind of speech in this sort of manner in order to obtain persuasion for this kind of activity—it is only when he can do all this and when he has, in addition, grasped the concept of propriety of time—when to speak and when to hold his tongue, when to use and when not to use brachylogy, piteous language, hyperbole for horrific effect, and, in a word, each of the specific devices of discourse he may have studied—it is only then, and not until then, that the finishing and perfecting touches will have been given to his science. But if in a man's speaking or teaching or writing he falls short in any one of these respects, he may indeed claim that he speaks by the rules of the art; but anyone who doesn't believe him is a better man than he is.[14]

Aside from alluding again more generally to the phenomenon of translation of theory into practice, which requires the invocation of tacit knowing in order to be rendered philosophically intelligible, Plato in this passage points to the specific theme of appropriateness—of knowing when to speak and when to remain silent, and of matching styles of discourse to the nature of the audience one is addressing—as an additional factor denoting the opacity of ordinary discourse. The exercise of judgment and connoisseurship in relation to one's audience constitutes the proximal moment out of which the distal moment of discourse emerges. All of the formally expressed protocols in the world concerning appropriateness would not do as a philosophically convincing notion of how discourse functions because we would still be faced with the problem of explaining how the gap between theory and practice had been bridged. There is also a problem of circularity affecting the choice of criteria utilized in judgment. Unless a sense of discernment and judgment is antecedently regarded as being present, the criteria selected in judgment will not make sense. The criteria of judgment have to be assumed before they can be postulated in order for their postulation to seem convincing. As we have seen, the philosophically most plausible strategy for avoiding both a vicious circle and an infinite regress at this point is to postulate a dimension of tacit knowing. It is this element that helps to make sense of the fact that discourse must "know" a lot more than it officially states in order for it to function as an adequate vehicle of communication.

Further philosophical support for the doctrine of tacit knowing is provided by Plato's *Meno*:

> *Men.* And how will you inquire, Socrates, into that which you do not know? What will you put forth as the subject of inquiry? And if you find what you want, how will you ever know that this is the thing which you did not know?

> *Socr.* I know, Meno, what you mean; but just see what a tiresome dispute you are introducing. You argue that a man cannot inquire either about that which he knows, or about that which he does not know; for if he knows, he has no need to inquire; and if not, he cannot; for he does not know the very subject about which he is to inquire.[15]

Plato argues that the traditional method for resolving perplexity by proceeding from problem to solution—engaging in the activities of problem formulation and problem solution—rests upon a paradox.

One either knows what one is looking for or one does not. If one knows, then the statement of the problem is pointless; if one does not, then the delineation of the problem becomes impossible.

Plato attempts to resolve this paradox by postulating the doctrine that "all inquiry and all learning is but recollection."[16] The very identification and diagnosis of this metatheoretical problem, however, is suggestive of the scope of tacit knowledge in our intellectual activities. It is just the vocabulary of "proximal" and "distal," or an equivalent set of terms, that is lacking in Plato. The prefiguration of directions in which to look for solutions to a problem that guides the formulation of the problem in the first place constitutes so many proximal moments that facilitate the articulation of the distal moment. One might even go so far as to say that Plato's notion of learning as recollection, aside from relating on the literal level to his doctrine of the transmigration of souls,[17] can also be interpreted as a metaphoric expression of the concept of tacit knowing. When one philosophically analyzes what takes place in the activities of intellectual inquiry and learning, these activities appear senseless without the prior postulation of a series of proximal moments that guide and limit inquiry. These proximal moments are denominated by Plato—"recollection," but "recollection" one could say simply refers to what has to be presupposed in order to render the current discourse intelligible.

Polanyi, taking his cue from Plato's discussion of the paradox of knowledge in the *Meno*, points to an additional ramification of tacit knowing. The term needs to be construed prospectively, as well as retrospectively. It is not just when as philosophical spectators we attempt to unravel a particular knowledge claim that we need to postulate a dimension of tacit knowing in order to make sense out of the claim. It is also the case that as actors attempting to expand the horizons of knowledge by resolving current perplexities we proceed through cultivation of "a tacit foreknowledge of yet undiscovered things."[18]

> It appears, then, that to know that a statement is true is to know more than we can tell and that hence, when a discovery solves a problem, it is itself fraught with further intimations of an indeterminate range, and that furthermore, when we accept the discovery as true, we commit ourselves to a belief in all these as yet undisclosed, perhaps as yet unthinkable, consequences.[19]

There are striking parallels between Polanyi's conception of the growth of knowledge and Kuhn's notion of how scientific advance always proceeds within the predetermined limits set by a large-scale paradigm. What Kuhn evinces as a sociological discovery about the way that individual scientific communities are structured—that they work in a highly conservative manner, pursuing the intimations of the reigning paradigms of their communities—is viewed by Polanyi as a necessary condition for the growth of knowledge generally. In the building up of knowledge, it is never a question of adding the previously totally unknown to the already understood and assimilated. The growth of knowledge proceeds, rather, in a circular manner, where, capitalizing upon the potential of the not-yet-fully-disclosed in what we conventionally take to be the already known, we generate a series of proximal moments that issue forth in more precise "distal" crystallizations of what we previously merely had a "tacit knowledge of." "The pursuit of discovery," Polanyi says, "is conducted from the start in these terms; all the time we are guided by sensing the presence of a hidden reality toward which our clues are pointing; and the discovery which terminates and satisfies this pursuit is still sustained by the same vision. It claims to have made contact with reality: a reality which, being real, may yet reveal itself to future eyes in an indefinite range of unexpected manifestations."[20]

To the extent that Kuhn, in the centrality that he assigns to paradigms in the structure of science, is making a philosophical point and not just a sociological one, the convergence with Polanyi runs deeper than that indicated in the preceding paragraph. If there never is under any paradigmatic dispensation, ancient or modern, a perfect fit between a paradigm and the facts that it seeks to explain and predict,[21] then the conservative bias of scientific communities is not just a function of sociological convenience (one does not need to redesign continually the socializing mechanisms of a scientific community) but is a matter of intellectual necessity. If there is no one-to-one correlation between particular components of a theory and individual facts or regions of fact, then the best way to ensure the ordered development of new facts and the disciplined testing of old facts is by retaining allegiance to a particular paradigm over an extended period. To have an ordered, cumulative, progressive universe to inhabit, we need to adhere conservatively to individual paradigms in the sciences for as long as possible. The lack of perfect fit between theory and fact that Kuhn talks about and the tacit dimension of knowledge that Polanyi describes—with perpetual movement from proximal "reserves" of cues to distal crystallizations—are both sets of factors that enable us to recognize and to better comprehend the elements of the "made" in the "given."

A further epistemological argument for postulating a tacit dimension to knowledge is suggested by Plato's Theory of Ideas. This familiar theory relegates the facts of the material world to an inferior ontological status, regarding them as mere copies of eternal Forms. This conception can be construed as a metaphoric and picturesque way of stating that so-called facts are theory dependent, that the world of theory is underdetermined by the universe of fact. An analogous point is suggested by Plato's labeling the highest form of knowledge the Good, rather than the True—with the True being a derivative form of knowledge from the Good. Plato perhaps means to suggest by this terminology the subordination of epistemology to ethics. There is an irreducible contingency in our categories of knowledge that can only be removed by placing them in the perspective afforded by our ethical categories, which decree that the particular ordering of truth and reality made possible and validated by our epistemological categories is good.

Plato's very broad conception of the political seems to be related to his theory of knowledge generally. Plato's stress on the priority of thought over fact predisposes him to become aware of the sheer element of arbitrariness, the factor of personal decision making, involved in the very structure of human personality. This leads him to extend the terms of the political vocabulary—including, especially, its cardinal term, justice—to the private realm as well.[22]

If theories are underdetermined by facts, then intersubjective, hard-nosed criteria for choosing between theories have to be supplemented by less easy to codify, more informal pragmatic criteria relating to elegance, economy, and theoretical and practical fecundity. These criteria, precisely because they help determine factual frameworks and are not determined by them, form part of a tacit lore that is transmitted in the course of carefully nurtured apprenticeships served by aspiring students under the tutelage of more experienced teachers.

Translated into the personal mode of human relationships, "tacit knowledge" presupposes the participation of new generations of initiates in the practices of judgment of an older generation. It is only through participation that a new generation of practitioners in any particular science or branch of knowledge is able to cultivate the skills in making judgments and exercising connoisseurship that are requisite for the application of tacit knowledge. "The transmission of knowledge from one generation to the other must be predominantly tacit."[23] Since in the end the acceptance of theories and forms of life must be understood as forms of commitment—and "you cannot formalize the act of commitment, for you cannot express your commitment non-committally"[24]—then society must foster participatory environments to enable sane, reasoned commitments to take place, which will ensure the reliable transmission of tacit knowledge and thus safeguard the further accretion of more concrete knowledge.

Participation and Tacit Knowledge in Plato

Now that we have seen what tacit knowledge is about and how it can be justified, let us examine its role in Plato's political thought. Once we recognize Plato's case for regarding explicit knowledge as an inadequate vehicle for formulating and communicating knowledge and truth, new light is cast on the issue of totalitarianism in the *Republic*. The ostensibly most odious totalitarian feature of the *Republic*—the medicinal lies—are not a deliberate instrumentality of the ruling class to deceive and dominate the lower class of the Republic society. They are, rather, a response to a metaphysical dilemma that affects the philosopher–kings as much as it does the artisans. The irremediable opacity of discourse can be compensated for in the confines of the guardian class by the close bonds that prevail between philosophical masters and philosophical initiates, which enable the initiates to absorb the tacit dimensions of knowledge (communicated in the interstices of conversation) in pauses, silences, omissions, and gestures. Perhaps it is the masses' necessary exclusion from this form of relationship that necessitates resort to medicinal lies.

Various lacunae in the *Republic* also testify to the indispensability of the theorist himself to effect an appropriate translation of theory into practice. The theorist as the living embodiment of tacit knowledge facilitates the smoothest possible transition between theoretical vision and concrete reality. For example, Plato's projection of the Republic society is replete with discussion of mechanisms of perpetuation that will ensure the stability of the class structure. These include eugenics, censorship of literature and the arts, a stratified educational system, and the myth of the metals. Nevertheless, there is only minimal confrontation as an analytically distinct question of how the original division into classes is to be accomplished. Presumably, the judgment and connoisseurship of the theorist would be crucial for yielding a just initial distribution into classes that would then be preserved through the methods Plato so amply describes.

Also, Plato is relatively silent on exigencies arising in the future, primarily disturbances of an international sort. The philosophical sensibility imbued with an awareness of, and responsiveness to, the teachings of tacit knowledge is ideally suited to fill this gap. The philosophical elite that receives training in the processes of tacit knowing (through the cultivation of dialectic) understands how the proximal and distal poles of knowledge stand in a dynamic relation to each other—so that the "distal" crystallization of one moment of action or insight becomes the "proximal," submerged pole sending off cues that help to orient us in a future situation. With their appreciation of the role of tacit knowledge, the philosopher–kings are in an ideal position to respond purposefully to new events if, and when, they arise.

It is possible to interpret the Republic society as being much more participatory than most commentators have hitherto remarked.[25] Plato's denial of given rational essences—his recognition of the assertion of power in the creation of human personality implied by both his Theory of Ideas and his very broad conception of the political discussed earlier—suggests that it is only through doing that we become. First one acts—with others, in the presence of others—and then one is. Participation becomes a major precondition for the formation of human personality. It is not a luxury, but a necessity, if a proper human self is to be formed.

That the self is in many ways a creation, a posit, means that a self that does not actively participate with others regarding matters of common concern is a literally impoverished and stunted self. In the process of self-creation (the only true conception of the formation of the self), large-scale interaction with others enables one to flex and extend one's sense of self—to fashion a sense of personal identity that is at once resilient, imaginative, and reliable. One might say that according to Plato we are rescued from inconsequence by constant interaction with others, which provides us with a common framework by which to test capabilities and ambitions. An isolated self is a self in the process of endless becoming because there is no external mooring in terms of which it can be, instead of incessantly become.

Participation with others regarding matters of common concern can be seen as an important feature of Plato's *Republic*. It is not just the ruling philosophical elite who are required to participate with each other in deliberation concerning public matters, and then to do the actual governing in the light of their deliberations.[26] The rigid class hierarchy in the *Republic* (the fashioning of separate living arrangements and life-styles for the guardians and auxiliaries on the one hand and the artisans on the other, with minimal circulation of personnel and ideas taking place between the classes) means that, in effect, Platonic society is composed of at least two separate, relatively self-contained minisocieties,[27] with participation being a major societal good at each level.

Platonic society appears as a tightly coordinated, cohesive unit only when viewed from the outside. Perceived internally, from the point of view of the members of such a society, what must seem of overriding importance is the insulated and disjointed nature of class relationships that only come together for purposes of presenting a united front, and then slip into mutual metaphysical nonrecognition pacts. Plato recognizes how in his ideal state the structure of disjointedness is working against the ideology of cohesiveness and unity and attempts to resolve this tension through the perpetration of the myth of the metals. The very fact that Plato has to resort to this myth suggests that there are other features about this society undermining his professed ideals of unity and class integration.

The very insulated and disjointed nature of the class structure suggests that within the confines of their own classes individuals will be thrown on each other to achieve whatever degree of social expressiveness and interaction they can muster. But "participation" is not just an adventitious sociological consequence flowing from Plato's structuring of his various classes. Participation at the organizational level of the class constitutes an integral part of Plato's design for his just society. Plato accepts Thrasymachus's challenge of showing the good of justice—how justice is an instrumental, as well as an intrinsic, good. The good of justice is happiness, which Plato defines in much more long-range terms than Thrasymachus. Happiness for Plato consists in the abolition of the tension between ambition and ability, where each person is doing that for which he is ideally suited, tapping internal stores of energy that are most truly expressive of the self. The abolition of this tension, the achievement of happiness, means discovering that optimal structuring of self that would make possible the release of a person's deepest drives and energies. Since the activity of structuring a self involves a residual element of arbitrariness that can never be totally factored out, the process of discovering the optimal structuring of a self involves participation with others for purposes of fashioning and perfecting one's own sense of being. The artisans and warriors in their way, just like the intellectuals at the top, are provided by Plato with an ideal class context to participate with others for purposes of mutual self-discovery and reinforcement of their most creative selves.

From the perspective that I am advancing here, Plato's understanding of how selves get formed remains continuous throughout the *Republic*. Participation forms as much a need of the auxiliary and artisan classes as it does of the guardian class. Their fixed structuring is only evident to the philosopher–shaper from the outside. From within each class, the specific structures of being defining each class[28] have to be arduously appropriated by each member of that class.

To the extent that one wants to say that Platonic teaching is being communicated through the medium of the dramatic clashes taking place within the dialogue rather than being directly identifiable with any particular position espoused by any one participant, the role of tacit knowledge becomes even more manifest. If Plato's message is to some extent a function of his medium, the dialogue form is uniquely structured to provide the reader with a shifting array of proximal and distal poles that yield unsuspected ironies and disclosures. If the dialogue form is meant to highlight the extent to which Socrates and Thrasymachus are both right in their approaches to justice—with, in each case, Thrasymachus's position serving as a proximal pole in order to be better able to appreciate the justice of Socrates' position, and Socrates' position serving as a proximal pole to be better able to elicit the appropriateness of Thrasymachus's position—then one could say that Socrates provides us with the ur-agent's perspective on justice and Thrasymachus gives us the ur-spectator's perspective on justice. To be an agent, an actor, in the world means that regardless of one's personal temperament and predilections one is engaging in activities that carry the implication that it is possible to change things for the better. To inhabit the role of actor means to deploy a set of assumptions and prospects that focus on the possibility of human improvement. Socrates, then, provides us with a delineation of justice from the perspective of an agent—and what the formal properties of the role of an agent are.

Thrasymachus, by contrast, defines for us what it means to be a spectator concerning justice. To be a spectator means to adopt a deflationary perspective toward the phenomena one is observing. It is to discount the pretensions and the self-characterizations of the actors one is studying, and to invoke more realistic standards of assessment than actors are prone to mobilize in their own behalf.

To be fully human means that one perennially has to shift from being an agent to being a spectator, and back again. People learn to cultivate the spectator stance not only in relation to other people's performances, but concerning their own actions as well. The full Platonic teaching, therefore, is addressed to instructing us how to play both roles. A just life and a just society consist in the formation of individuals who can absorb the transitional tensions involved in shifting from one role to the other.

Adopting the perspective of tacit knowledge—that a proximal pole is necessary to generate and justify knowledge—reveals an unexpected irony in the structuring of Plato's argument. If one juxtaposes

Plato's attack against the poets with his endorsement of the theoretical vocation (and uses the latter as a "proximal" pole from which to launch a deeper reading of the former) a more democratic gloss emerges upon Plato's political theory. There is an ambiguity surrounding Plato's ultimate commitment. Is it to theorizing—the pursuit of interconnections as an activity—which is literally endless, all resting places being merely temporary and provisional in character, a result of flagging energies, or is Plato's ultimate commitment to a specific content yielded by theoretical activity, that is, the substantive theory of justice outlined in the pages of the *Republic*? Plato's anathema against the poets suggests that the former is the case. In many key respects, poetry, and artistic creation generally, resemble theoretical activity in that they each involve the pursuit of interconnections. A major difference between theoretical activity and artistic endeavor is the degree of self-consciousness evinced at each stage in the fashioning of the final product—philosophical argument and work of art. The appeal at all stages in the elaboration of a philosophical argument is to neutral, impersonal criteria of inference and judgment, whereas in artistic activity the connections are mainly drawn intuitively and unconsciously.

However, as we have seen, Plato would acknowledge that the rules in accordance with which transitions in argument are negotiated in philosophy are not ironclad, but are, to some extent, fluid and discretionary in character. Theories are underdetermined by facts, so that logical connectives between different layers of theoretical statement as well as the pattern of inference leading from a certain structuring of the facts to a particular articulation of theory are all equally underdetermined by facts.

The juxtaposing of the lauding of theoretical activity with the castigating of the work of the poets, therefore, tells us that there might not be something genuine in the offensive against the poets. Theory as intellectual product that issues forth in a close monitoring of the poets might not represent a settled Platonic conviction, but is inserted for more exigent reasons relating to the particular sensibilities of Plato's immediate audience. The defense of the philosophical vocation might be intended to contain and drastically limit the implications of Plato's attack against the poets. The tacit knowledge present in the interstices of the argument of the *Republic* itself might subvert a literal reading of it.[29]

The Allegory of the Cave captures most fully the relationship between philosophy and tacit knowledge and the democratic political implications that follow from that relationship. If the pursuit of philosophical reasoning eventuates in an enhanced appreciation of the role of tacit knowledge, then philosophical reasoning itself ends up in a movement of recoil rejecting philosophy and recommending the sphere of action as the appropriate arena for the mobilization and investment of human energies. If pushing philosophical argument to its furthest possible reaches leads to a recognition of how limited, submerged, and contextual the bases of justification are, then the Allegory of the Cave suggests that Plato might be willing to take the additional step of declaring that the realm of philosophy itself, by probing human limits, ends up experiencing their impact more fully than nonphilosophical domains of inquiry and can therefore paradoxically point to the realm of action as the most appropriate setting for the deployment of human energies. Almost after the manner of Santayana,[30] one could say that the Allegory of the Cave captures Plato's sense of why, on philosophical grounds, it is misguided to be a philosopher. The philosopher returns to the realm of shadows, to the cave, not just because he seeks to be a public benefactor or because he declines to be ruled by someone inferior to himself, but also and most importantly because the return is a central part of the message of his communion with the blazing sun—the realm of Ideas, and, especially, the highest Idea, the Form of Goodness. The ethical implications of remaining permanently open to new possibilities and never losing sight of the provisional character of justification (the conceptual core of tacit knowledge) propel one in the direction of practice, and more specifically in the direction of democratic practice, where the openness and the provisionalness can become institutionalized and be transmitted as a cultural inheritance. A reading of the Allegory of the Cave in the context of Plato's skeptical tenets and his arguments in favor of tacit knowledge leads to a dual displacement, a dual subversion, in Plato's political thought: Practice replaces theoretical exploration as the highest form of human life, and democratic political institutions replace authoritarian ones as the richest exemplification of a life of practice.[31]

Taking the dialogue form of the *Republic* seriously as a communicator of meaning—and reading the work in a skeptical, democratic, participatory light—suggests further ironic possibilities in juxtaposing Socrates with Thrasymachus. Thrasymachus's enterprise appears radically self-defeating. By postulating a pragmatic, rather than a cognitive, foundation for justice, does it not make the most sense to promulgate natural-law absolutes within one's society, and for people collectively to act as if they were true? Does this not redound the most to everyone's benefit in the long run? Does it not lead to the least exploitation, the least "injustice" by a common, intuitively accepted standard? So might not one say that if Thrasymachus is right about the pragmatic foundation of justice, then he is wrong in his conclusion? Might it not be the case, therefore, that Plato, the philosopher, on the surface arguing against skepticism, is philosophically wrong but pragmatically right, while Thrasymachus, the pragmatist, scornful of the claims of philosophy, is philosophically right but pragmatically wrong? Each protagonist in the dialogue would then be right in the area that matters least to him. This very formulation, if it seems at all correct, would provide a vindication of tacit knowledge. The concept of tacit knowledge reminds us that the ironic shadow cast by a particular statement, which reflects the sense in which the statement remains connected with the "proximal" pole of discourse, might be more "true" than a literal construal of the statement itself.

Tacit knowledge makes its presence felt most palpably in the *Phaedrus*, which can be read as an attempt to delineate the relationship between love and discourse. On the surface, the dialogue appears to be split down the middle. Socrates' First Speech, which occupies a central place in the dialogue, is concerned with the nature of love; his Second Speech, until the end of the dialogue, addresses the nature of discourse. Does the *Phaedrus* then really consist of two semi-independent halves, the first devoted to the nature of love and the second concerned with the nature of true discourse? Or is there an underlying connection between the two portions of the dialogue? What is the relationship between love and discourse?

The connection between the two halves of the dialogue might be formulated as follows: The only rationally defensible mode of communication, dialectic—which attempts to institutionalize the teachings of tacit knowledge by never allowing us to lose sight of the proximal pole of discourse, so that we constantly attempt to bring to the forefront of consciousness matters relating to such issues as the translation of theory into practice, of appropriateness generally, the hidden premises and assumptions of the statements that we make, and the suppressed implications to which they lead—is also the only mode of communication possible between lovers. In fact, it is only this type of communication that establishes love as a possible form of human relationship. Ordinary discourse in all its forms, written or spoken, descriptive or hortatory, is manipulative, and subversive of the possibility of love. Only dialectic is tentative and exploratory, and capable of addressing and accommodating the other person as an end and not merely as a means. The person who communicates with himself/herself dialectically, who is a pursuer of truth and wisdom in the Socratic sense, can broaden the circle of conversation to include another human being without either sacrificing the integrity of the self or the dignity of the other.

The reversal of roles between lover and nonlover in Socrates' two speeches underscores the relationship between love and discourse. In his First Speech, Socrates equates love with domination: "So the lover will not willingly endure to have his beloved stronger or an equal but will continually strive to make him weaker or inferior."[32] The appropriate type of person to whom the beloved should have surrendered, therefore, is the non-lover, rather than the lover: "He [the beloved] should not in the first place have yielded to a lover, to a man necessarily out of his mind; a non-lover, a man perfectly in his senses, is what it should have been."[33] In his Second Speech, Socrates redefines the lover, so that he assumes many of the personality characteristics of the nonlover in the First Speech: "He [the true lover] gazes upward as though he were a bird and cares nothing for what is here below, so that he is accused of being mad. I have shown that this, of all forms of divine possession, is the best and has the highest origin, both for him that has it and for him who shares in it; and that the man who partakes

of this madness and loves beauty is called a lover."[34] This true madness can be cultivated only by the philosopher: "For to be a man one
must understand the content of a general term, leaving the field of
manifold sense-perceptions, and entering that in which the object of
knowledge is unique and grasped only by reasoning. This process is a
remembering of what our soul once saw as it made its journey with a
god, looking down upon what we now assert to be real and gazing
upwards at what is Reality itself. This is clearly the reason why it is
right for only the philosopher's mind to have wings; for he remains
always, so far as he can, through memory in the field of precisely those
entities in whose presence, as though he were a god, he is himself
divine. And if a man makes a right use of such entities as memoranda,
always being perfectly initiated into perfect mysteries, he alone becomes truly perfected. He separates himself from the busy interests of
man and approaches the divine. He is rebuked by the vulgar as insane,
for they cannot know that he is possessed by divinity."[35]

The true lover in Socrates' Second Speech is the philosopher,
hungering for communion with an eternal realm of Ideas. All other
forms of madness, including the ordinary state of being in love, are
pale copies of this highest form of madness. They are in a sense
substitutes for the all-encompassing intellectual experience that we
crave. Plato's nonlover of the First Speech, immersed in his own
special otherworldly concerns, has now been redescribed as the highest form of lover. It is precisely at this point that the transition is
negotiated between the focusing on love in the first half of the dialogue and the concentrating on discourse in the second. The intellectual protocols imbued with an awareness of the tacit dimension of
knowledge that facilitate engagement in dialectical discourse also
create the possibility of love. Only someone for whom words are as
much an instrument of self-awareness as they are of communication
with others and mastery can achieve a nonmanipulative relation with
the other. The tact and restraint of Plato's philosophically mad lover
promote the achievement of true love.

Part of Plato's criticism of the Sophists in the *Phaedrus* is that they
elevate what Plato also takes to be the descriptive condition of most
discourse as manipulative into a normative status as well, a limit that

discourse cannot transcend. This overlooks the possibility of tacit knowing—and of how a reading out of the intimations of this process creates the intellectual infrastructure for dialectical thought and speech. "In his lover," Plato says, the lover "beholds himself as in a mirror."[36] Given the reversal evinced by Socrates' Second Speech, we can say that the mirror image returned to the lover is that of a coordinate center of freedom, confronting its beloved in its aspect of freedom. The shock of recognition comes when it is *two* human beings who are engaged in the perpetual task of taking risks and taking flight that constitute the Socratic art of dialectic.

Participation and Tacit Knowledge in Machiavelli

The Prince of Machiavelli can be viewed as the enactment of a "revisionary ratio" on Plato's political philosophy.[37] Machiavelli's innovative twist on Plato's political theory consists in proposing the notion that it is not merely something as subjective and variable as a particular intellectual sensibility—the philosophical—that displays a radical openness toward the future. There is a whole sphere of activity, a unique form of life, that betrays a comparable openness, namely, the political. One can read *The Prince* as an announcement and elaboration of this theme. The opening wedge facilitating Machiavelli's political theorizing in relation to his awesome predecessor, Plato, might be his insight into how a whole objectified form of activity substitutes for the cultivation of a particular personality type in Plato. In what follows I would like to illustrate how tacit knowledge is exemplified in Machiavelli's political thought on three different levels: overt text; structure and tenor of political teaching; and presuppositions of argument. I shall address each of these areas in turn.

Overt Text

Two significant references to tacit knowledge are contained in the Letter of Dedication to *The Prince*. The first is that in addressing

Lorenzo de' Medici, Machiavelli says, "Now, I am anxious to offer myself to Your Magnificence with some token of my devotion to you."[38] While this elaborate circumlocution is intended to convey subservience, the pointed insertion of "to offer myself" at the beginning of the sentence might be taken as a subtle reminder to Lorenzo that however wonderful the "little book" is that Machiavelli is presenting to him it constitutes a mere abridgement out of the more profound stores of knowledge and enhanced capacity for nuanced judgments residing in the theorist—Machiavelli—himself. The phrasing in this passage is suggestive of Machiavelli's awareness that all books can be read as "advertisements for myself," and may be intended to nudge Lorenzo into experiencing a comparable insight and acknowledging that the living embodiment of the knowledge only necessarily partially reflected in *The Prince* is found in Machiavelli himself.

A second ramification of tacit knowledge is contained in Machiavelli's characterization of his audience. Machiavelli continues to address Lorenzo in the Letter of Dedication by stating, "And although I consider this work unworthy to be put before you, yet I am fully confident that you will be kind enough to accept it, seeing that I could not give you a more valuable gift than the means of being able in a very short space of time to grasp all that I, over so many years and with so much affliction and peril, have learned and understood."[39] Machiavelli here designates his audience as consisting of political upstarts, individuals who have very limited resources under all the traditional headings of political leadership—and who are unlimited only in the political ambitions they harbor. Machiavelli is confronting a generation of political actor that is trying to do everything on a shoestring. They are short of knowledge, learning, experience, money, influence, inherited wealth and status, and time—during which to attempt to compensate for all the other deficiencies. Given this delineation of his audience, Machiavelli obviously does not expect to enable them to overcome all these drawbacks through the precepts contained in one short book. For one thing (as we will see shortly) Machiavelli is aware of the paradox that one can communicate knowledge and wisdom only to the already knowing and wise. For another, the debilitating circumstances are so multiple and mutually reinforcing that Machia-

85

velli's advice, however practically formulated, is bound to appear abstract and ethereal to these political actors. Machiavelli is therefore relying on tacit knowledge (and primarily its incarnation in the theorist himself) to provide the needed context for application, which he stresses is absent in members of the audience themselves.

A third area in the text where tacit knowledge is being assumed are the numerous places where Machiavelli surrounds his practical advice with qualifying phrases, adjectives, and adverbs. The following is a detailed, but by no means exhaustive, list of examples (emphasis added throughout):

"Far fewer difficulties" (p. 33)

"It is reasonable that . . ." (p. 34)

"Disorders arise *chiefly* because . . ." (p. 34)

"They are not lost *so* easily" (p. 35)

"One of the best, most effective expedients . . ." (p. 36)

"From this we can deduce a general rule, which never or *rarely* fails to apply." (p. 44)

"A man who becomes prince with the help of the nobles finds it *more* difficult . . ." (p. 67)

"The people are *more* honest in their intentions . . ." (p. 68)

"The most that *can* happen to a prince . . ." (p. 68)

"There is another consideration rightly to be borne in mind . . ." (p. 71)

"But few rulers have the ability to do so" (p. 86)

"This is because taking everything into account . . ." (p. 92)

"Therefore one must be a fox in order to recognize traps and a lion to frighten off wolves." (p. 99)

"So it follows that a prudent ruler cannot and should not honor his word when it places him at a disadvantage and when the reasons for which he made his promise no longer exist." (pp. 99–100)

"You must realize this: that a prince, and especially a new prince, cannot observe . . ." (p. 101)

"One of the most powerful safeguards a prince can have against conspiracies . . ." (p. 103)

"From this can be drawn another noteworthy consideration:" (p. 106)

"A prince who wants to maintain his rule is *often* forced not to be good" (p. 108)

"On the other hand, there is less need for a prince to be afraid" (p. 111)

"It is impossible to give a final verdict on any of these policies, unless one examines the particular circumstances of the states in which such decisions have had to be taken. Nonetheless, I shall as far as possible discuss the matter in generalizations." (p. 114)

"It will be found that a prince *far more easily* wins the friendship . . ." (p. 118)

"So then as before *it would have been safer* for her to have avoided the enmity of the people than to have had fortresses." (p. 119)

"So, *all things considered*, I commend those who erect fortresses and those who do not." (p. 119)

"And yet everyone, for all *this diversity of method*, can reach his objective." (p. 131)

This proliferation of qualifying terms and phrases registers Machiavelli's awareness of an unbridgeable gap between theory and practice that can never be entirely closed from the side of theory—by further theoretical refinement and specification. It is only by acknowledgment of a tacit dimension to knowledge, the recognition of proximal poles that facilitate distal crystallizations in action, that we can render the processes of rational action and decision making intelligible.

A fourth example of the animating presence of tacit knowledge on the level of overt textual argument in *The Prince* is found in the chapters where Machiavelli examines how a prince should relate to his personal staff and how he must shun flatterers.[40]

Here is an infallible rule: a prince who is not himself wise cannot be well advised. . . . But when seeking advice of more than one person a prince who is not himself wise will never get unanimity in his councils or be able to reconcile their views. Each councillor will consult his own interests, and the prince will not know how to correct or understand them. Things cannot be otherwise, since men will always do badly by you unless they are forced to be virtuous. So the conclusion is that good advice, whomever it comes from, depends on the shrewdness of the prince who seeks it, and not the shrewdness of the prince on good advice.[41]

There is an irredeemable circularity attached to the concept of receiving good advice that can only be abrogated by acknowledging a tacit dimension to knowledge, which enables us to exercise a connoisseurship over areas of knowledge and regions of experience to which we have not been previously exposed. By a proper "feel" for how what we already know might be extended (and might be managed to lead to favorable consequences in the future, which is achieved by building up within ourselves a "proximal" pole of knowledge, consisting of these unconscious extensions and extrapolations), we can break out of the apparently vicious circularity that in order to know we must already know, in order to receive good advice we must already be wise.

Structure and Tenor of Political Teaching

Machiavelli's concrete political advice throughout *The Prince* is structured after the manner of tacit knowledge. He wants his political actor constantly to discern the signals of his environment in such a way as to be poised on the brink of successful action. The content of appropriately aimed and planned action cannot be legislated in advance. It is not just that the nuances of possible action as perceived by an actor in the throes of decision making transcend even the most refined and sophisticated theorizing. An additional factor that explains why Machiavelli's political advice never aspires to a higher epistemological status than what Michael Oakeshott has called "safe assumptions"[42] is that the intellectual bases for knowledge and for action remain partially submerged, constituting what Polanyi calls "proximal" poles, so that what is known and acted upon becomes more fully disclosed to the actor only in the moment of action itself. Some of the major guidelines Machiavelli sets for his political actors represent an attempt at self-conscious distillation of the teachings that the structuring of the field of action in accordance with the principles of tacit knowledge yields. If "distal" crystallization in thought and action always emerges out of never fully severed dialectical interaction with partially inchoate "proximal" poles of awareness, then a premium is placed on acting (doing) as a tool of knowledge and expanded awareness. Therefore, the overall orientations of the political actor should be controlled by the notions that "existence precedes essence,"[43] and that will is primary over intellect. The following are seven examples from Machiavelli's text of political advice manifesting these larger principles:

1. In chapter six, which deals with Machiavelli's central theme of "new principalities acquired by one's own arms and prowess," Machiavelli says that "a prudent man should always follow in the footsteps of great men and imitate those who have been outstanding. If his own prowess fails to compare with theirs, at least it has an air of greatness about it. He should behave like those archers who, if they are skilled, when the target seems too distant, know the capabilities of their bow and aim a good deal higher than their objective, not in order to shoot so high but so that by aiming high they can reach the target."[44] Machiavelli is here recommending a conscious strategy of overreaching— doing, for the sake of learning what one can do—as an appropriate course of conduct for the political actor to follow. By self-consciously imitating great men, one gradually gains access to the series of "proximal" cues and promptings that facilitate heroic action, and, in the course of time, one might also become capable of great deeds.[45]

2. As a way of ensuring reliable responses from one's subjects in times of crisis, Machiavelli recommends that the prince accustom his subjects to doing things for him, rather than conferring undue benefits upon them. "The nature of man is such that people consider themselves put under an obligation as much by the benefits they confer as by those they receive."[46] Since the character of an action remains fluid until the moment of doing, setting in motion a whole train of people's doing for you will more reliably orient them in a moment of crisis than counting upon their properly appreciating and interpreting the bursts of generosity that you have displayed toward them.

3. Machiavelli advocates constant military exercises—"So he [the prince] should never let his thoughts stray from military exercises, which he should pursue more vigorously in peace than in war"[47]—not because he is a militarist, but because of the political repercussions upon individual political actors of military training. The vigilance that sustained military exercises evokes nurtures a readiness to act and a responsiveness to even relatively remote cues and signals that facilitate ultimate political success.

4. In the concluding paragraph in the chapter on the role of Fortuna in human affairs a similar emphasis on doing is expressed: "I hold strongly to this: that it is better to be impetuous than circumspect; because fortune is a woman and if she is to be submissive it is necessary to beat and coerce her. Experience shows that she is more often subdued by men who do this than by those who act coldly. Always, being a woman, she favours young men, because they are less circumspect, and more ardent, and because they command her with greater audacity."[48] There is a premium on simply acting rather than remaining passive because even though the larger constellation of historical forces—the "geological factors in politics," the secular trends—are elements over which we exercise no immediate control, every "distal" crystallization in action contributes toward the shaping of new "proximal" poles that influence the articulation of further action. Acting in the present helps to create new fields of action in the future, leading to a redesigning of new limits for oneself and for others.

5. The delineation of political decision making as the choice of the lesser evil ("Thus no government should ever imagine that it can adopt a safe course of action; rather, it should regard all possible courses of action as risky. This is the way things are: whenever one tries to escape one danger one runs into another. Prudence consists in being able to assess the nature of a particular threat and in accepting the lesser evil")[49] suggests that the embeddedness and invisibility of huge chunks of the field of action disbar us from ever choosing decisive good over decisive evil. If action is as much constitutive of knowledge as it is based on knowledge, then the values to be assigned to action remain permanently fluid, always subject to the meaning-conferring effects of later actions. We must, therefore, learn how to

make judgments in a world where judgments are continually being revised in the light of later actions and later judgments. Acclimating oneself to making judgments on the wing forms an essential precondition for effective political action.

6. Machiavelli's delineation of two systems of morality—public and private, which can never be totally coordinated with each other, aside from the literal implications of the doctrine that I will consider shortly—can also be read as a metaphoric expression of an insurmountable tension between proximal and distal poles of knowledge. The unbridgeable distance between public and private morality is suggestive of the preordained failure of any attempt to rationalize totally the bases of action. To act in the world always means to be working out of an at least partially tacit context that transcends one's previously formulated statements of principle. Only if one interposes a realm of tacit promptings and cues between one's officially adopted principles and the sphere of action does the concept of rational action become intelligible. All of *The Prince* might thus be read as a theoretical defense of tacit knowledge.

7. The complex interweaving of deterministic and indeterministic strands of argument in Machiavelli's thought is modulated by reliance on tacit knowledge. Of the four key terms in Machiavelli's political vocabulary—Fortuna, Necessita, Opportunita, and Vertu—the first two connote determinism and the last two point to a large role carved out for human interventionism in human affairs. The concluding paragraph in the chapter summarizing the career of Cesare Borgia (chapter seven) betrays an almost schizophrenic split between attributing Borgia's ultimate failure to a malicious Fortuna ("his plans were frustrated only because Alexander's life was cut short and because of his own sickness")[50] and accusing him of a lack of political Vertu ("The duke only deserves censure regarding the election of Pope Julius, where he made a bad choice. . . . The duke's choice was a mistaken one; and it was the cause of his ultimate ruin").[51] Finally, in the chapter specifically devoted to the question of how much of human affairs are governed by fortune and how much by indeterministic elements, Machiavelli invokes a contradictory set of metaphors—Fortuna as a raging, overflowing river and Fortuna as a woman that can be beaten and

coerced into submission—and leaves the fundamental issues unresolved.[52]

The nature of tacit knowing provides an important gloss on the issue of determinism versus indeterminism in Machiavelli's thought. Prospectively (before we act), given the at least partially tacit context in which human action proceeds, our very engagement in action presupposes indeterminism. After the action is taken, we are able (from a spectator's perspective) to render more self-conscious the "proximal" pole of action, and are thus able to project mediating causative links that we were oblivious of before. The concept of tacit knowledge thus makes us aware that human life consists of a plurality of irreducible voices or perspectives, which grows out of our futile attempt to render perfectly luminous to consciousness the bases of our actions.

Once we recognize how tacit knowing imbues the very structure and tenor of Machiavelli's political teaching in *The Prince*, we have a revised basis for delineating the intertextual relation between *The Prince* and the *Republic*. One could say that *The Prince* constitutes an extended commentary on Plato's Allegory of the Cave. If the contemplation of the lessons of philosophical reasoning leads to a recoil from philosophy into the realm of action, then a new dignity attaches itself to the political realm as the preeminent sphere of heightened, self-conscious, heroic action. Juxtaposing *The Prince* to the Allegory of the Cave, we could say that Machiavelli sees political activity as the secularization of philosophy. Philosophical inquiry in its most self-conscious moments emphasizes the role of tacit knowledge in accounting for the knowledge claims that we make, but tacit knowledge, as an actual form of knowing, and not just as a philosophical concept, is most fully exemplified in political activity. Tacit knowledge is endemic to the political realm in the senses illustrated by my analyses of Machiavelli's text above. The political, from this perspective, represents the consummation of philosophy.

One could also say that the implicit critique of the *Republic* contained in *The Prince* is that the reified constructs, the ideal projections, found in the *Republic* constitute so many futile attempts to identify a conceptual residue after the relationship between explicit principle and tacit knowledge has been worked out. Since, according to Machiavelli, there is no such remainder, all that is left is what Plato at one point calls "the commonwealth within" that is without walls and without a permanent structure, consisting mainly of an indefatigable openness and a repertoire of assiduously cultivated flexible and adaptive responses.

The approach to *The Prince* that I am emphasizing also helps us to see the extent to which *The Discourses* constitutes a complementary work to it. Instead of there being a problem of two Machiavellis, one who favors principalities in *The Prince* and another who extolls the virtues of republics in *The Discourses*, we are now in a better position to appreciate the extent to which *The Discourses* completes the argument of *The Prince*.[53] *The Prince*, as it were, constitutes an epistemology for which *The Discourses* provides the appropriate political theory. If the bases of political knowledge (as of all other forms of knowledge) are tacit, then it is primarily through participation with others in common political practices that we cultivate and test the ability to discern the "proximal" cues and make the appropriate moves within the political terrain. If these sorts of abilities are refined through experience, then a one-to-one relationship with a teacher who is already adept at political decision making would be insufficient to foster these abilities. A participatory praxis where members of the political society both contribute to and learn from the formation of the political society they mutually create seems like the most appropriate institutionalization of the teachings of tacit knowledge. A republican political setting replicates in institutional form the continuity between making, knowing, learning, and teaching emphasized by tacit knowledge.[54]

Also, the idea of a balancing of opposites emphasized by republican political institutions ("the laws that are favorable to liberty result from the opposition of these parties [the nobles and the people] to each other"[55]—coheres very well with the notion of tacit knowledge as the ultimate basis for our knowledge. The idea of tacit knowledge suggests that for every action undertaken and for every concept held to be true we can never fully explicate and justify by reasoned argument our pursuit of the action or our adoption of the concept. An unbridgeable skepticism underlies all our actions and concepts, and tacit knowledge can be seen as a formalization of the principles of a viable skepticism. Since, on an explicit level, one confronts the problem of formulating skepticism so that it does not become self-refuting, skepticism is encoded in a tacit dimension as a way of circumventing the problem of consistency. The principle of balance central to republican political institutions can from this perspective be viewed as a way of generating a modicum of political certainty out of skepticism. The principle of balance constitutes a mechanical test whereby in the absence of secure knowledge a society can assign relative weights to the claimants appearing before it.[56]

Presuppositions of Argument

An additional perspective to bring to bear on *The Prince*, motivated by an awareness of the large animating presence of tacit knowledge within the work, is to examine *The Prince* itself with its major substantive arguments as a reflection of tacit knowledge. How can one read *The Prince* so that it bespeaks a richer revolutionary import than it openly articulates? What are the submerged "proximal" metaphysical cues that facilitate the "distal" tactical and strategic formulations found in *The Prince*?

1. The structure of Machiavelli's argument in *The Prince* (and to some extent also in *The Discourses*) is predicated on the assumption that reason is subservient to the passions, that the ends of life are dictated by our passions, with reason being limited to finding the most expeditious means for attaining the ends that they dictate. Machiavelli's political discourse seems hypothetical in character. He appears to be telling the new actors on the Italian political scene, "If these are your ends in life (political power, glory, etc.), then these are the safest means toward their attainment." Nowhere in *The Prince* does Machiavelli address the problem of the ends of action themselves. He employs his political argument in the manner of reasoning—taking certain ends for granted and noting certain calculations with regard to them.

2. With regard to the puzzling question of whether Machiavelli's conception of political time is cyclical or linear, one might say in

addition to the approach suggested in the previous section of this chapter that Machiavelli discerns a mode of human existence (with the passions predominating over reason) in which the content of human life gets continually used up as previous exertions of will become actualized. The substance of human life then gets replenished by new assertions of will that in turn get "used up." From the point of view of ancient and medieval conceptions of human nature, which advocated well-defined, universal ends for man, the process appears hopelessly enervating and cyclical. It remained for Hobbes to articulate and rationalize the progressive element inherent in the image of human nature pulsating beneath the surface of Machiavelli's writings. The shadows of older conceptions of human nature are corroded by Hobbes's extremely nominalistic metaphysics, and we are left in Hobbes with an image of perpetual human striving that stretches forward into eternity.

3. A characteristic point of Machiavelli's, reiterated throughout his political writings, a point that is captured in a quotation such as the following from *The Prince*:

> But men are so imprudent that they take up a diet which, as it tastes good to start with, they do not realize is poisonous, a point I made before when talking about wasting fevers.

> The prince who does not detect evils the moment they appear is lacking in true wisdom; but few rulers have the ability to do so. If we consider what was the start of the downfall of the Roman empire, it will be found that it was simply when the Goths started to be hired as mercenaries. To that small beginning can be traced the enervation of the forces of the Roman empire. And the Goths inherited the prowess which the Romans lost.[57]

This characteristic point of Machiavelli's about princes' lack of foresight carries systematic implications for a major theme of ancient and medieval political thought. Both Plato and classical Christian thinkers believed that (at least with regard to a small minority of philosophers or saints) no dichotomy was present between human nature and the requirements of virtuous action. It remained for Machiavelli in the passage cited (and in numerous others like it) to point to an unbridgeable gap between human nature, with its customary inertia and inflex-

95

ibility, and the requirements of successful political action. Machiavelli, confronting only this world and not the next—and considering only mundane affairs and not supramundane realities—had the audacity to issue forth with a blanket indictment of human nature.

4. According to Machiavelli, the asymmetry between a radically deficient human nature and the requirements of politics can be remedied through the interposition of something artificial. The major medium through which this asymmetry can be overcome is the Machiavellian artificial political intelligence codifying the intimations of tacit knowledge manifested throughout *The Prince*. This intelligence is artificial in the sense that through highly self-conscious, sustained effort it is able to mobilize that constant foresight and sensitivity to possible alternatives that even the most active political intelligences merely stumble upon from time to time. Machiavelli's political precepts in *The Prince* constitute so many memos from the arctic zone, where the political temperature is always below freezing, and the mobilization of vigilance is a constant necessity.

A second artificial mechanism prominent in Machiavelli's political teaching is a reliance on fear in establishing political relationships with one's followers.[58] Part of Machiavelli's discrediting of the extremes of love and hatred as dominant emotions regulating one's relationships with one's followers has to do with the uncontrollable, sheerly spontaneous nature of both emotions. Love and hatred simply well up within one. One responds to their promptings or one ignores them, but the emotions themselves are subject to little direct human intervention and control. In contrast to love and hatred, fear is preeminently the artificial, the calculating emotion. Fear is very often ancillary to our reasoning and calculating processes, serving as a goad to those processes and being mobilized by them as a spur to further calculation. Fear arises and can be subdued through calculation. Machiavelli wants relations between the prince and his subjects to be governed by it rather than by the more spontaneous emotions of love and hatred.

There is an important structural affinity between the way social-contract theorists diagnose the human condition and present a remedy for it and the analysis of the human condition and the remedy for it that we have just found in Machiavelli. For social-contract theorists as well, there is an unbridgeable gap between human nature and the requirements of successful political action. Man in the state of nature displays an inordinate selfishness that makes him ill-equipped for any sustained interaction with his fellows. Man's inordinate selfishness itself can be construed as a subcategory of the larger flaw diagnosed by Machiavelli: man's limited flexibility. In the state of nature man does not know how to be selfish in the properly self-correcting way—in order to preserve himself and to maximize his happiness and well-being. The remedy, for social-contract writers (as for Machiavelli), is the interposition of something artificial for man's built-in limitations. For these writers, it is the artificial social contract that enables man to overcome his finite intelligence and capacity for sympathy.[59] The structural model for liberalism's reliance on institutional tinkering to remedy the flaws of human nature is found in Machiavelli.

5. Another important systematic difference between Machiavelli and his predecessors is that in *The Prince* an irremediable breach opens up between appearance and reality. Unlike Greek and Christian thought, where appearance serves as either a reflection of or a gateway to a higher reality, for Machiavelli appearance becomes the sole reality. A familiar passage contains the flavor of what I have in mind:

> I know everyone will agree that it would be most laudable if a prince possessed all the qualities deemed to be good among those I have enumerated. But, human nature being what it is, princes cannot possess those qualities, or rather they cannot always exhibit them. So a prince should be so prudent that he knows how to escape the evil reputation attached to those vices which could lose him his state, and how to avoid those vices which are not so dangerous, if he possibly can; but, if he cannot, he need not worry so much about the latter.[60]

Unlike Greek and Christian thought, where our ordinary sense experiences and our passage through this "vale of tears" point to something beyond themselves, for Machiavelli all connection has been severed between the realm of appearance and any kind of higher reality. In this systematic divergence from his predecessors, there is also manifested a systematic link with his successors in the Western liberal tradition. Machiavelli's assessment of the relationship between appearance and reality prefigures the intellectual reversal accomplished by British empiricism. Instead of sense experience being a pale reflection of a higher reality—as it is in different ways in both Greek and Christian thought—it is itself constitutive of reality. The building blocks in our whole edifice of knowledge and truth are composed ultimately of sense experiences, supplemented by laws of logic and rules of inference.

6. Machiavelli's rehabilitation of the distinction between public and private as a central dichotomy of his political thought represents an important break with Plato and with Christian thought, and forms a major element in the foundations of modern liberalism.[61] Plato throughout the *Republic* works with a conception of politics as an omnipresent human phenomenon, one that is not restricted to what takes place in the public sphere. An analogy between the just soul and the just commonwealth dominates the *Republic*. According to Plato, politics does not arise in a determinate historical and social context as a response to a preexisting situation of conflict between men. Instead, it emerges whenever human beings attain to that degree of self-consciousness that allows them to perceive that acting in recognizably human ways nearly always involves the subordination of certain aspects of self to others. Since the very activity of structuring, divorced from historical or social setting, is regarded as a manifestation of the political—of the exertion of power—politics emerges as a kind of primary datum in human experience, affecting equally the private as well as the public sphere.

To the extent that early Christianity develops beyond a mere eschatology to making certain interim accommodations with the world, it puts forward an ethical position in late antiquity and the early middle ages inspired by the Platonic notion of a seamless web of human exertion of power across all spheres of activity, from the most intensely private to the most ornamentally public. All of these exertions of power are subject to church intervention and regulation.

By contrast, liberal political thought, starting with Hobbes, builds upon and rationalizes a rigid distinction between "public" and "private." According to this view, politics emerges as a kind of second-order human activity, concerned with reconciling competing claims of private interest. Political activity arises only under a determinate set of historical circumstances, where territorial cohesiveness and the extent of interdependence among different segments of a population have become sophisticated enough to warrant the institution of regularized procedures for the containment of conflict. Politics addresses itself initially to procedural questions, staking out certain ground rules for the mitigation of conflict, while leaving untouched the whole range of substantive questions having to do with the inherent justness of the claims clamoring for resolution in the first place.[62] Political activity appears on the human scene to facilitate the pursuit of private interest, not to institute a regime of truth.

Machiavelli points to a systematic connection with his successors—and establishes a systematic break with his predecessors—in the centrality he attaches to the public–private distinction in his many discussions of morality. The following is a characteristic passage:

> And then, he must not flinch from being blamed for vices which are necessary for safeguarding the state. This is because, taking everything into account, he will find that some of the things that appear to be virtues will, if he practises them, ruin him, and some of the things that appear to be wicked will bring him security and prosperity.[63]

There appear to be complex reasons leading Machiavelli to search for a new basis for morality in the public realm. One factor seems to be that referred to in the passage cited. In the private realm, a more straightforward relationship exists between means and ends than is the case in the public realm. One can feel love or kindness toward another human being, and the effects of one's actions toward that person might objectively be described (and experienced by that second person himself) as manifesting love or kindness. Where the welfare of states is involved, and not that of individuals, personal uprightness is no guarantee of a morally praiseworthy result. The causal network in which a particular move by a political actor is set might be so complex that the outcome of action bears only a slight resemblance to the motivation that accompanied it. It is possible to interpret this aspect of Machiavelli's argument after the manner of Sheldon Wolin in *Politics and Vision*[64] as calling attention to the complexity of the means–end relationship in politics.

Another possible way of construing this dimension of Machiavelli's scruples concerning the adequacy of the private moral code[65] in the public sphere is in accordance with Stuart Hampshire's discussion in his essay "Public and Private Morality," where he states that the magnitude of public decision making inevitably gives rise to a wholly different set of considerations as relevant. This is the way Hampshire delineates the Machiavellian transition from private to public morality:

(a) Public policy is a greater thing, as Aristotle remarked, and an agent in the public domain normally has responsibility for greater and more enduring consequences and consequences that change more men's lives.

(b) Violence, and the threat of violence or of force, have always been in prospect in public life and in the execution of public policies. In the normal run of things the moral problems associated with the uses of force, and with war and violence, do not now arise in private life. The occasional use of violence, and the normal uses of force and of threats of force, introduce their own moral conflicts.

(c) In modern politics, and particularly in a democracy, one is reasonably required to protect the interests of those whom one in some sense represents, whether they be one's followers in a party or fellow citizens. There are obligations and duties specifically attached to representative roles.[66]

As a result of all these elements, Hampshire suggests, "Machiavelli implied that morality in politics must be a consequentialist morality, and the 'must' here marks a moral injunction. A fastidiousness about the means employed, appropriate in personal relations, is a moral dereliction in a politician, and the relevant moral criterion for a great national enterprise is lasting success; and success is measured by a historian's yardstick: continuing power, prosperity, high national spirit, a long-lasting dominance of the particular state or nation in the affairs of men."[67]

A third factor influencing Machiavelli's deliberations concerning the content of a public morality is suggested by the following famous passage:

The gulf between how one should live and how one does live is so wide that a man who neglects what is actually done for what should be done learns the way to self-destruction rather than self-preservation. *The fact is that a man who wants to act virtuously in every way necessarily comes to grief among so many who are not virtuous.* Therefore, if a prince wants to maintain his rule he must learn how not to be virtuous, and to make use of this or not according to need.[68]

This passage highlights Machiavelli's discovery of the significance of the social—of the existence of brute, irreducible others—and of the theoretical implications that follow when the dimension of the social is taken seriously. A political theoretical ontology that takes seriously the existence of others has to consider how the motivational calculus of one individual is irretrievably affected by the mere fact that motivational calculations are undertaken in the context of a mass of other people engaging in similar calculations. What this leads to, according to Machiavelli, is the need to pitch the code of public morality to the lowest common denominator of public behavior, as a defensive reaction against the unfairly aggrandizing impulses of others. To take the existence of multiple others seriously means, according to Machiavelli, that one has ultimately to revise the set of moral precepts appropriate for the public sphere.[69]

One might raise at this juncture the question of whether indeed Machiavelli's code of public morality is a bona fide moral code, or whether it is simply a whitewash for whatever courses of action statesmen choose to undertake. It seems to me that a persuasive answer to this question comes from Machiavelli's discussion of the career of Agathocles the Sicilian, where we not only discover that Machiavelli's code of public morality is a genuine moral code but what its foundational principle is. Here is Machiavelli on Agathocles:

> Agathocles, the Sicilian, not only from the status of a private citizen but from the lowest, most abject condition of life, rose to become king of Syracuse. At every stage of his career this man, the son of a potter, behaved like a criminal; nonetheless he accompanied his crimes with so much audacity and physical courage that when he joined the militia he rose through the ranks to become its commander. After he had been appointed to this position, he determined to make himself prince and to possess by force and without obligation to others what had been voluntarily conceded to him. He reached an understanding about this ambition

of his with Hamilcar the Carthaginian, who was campaigning with his armies in Sicily. Then one morning he assembled the people and Senate of Syracuse, as if he meant to raise matters which affected the republic; and at a prearranged signal he had all the senators, along with the richest citizens, killed by his soldiers; and when they were dead he seized and held the government of that city, without encountering any other internal opposition. Although he was twice routed and even besieged by the Carthaginians, not only did he successfully defend the city, but leaving some of his troops to defend it, he invaded Africa with the rest, and in a short time lifted the siege and reduced the Carthaginians to severe straits. They were compelled to make a pact with him, contenting themselves with the possession of Africa and leaving Sicily to Agathocles. So whoever studies that man's actions will discover little or nothing that can be attributed to fortune, inasmuch as he rose through the ranks of the militia, as I said, and his progress was attended by countless difficulties and dangers; that was how he won his principality, and he maintained his position with many audacious and dangerous enterprises. Yet it cannot be called prowess to kill fellow citizens, to betray friends, to be treacherous, pitiless, irreligious. These ways can win a prince power but not glory. One can draw attention to the prowess of Agathocles in confronting and surviving danger, and his courageous spirit in enduring and overcoming adversity, and it appears that he should not be judged inferior to any eminent commander; nonetheless, his brutal cruelty and inhumanity, his countless crimes, forbid his being honoured among eminent men. One cannot attribute to fortune or prowess what was accomplished by him without the help of either.[70]

In order for a code of public morality to be a genuine one and not merely a whitewash, there have to be some actions within it that are forbidden on moral, and not merely prudential, grounds. Some courses of action have to be ruled out not just because they lead to undesirable consequences, but because they are intrinsically wrong. The passage cited suggests that for Machiavelli the code of public morality contains at least one precept that can be characterized in this way, and this precept appears so important to Machiavelli that one might want to designate it the foundational principle of public morality. What evokes Machiavelli's most bitter denunciation of Agathocles is not his resort to killing, but to *excessive* killing. It is not that Agathocles killed others in order to arrive at his position of preeminence that irks Machiavelli, but that he killed more people than he strictly had to in order to achieve this result. It is the violation of a principle of economy—of not tailoring means to make them exactly commensurate with ends—that arouses Machiavelli's moral ire. One might say therefore that according to Machiavelli wherever the principle of economy is violated, this not only constitutes an imprudent act, but an immoral one as well. It is wrong in its own right—and not just for the untoward consequences it might bring. The principle of economy would appear to be the foundational principle in the public realm that corresponds to the Golden Rule in the private realm.

The distinction between public and private thus appears to be central to Machiavelli's political teaching—establishing a clear break with Plato and the Christian past and foreshadowing a significant connection with the liberal future. In fact there is one passage in *The Prince* that moves beyond an application of the public–private distinction in the moral sphere to an invocation of that distinction in a way that straightforwardly resembles its employment by the social-contract writers.

> A prince should also show his esteem for talent, actively encouraging able men, and paying honour to eminent craftsmen. So he should encourage his citizens, enabling them to go peaceably about their business, whether it be trade or agriculture or any other profession. One man should not be afraid of improving his possessions, lest they be taken away from him, or another deterred by high taxes from starting a new business. Rather, the prince should be ready to reward men who want to do these things and those who endeavour in any way to increase the prosperity of their city or their state.[71]

Participation and Tacit Knowledge in Hobbes

The Status of Hobbes's First Principles

Hobbes is confronted with a dilemma in his adaptation of what he takes to be scientific method to politics. One of the two dominant scientific methods Hobbes follows in his pursuit of a scientific approach to political questions is a deductive, geometric method that involves working out the implications and interconnections of his basic axioms.[72] However, the status of these basic axioms themselves is not resolved by geometric method. Hobbes is therefore faced with the problem of justifying his basic axioms and proving them worthy of the privileged epistemological status they enjoy within his system.

There are at least two references in *Leviathan* that can be construed as responses to this basic question. One occurs toward the end of the Introduction: "He that is to govern a whole nation, must read in himself, not this or that particular man; but mankind: which though it be hard to do, harder than to learn any language or science; yet when I shall have set down my own reading orderly, and perspicuously, the pains left another, will be only to consider, if he also find not the same in himself. For this kind of doctrine admitteth no other demonstration."[73] Another possible attempt at resolution of the basic question concerning the status of the initial axioms of *Leviathan* can be found in Hobbes's discussion of the role of universities: "For seeing the Universities are the fountains of civil and moral doctrine, from where the preachers, and the gentry, drawing such water as they find, use to sprinkle the same (both from the pulpit and in their conversation), upon the people, there ought certainly to be great care taken, to have it pure, both from the venom of heathen politicians, and the incantation of deceiving spirits. And by that means the most men, knowing their duties, will be the less subject to serve the ambition of a few discontented persons, in their purposes against the state; and be the less grieved with the contributions necessary for their peace, and defence; and the governors themselves have the less cause, to maintain at the common charge any greater army, than is necessary to make good the public liberty, against the invasions and encroachments of foreign enemies."[74]

First principles in a deductively formulated political theory appear on the verge of being impaled on the horns of a dilemma. If these first principles are acknowledged as intuitively self-evident by the members of the theorist's society, then the deductive method was unnecessary; if there is disagreement concerning first principles and coercion is necessary to ensure their dissemination and acceptance, then the deductive approach is impossible—it cannot achieve its intended result. However, there is a third possibility, involving tacit knowledge and participation, which renders Hobbes's argument much more coherent.

The office of the sovereign representative, according to Hobbes, can be rationally reconstructed as following upon the consent of the governed. There is a very tight conceptual connection between authority and consent that results from Hobbes's radically nominalistic epistemology and metaphysics. Hobbes says, as we have seen, that "there is nothing in the world universal but names; for the things named are every one of them individual and singular."[75] Two pages later he goes on to add that "truth consisteth in the right ordering of names in our affirmations." The radical nominalism expressed in these passages suggests that for Hobbes what there is depends in a crucial sense on our naming of it. Prior to our naming of things, there exists only an indeterminate flux of experience. There is, strictly speaking, no objective, external world in terms of which individual statements about experience can be either verified or falsified until this "objective world" is constituted by us in acts of speech, of naming.

Hobbes's nominalistic epistemology enables him to achieve two objectives that are fundamental to his political theory: to justify on philosophical grounds the role of the sovereign, without whom no stable patterns of meaning would emerge between men; and to show that since without the creation of sovereign authority no ordered communication between men would be possible, then the basis of sovereign authority is consent. The existence of sovereign authority forms a precondition of our world as we know it, and therefore consent in the formation of sovereignty can be formally, rationally reconstructed.

Hobbes's elucidation of the relationship between authority and consent, showing them to be two sides of the same coin—the idea of consent presupposing the idea of authority, and the most persuasive analysis of "authority" being one that shows it rooted in consent—is a classic instance of Hobbes's resoluto–composite method at work. Once the ostensibly antithetical concepts of "authority" and "consent" are decomposed into their most fundamental elements and reconstituted on their basis, the dialectical relationship between the two concepts is disclosed, and instead of being seen as antagonistic, they are revealed as being almost mutually supportive.

The first principles of *Leviathan* are thus skeptical principles: "There is nothing in the world universal but names; for the things named are every one of them individual and singular"; "Truth consisteth in the right ordering of names in our affirmations." In order for them not to be vulnerable to the charge of self-refutation (What is the status of these first principles themselves? Can they be justified in terms of the reasoned notions they lay down? Can a theory about *all* names in a language itself be justified in terms of that theory? Would this not be to move in a vicious circle?) a strategy must be found to contain the scope of skepticism so that the issue of the self-refuting character of extreme skepticism would not arise. The idea of tacit knowledge, from this perspective, becomes a presupposition of Hobbes's argument in *Leviathan* because it allows him to formulate his first principles in an unproblematic way. "Tacit knowledge" emphasizes that the bases of knowledge and of action are always partial and contextual. The formulation of skeptical first principles themselves constitutes "distal" crystallizations out of the submerged "proximal" moments that delimit their import and convert the "distal crystallizations" into something other than what they appear on the surface. Skeptical premises as "distal" statements rooted in a "proximal" substratum can never be as extreme as they officially "stretch" on the surface. The tacit dimension of knowledge holds their conceptual content in check, and underlines their instrumentalist character as enabling us to do certain things in the world—in Hobbes's case, to justify sovereign political authority.

If Hobbes's political teaching is grounded in tacit knowledge (which, as Polanyi emphasizes, can only be transmitted in a participatory manner, with personal communications networks established between teachers and students)[76] then the import of the passages cited earlier about the role of the universities and the function of the gentry and the clergy in society becomes clearer. Hobbes's political teaching, even though it emphasizes stasis and a formal act of authorization and representation without further periodic checks as being sufficient to preserve the legitimacy of civil society, nevertheless is crucially dependent upon the nurturing and maintenance of extrapolitical participatory frameworks in which the tacit lore sustaining the plausibility of the first principles can be upheld. Students must participate in a learning relationship with teachers in order to absorb the truths of nominalism. When these students, in turn, become the teachers of the masses from the pulpits and in exercising the perquisites of aristocratic landholding, they must suitably tailor the teaching of the inherently limited bases of political justification to the masses so as to evoke a geniune recognition on their part of the legitimacy of the political order currently prevailing.

Hobbes's Metaphysics and Participation

There is a subversive underside to Hobbesian thought that is in tension with the understandings of politics, representation, and the priority assigned to the theory of political obligation over the theory of justice[77] that one finds expressed in his thought. The conception of politics as an external, social phenomenon—the stress laid on mechanisms of representation in both theory and practice—and the priority assigned to the concept of political obligation over justice all lead to a rejection of participation as a principal organizing category for responding to human needs in politics. However, certain key metaphysical elements found in Hobbes's thought point to "participation" as an appropriate complement to the tendencies implicit in these metaphysical ideas. It is to an examination of these tensions that I now turn.

In his demystification of the idea of authority and his rooting it in consent, Hobbes, on one level, accomplishes a reversal in relation to Plato's thought.[78] Instead of having the exercise of political authority depend upon an antecedent cultivation of reason, merging together the vocations of philosopher and king, Hobbes shows that one cannot engage in a reasoning process at all without presupposing sovereign authority that provides us with the stable counters to manipulate in reasoning. Instead of reason serving as the basis for the exercise of political authority, as in Plato, Hobbes shows that reason itself is grounded upon an antecedently created authority.

Hobbes's idea of authority not only has an external reference in terms of justifying his concept of political obligation, but it has an internal reference as well. It provides the missing metaphysical underpinning for his conduct of the activity of political theorizing.

For all of *Leviathan*'s systematic aspirations and achievement, the argument of the book remains strangely silent and incomplete. Plato, at least, refers to a capacity of reason (which he summarizes by the term "dialectic") that can account for the creative, synthesizing activity of mind exhibited in the *Republic*. Hobbes, in his moral psychology, however, traces the origins of our ideas to sense experience, and provides a generally incremental analysis of how our more abstract concepts and thought processes get built up from an original stock of sense data. Hobbes's account of the self makes no allowances for the creative, synthesizing functions of mind manifested in *Leviathan* itself. However, his concept of authority as being antecedent to reasoning does make sense of the theorizing activity found in the book.

Hobbes's rooting of the very possibility of rational argument in the existence of authority—and the resolution of the metatheoretical problem of where the theorizing activity exhibited in *Leviathan* comes from, and how it can be justified—issues forth in the thesis of what I have elsewhere called "power as rationality."[79] If the ultimate foundation for the exercise of human reason rests upon what from an absolutist philosophical perspective can only appear as an arbitrary allocation of words and their significations, then the paradox emerges that instead of "power" and "rationality" being antithetical conceptions, as our conventional discourse would have it, power emerges as the distinct form of human rationality—the very syntax, as it were, through which rationality gets expressed. Hobbes's setting forth of the relationship between reason and political authority leads to an understanding of human nature as being radically discontinuous, with conceptual frameworks employed for interpretation having epistemological priority over the events, ideas, feelings, volitions, and so on, interpreted. "We are what we choose to read ourselves to be" might serve as the motto for the understanding of human nature implicit in Hobbes's theorizing of the foundations of reason. This understanding establishes the basis for a reversal of our ordinary grasp of the nature of power. Instead of power being viewed as an irrationalist intrusion into a rationally connected network of understandings and relationships (the exertion of power as overturning norms of involvement and relationship between individuals and between nations), power is seen from this perspective as a dominant mode for establishing continuity itself. According to this view, it is only through the exertion of power that we have an enduring presence even to ourselves.

The idea of power as the distinct mode of human rationality carries momentous consequences for the theory and practice of political participation. The greatest ontological burden that human beings shoulder according to the subversive underside of Hobbes's thought is that it is power that holds us together, that gives us our recognizable human identity. The only thing that can redeem this insight (and confer a certain amount of grace on human living) is the sharing of this insight with others in participatory frameworks. Participation, as it were, takes the sting out of being human.

The Two Political Epistemologies of Leviathan

There are two political epistemologies in *Leviathan* issuing forth in two models of political action, the aristocratic and the conventional. Participation and tacit knowledge are important in both of them. We have already seen how in his conventional model of political action—where human life is experienced as "a tension between pride and fear; each of these primary passions elucidates the character of the other, and together they define the ambivalent relationship which men enjoy with one another"[80]—participation and tacit knowledge are presupposed in the processes of inculcation of the primary metaphysical norms that render existing political arrangements legitimate and are also insinuated by the subversive underside of Hobbes's thought. The aristocratic political epistemology yields an alternative model of political action, with a suitably differentiated version of participation and tacit knowledge. What is Hobbes's aristocratic political epistemology and where is it to be found?

Such a political epistemology is suggested by his philosophy of religion. Hobbes resolutely defines monotheistic God-talk as being self-referential in character: "For the nature of God is incomprehensible; that is to say, we understand nothing of what he is, but only that he is; and therefore the attributes we give him, are not to tell one another what he is, nor to signify our opinion of his nature, but our desire to honour him with such names as we conceive honourable among ourselves."[81] What motivates this conclusion? Why could he not have said simply that the religious doctrine of monotheism constitutes a denial of the literal ascription of any set of attributes to God— so that all such attributes, omnipotence, omniscience, and benevolence, for example—have to be construed metaphorically? What necessitated Hobbes's taking the additional step of saying that the attribute terms are really disguised self-referential statements, ways of praising God (giving vent to our human need to exalt him and to point to the overwhelming distance separating us from him) couched in the form of descriptions of him?

It seems to me that one factor driving Hobbes to this extreme formulation is a logical perplexity surrounding monotheistic doctrine, which carries important implications for skeptical positions in philosophy generally. To the extent that the attempt is made to have the conceptual core of monotheistic theology—the denial of attributes to God—refer to and in some way delimit our understanding of God himself (and not just, in Hobbesian fashion, amount to a reflexive acknowledgment that the point of such talk is to honor him rather than to say anything meaningful about him) the problem of consistency emerges. The proposition that none of our imputations of particular attributes to God is to be construed literally because of the unbridgeable conceptual distance that separates us from him cannot be consistently formulated without also undermining the possibility of formulating this very sentence itself. If we cannot know, then we also cannot know that we cannot know. How can it be stated in a balanced and coherent philosophical idiom that the concepts of omnipotence, omniscience, and benevolence articulate particular meanings in relation to God, yet fail to apply to *him*? Our denial in the second half of this question disbars us from the degree of knowledge required to secure the first half of the question. I believe that it is the logical dilemma which Hobbes confronts in stating a non-self-refuting version of monotheism that leads him to excise God altogether from the equation and to give us his anthropocentric reading of monotheism. The fate of monotheism in theology thus prefigures (and parallels) the career of skepticism in philosophy.[82]

The self-refuting nature of monotheistic theology—to the extent that its terms are interpreted literally—constitutes the central phase of Hobbes's critique of religion. Yet, in his political philosophy, which is founded in varying ways upon his skeptical epistemology, the consistency and rigor displayed in the philosophy of religion are absent, and the problem of how to accommodate the self-refuting nature of extreme skepticism in his political theorizing is not even confronted.[83] I have already summarized Hobbes's formulation of his nominalism: There is "nothing in the world universal but names; for the things named are every one of them individual and singular. . . . Truth consisteth in the right ordering of names in our affirmations."[84] To the extent that one assigns priority to Hobbes's nominalism over his empiricism ("There is no conception in a man's mind, which hath not at first, totally, or by parts, been begotten by the organs of sense. The rest are derived from the original")[85] so that particular sense impressions exert the constraints that they do upon the body of statements that we regard as correct only within the context of a prior naming process that has led us to "parcel up" the world and identify discrete particulars within it in such a manner that the discrepancies between these sense-data statements and the rest of our statements emerge, Hobbes confronts the problem of consistency. If skepticism is correct, if the "naming process" is all, then how can this idea be regarded as true without it also undermining the possibility of stating this very idea? Aside from the problem of circularity referred to earlier, there is also a straightforward problem of consistency. The statement that a "naming process" is all cannot be justified in its own terms. A central problem then becomes how one can adhere to skepticism and be able to state it as a coherent philosophical notion. The problem concerning skepticism parallels the problem with monotheism. In the latter, the impossibility of formulating the two halves of monotheistic doctrine—that God is wholly other, and that he is omnipotent, omniscient, and benevolent in ways that we cannot conceptually grasp—leads Hobbes to an anthropocentric reformulation of the doctrine so that its referential parameters never extend beyond man; and with regard to skepticism, the analogous dilemma would seem to invite an anthropocentric interpretation. If skepticism seems philosophically inescapable and yet one cannot state a non-self-refuting version of it, the resolution again seems to be not intellectual but some deepening of the humanistic dimension—in this case, an enactment of skepticism through the fostering of participatory structures throughout society.[86]

Hobbes, however, does not follow through in his political philosophy on the same strategy of argument that he exhibits in his philosophy of religion. Hobbes's grappling with the problem of stating a consistent version of skepticism is evidenced by his resorting to the hypothetical construct of a social contract to justify the establishment of civil society. However, as we saw in Chapter Two, the proto-Kantian, transcendentally deductive mode of justification Hobbes pursues in his contractarian theorizing withholds from view the radically egalitarian, participatory implications inherent in his skepticism. Nonetheless, even on this level of political theorizing the structure of tacit knowing is exemplified in Hobbes's thought in the sense that the hypothetical construct of a state of nature constitutes a partially suppressed proximal pole of argument that facilitates the articulation of the distal pole, the social contract, pointing to universal acquiescence to political authority.

What I have presented so far, however, is only one-half of Hobbes's political doctrine. The need for a supplementary half is suggested by those elements of social-contract theory that I have already summarized. The problem here is reminiscent of the problem in Platonic interpretation of closing the gap between the mechanisms of perpetuation of theoretically defined and defended political arrangements and initiating those arrangements themselves. The whole game-theoretic outlook that facilitates the triumph of the institutional status quo over the state of nature and lone defiance[87] presupposes an environment where coordinated social interaction is possible, so that the consequences of deviating from societally approved schemes of preference are palpable to all. However, Hobbes's problem, both historically (in writing during a time when traditional political order had become deranged and some of the competitors for political power relish the need for periodic disorder) and theoretically (in providing a justification for political authority from the ground upward, engaging in an intellectual *creatio ex nihilo* that takes nothing for granted by way of existing arrangements), is also to be able to account plausibly for the *establishment* of his vision of a properly ordered society. In terms of the aspirations of his political theory, it is at least as important for him to provide a satisfactory resolution of the problems of the first generation—of institution—as it is to account for his image of a just society itself, and the mechanisms by which it will be reproduced from generation to generation.

As Michael Oakeshott has pointed out, Hobbes is as much concerned with cultivating a personality type concerned with honor as he is with those devoted to the ends of survival or prosperity.[88] Hobbes says, "That which gives to human actions the relish of justice is a certain nobleness or gallantness of courage, rarely found, by which a man scorns to be beholden for the contentment of his life to fraud, or breach of promise. This justice of the manners, is that which is meant, where justice is called a virtue; and injustice a vice."[89] In the previous chapter, Hobbes refers to two emotions that can counteract the inherent weakness of covenants (that they rely on "the force of words"). The first emotion is fear, "a fear of the consequence of breaking their word." The second emotion is glory, "a glory, or pride in appearing not to need to break it."[90] Hobbes identifies magnanimity with just conduct that springs from "contempt" of injustice, and he recognizes that men are sometimes prepared to lose their lives rather than suffer some sorts of shame.[91] Hobbes also says that "magnanimity is a sign of power."[92]

How does Hobbes account for—rationally reconstruct—the first steps in the transition from a state-of-nature society to a social-contract society? The implicit Hobbesian answer suggested by the quotations above is that some members at least of the original society have to be of a sufficiently magnanimous temperament that they are willing to take unprecedented risks for the benefit of all, even though the mechanisms of mutual calculation and restraint designed to limit the scope of those risks are not yet in place. The mechanism of calculation is institutionalized only when the society of the social contract is established. In accordance with what motivational factors does one break into this circle and begin to act on the basis of the new prudential principles—before the social-contract society is established—as a way of fostering the creation of the new society?

It is at this point that the political epistemology suggested by Hobbes's philosophy of religion comes into play. The fate of monotheism in religion prefigures the fate of skepticism in philosophy. The parallel problems of formulating a consistent version of monotheism and a non-self-refuting version of skepticism lead to a recognition that certain limiting statements in theology and philosophy—statements denoting the reaching of a limit of the rationally expressible—propel one to acknowledge a tacit dimension to knowledge. The dense undercurrent of certain limiting statements that inhibits their future rational unraveling serves as a cue for action-oriented translations of those statements. To use the vocabulary borrowed from Polanyi, these statements serve as heightened "proximal" poles for facilitating new "distal" crystallizations in thought and action. The movement of reflexiveness and recoil that Hobbes evinces in his construal of monotheism—so that the conceptualization of the term has a human center and trajectory—becomes a paradigm of tacit knowledge. The translation of a rationally irresolvable thought statement into a humanly compassable action statement becomes for Hobbes's natural aristocracy the model for the structuring of the field of action generally. To convert the monotheistic thought statement into an action statement with a human center is to generate a series of previously unimagined possibilities concerning the organization of life in this world. The image of tacit knowledge figured in this formulation of Hobbes's political epistemology cues his aristocratic political actors into seeing that all knowledge partakes of an element of risk taking, of gesturing toward the future, by way of both disclosing and imparting a content to that future. The initial steps taken toward the establishment of the social-contract society are strictly continuous with the steps needed to ensure the advancement of knowledge generally.

Participation for Hobbes's political aristocracy—just like participation for Plato's philosopher–kings—is largely a restricted affair, confined to immersion in contemplation in large themes and issues and conversations with a set of like-minded individuals. This sort of restricted participation renders possible political action fashioned in the idiom of truth (that in an unrehearsed, unimpeded search for knowledge and truth we get thrown back on the resources of action, of doing) to break the impasses of knowledge. The daring, innovative action of Hobbes's political aristocrats in dramatizing a new mode of social-contractarian being by way of making its institutionalization palatable is action cast in the idiom of truth. The more literal, communitarian types of participation of the average members of the Leviathan state (attending church in relatively large groups on Sunday, and getting their mores of obedience to state authority reinforced) lead to political actions fashioned in the idiom of approximation—collectively agreeing to inhabit a world—and confer upon it a certain degree of stability, which in its fidelity to the shape and structure of tacit knowledge constitutes a making in the idiom of truth. The tacit knowledge of the political aristocracy enables them to create by taking risks. The tacit knowledge sustained by the extrapolitical participatory outlets of the Leviathan state enables its average members to recognize its arbitrary political structures as a function of the limits to knowledge and to truth pertaining to the human condition generally, and thereby to invoke an ideal human community as the ultimate participatory sanction for the particularistic loyalties these citizens exhibit.

Conclusion: Skepticism, Tacit Knowledge, and Participation

Tacit knowledge offers a most promising solution to the problem of formulating a non-self-refuting version of skepticism. If the arguments in favor of extreme skepticism (such as those adduced earlier in this chapter from Plato) seem convincing, and yet extreme skepticism cannot be stated without also negating itself, then the solution lies, as we have seen in Hobbes, in our acknowledging that we have reached a limit of thought. This means that extreme skepticism has to be seen as a "proximal" pole that enables us to do certain things in the world—such as Hobbes's aristocratic political actors imbibing from it the daring to fashion a new mode of coordinated societal living. Tacit knowledge "dissolves" skepticism as an issue in philosophy because it places it in a context where our paradigms of knowledge are statements that are more "knowing" than anything they can directly justify. Skepticism, too, paradoxically has to be believed before it can be known.

What makes the modern age so resistant to this solution of the problem of skepticism is that its chief characteristic is a proliferation of the phenomenon of self-consciousness. A major difference between antiquity and modernity is the diffusion of the activities and products of elite consciousness, such as Plato's skepticism, among a broad mass of the population, so that what in previous ages constituted a rigid distinction between elite and mass consciousness becomes blurred as modernity advances. It is not the content of speculation and insight (as the remarkable continuity between Plato and Machiavelli and Hobbes demonstrates) that distinguishes the modern age from those that preceded it, but rather the diffusion of speculation and insight among a broad mass of the population.

Incipient self-consciousness makes tacit knowledge appear archaic and obscurantist. And yet an overweening self-consciousness that considers itself part of the solution and refuses to see itself as part of the problem just intensifies the problem. The moral and epistemological conundrums that are generated by a skepticism that continually calls itself into question at the same time that it attacks everything else gives rise to the phenomenon described by Polanyi at the beginning of his book[93] of thought not being able to certify action and of action being disjointed from thought. The distinctive cultural style of modernity is irredeemably schizophrenic—an "extreme critical lucidity" and "an intense moral conscience" that rarely seem to coalesce.

Given the pervasiveness of self-consciousness, whereas previously it was a symbol that might have liberated us, now it appears to be a form of activity. The concept of God as the ground of being serves as an ultimate reminder of the tacit structuring of all knowledge. An unfathomable God (when he is widely accepted) functions as a kind of cosmic "proximal" pole underscoring the partial, limited scope of justification in knowledge and in action. The heightened self-consciousness of modernity, however, seems to place a premium on a form of activity as a fitting restorative mechanism for the modern astigmatism.

Creating more and more societal frameworks where human beings can participate in the decisions that affect their lives presents the most valid promise of wholeness that modernity can offer. Participation helps all to see that in a very real sense it is the future that determines the past—with each contribution by a member of a particular participatory network on either the level of thought or action being held hostage by later developments and later fusions with the thoughts and actions of others.

Also, participation on the specifically political level of decision making (which today includes such historic preserves of private decision making as the workplace) affords human beings access to the only kind of objectivity that they seem capable of attaining. If tacit knowledge teaches us that knowing is inseparable from doing, then the more grandiose the doing, the more secure the knowing. By collectively inhabiting a natural world and deliberately fashioning together social and political ones, we are granted new access to the givens of our lives through the agency of what we collectively create. Political participation in a broad sense makes us more reliable trustees for the human and natural orders—the permanently present and never fully fathomable "proximal" poles that facilitate our "distal" creativeness.

CHAPTER 5

The Role of Tacit Knowledge in the Argument of Federalist Number Ten

The Emergence of "Method"

The nature of the problem that Madison proposes to solve in Federalist Number Ten is posed in the idiom of classical political philosophy. "The instability, injustice, and confusion introduced into the public councils," Madison writes, "have, in truth, been the mortal diseases under which popular governments have everywhere perished, as they continue to be the favorite and fruitful topics from which the adversaries to liberty derive their most specious declamations."[1] Madison thus defines his problem by invoking a cyclical conception of political time. Democratic regimes always have been doomed to political instability by the factious predominance of their public councils, which causes the political pendulum to swing in a completely opposite direction and leads to the establishment of tyranny as the only means for restoring political order.

As the solution to the problem of staving off indefinitely the destabilizing forces of cyclical political time, Madison resorts to a method that he believes has been overlooked by previous political writers and practitioners. The method consists in the forms of institutional manipulation that enable a designer of states to convert a direct democracy into a republican regime, emphasizing the strategic decision-making role played by political representatives and the prospect of a mutual restraining and cancellation process emerging to blunt the force of factious incursion against the public good that a large society characterized by political representation affords.

When viewed phenomenologically, "method" might be described as a means of being able to discover in the homely materials of one's problem a clue to its solution. Without having to import entities from outside the framework of one's problem, one is able to fashion a solution. Hobbes in *Leviathan* can rightfully be regarded as one of the modern progenitors of the idea of the supremacy of method. A delineation of the economy of the human psyche in which the passions predominate over reason can yet be rendered compatible with the achievement of civil peace if the devaluation of reason announced by the doctrine of the paramountcy of the passions issues forth in an assessment of the role of reason as the "scout of," as instrumental to, the passions.[2] Hobbes appears to be indebted to Machiavelli for the notion that large groups of men (in contrast to isolated individual men) constitute a different gestalt, a new order of magnitude, for the theorist to reckon with.[3] The multitude of passionately driven men populating the state of nature bent on limitless aggrandizement of the self at the expense of others comes to recognize in the course of time—and this very perception marks the birth of instrumental reason—that only by engaging in a movement of limited recoil and allowing themselves to be guided by this newly forming region of "rationalized passion" called prudential or instrumental reason can they most reliably attain the goals of maximizing pleasure and minimizing pain dictated by their passions. Otherwise, the movement toward overwhelming human assertiveness gets quickly converted into an orgy of mutual human self-destructiveness.

Machiavelli's political thought also serves as one of the significant early modern antecedents for Madison's deployment of "right method" as a solution to his problem. The key weapon in the armory of Fortuna, which she uses to defeat even formidable displays of political Vertu, is Necessita. The aspect of Fortuna that very often impinges on the political actor in the moment of action is a malicious fortune, a constricting necessity that limits the actor's options and overpowers his initiatives. Machiavelli emphasizes in both literal and metaphoric ways that enemies must learn to use each other's weapons. A general compelled by fortune exhibiting its guise of necessity to fight an opposing army should attempt to mobilize necessity to defeat necessity. He should select terrain for battle (such as positioning his soldiers with their backs to the sea) so that his soldiers are forced to fight, to invest all of their energies in the vanquishing of the opponent. At the same time, the general should strive to have his opponent's soldiers placed in a position where they do not have to fight, where escape routes remain open. In this manner, a successful general learns to mobilize necessity to defeat necessity.[4]

Analogously, as the pervasive principle in his political thought, Machiavelli argues throughout *The Prince* for the importance of the political actor tailoring his actions to conform to a principle of economy—to engage in the least mobilization of effort and violence compatible with the achievement of his strategic results. Machiavelli, as we have seen, condemns Agathocles the Sicilian for engaging in excessive violence—killing more people than strictly necessary for acquiring and maintaining himself in power.[5] Most of the individual strategic and tactical precepts found in *The Prince* can be subsumed under the broader notational principle of economy. An example of this indirect reliance on the principle of economy is to be found where Machiavelli advocates that a prince should govern his relations with his subjects on the basis of fear rather than have such relations predicated on the extreme emotions of hatred or love.[6] Love and hatred, being extreme, are more nearly spontaneous emotions than fear, a supremely calculating emotion. Since fear as an emotion regulating a prince's relations with his subjects is more often under his control than either love or hatred, it behooves the prince in following the principle of economy (in deploying only what is strictly necessary) to achieve his results to establish his relations with his subjects on the basis of fear rather than allowing the relations to be grounded in love or hatred. Thus, the dominant notion of mobilizing necessity to defeat necessity in Machiavelli's thought, which issues forth in the regulative principle of economizing one's actions and the myriad specific precepts that it spawns, constitutes an early prefiguration of the idea of method—utilizing the homely and unpromising materials that form the basis of one's problem as the key to its solution.

While the search for a right method to solve one's problems seems distinctly modern, my conceptualization of what is involved in a stress on method manifests important continuities with the ancient and the medieval idea identified by Lovejoy in *The Great Chain of Being* as the principle of plenitude.[7] According to this principle, there are no lacunae in nature or in being. "The range of conceivable diversity of kinds of living things is exhaustively exemplified [in the universe]."[8] The idea of method can be viewed as a secularization of the principle of plenitude. The natural and social orders harbor no gaps. From the deceptively constricting materials that go to constitute the nature of one's problem, one can unravel new motifs and possibilities that facilitate the resolution of the problem.

There is a more radical phenomenological approach that one can take to the idea of method. According to my first account, "method" consists in fashioning out of the homely materials that go to constitute the nature of one's problem a means to its solution. The solution is only implicitly present in the entities going to compose the nature of one's problem. The precise configuration of the solution still has to be teased out of the initial materials by the imaginative investigator or theorist. According to the (second) approach that I am presenting now, "method" simply refers to the way(s) a problem is institutionalized so that it can be preserved in its original form as a problem without requiring or provoking solution. From this perspective, the very institutionalization of a problem involves a distancing and containment process that staves off the need for a solution indefinitely. The problem gets played out by being reenacted continually and never needs to be solved in a more overt, official sense. From the current vantage point, to speak of a solution in a context where emphasis is being placed on the search for and application of "right method" is methodologically redundant.

Madison's problem in Federalist Number Ten is twofold: epistemological and practical. Epistemologically, no group tendering claims in the political arena can demonstrate the superior wisdom or justness of its claims in contrast to those of its adversaries and competitors. Madison adopts a Hobbesian and Augustinian view concerning the tainted and limited character of reason: "As long as the reason of man continues fallible, and he is at liberty to exercise it, different opinions will be formed. As long as the connection subsists between his reason and his self-love, his opinions and his passions will have a reciprocal influence on each other; and the former will be objects to which the latter will attach themselves."[9] Madison confronts the dual problem of not being able to adjudicate rationally between the competing claims of different groups and of not being able to contain the power conflicts that result when rational resolution of an absolutist sort has been ruled out. What he proposes to do at this point can be conceptualized simply by saying that he institutionalizes the conflict. He encases it in a more remote setting than that of its original enactment, spearheaded by surrogate advocates, called representatives, in lieu of the original combatants who pressed their claims initially. The transfer of locale and substitution of personnel (the distancing occurring on both levels) allows the conflict to continue without its becoming destructive of either the persons or interests of the original competitors or the institutional structures formed to house and contain their conflicts. From this second phenomenological perspective, the number and diversity of the original combatants is to be seen as a feature of the original conflict situation itself, which is simply transferred to an institutionalized setting and is not an innovation conjured up from the initial materials defining the nature of the problem.

Madison's approach reduces itself to postulating the idea of balance as the appropriate resolution to both his epistemological and power perplexities. "The influence of factious leaders may kindle a flame within their particular States but will be unable to spread a general conflagration through the other States. A religious sect may degenerate into a political faction in a part of the Confederacy; but the variety of sects dispersed over the entire face of it must secure the national councils against any danger from that source. A rage for paper money, for an abolition of debts, for an equal division of property, or for any other improper or wicked project, will be less apt to pervade the whole body of the Union than a particular member of it, in the same proportion as such a malady is more likely to taint a particular county or district than an entire State."[10] What contains religious and political factions is simply their having to confront within a unified institutional setting countervailing factions of an equally insistent sort, which ensures that the residue of deliberation and policy that results from their interaction will more closely approximate to the public interest than any faction's special advocacy taken by itself would. In short, it is the balance struck between opposing forces in an institutionalized setting that serves as the surrogate for Madison for both epistemological certainty and preponderance of power enjoyed by any would-be combatant. In a knowledge and power vacuum, "balance" assigns rewards and distributes penalties. The idea of balance becomes a shorthand way of expressing the primacy of the institutional structure in the achievement of an interim peace.

The idea of method in my second sense as an institutionalization of a problem betrays strong continuity with the notion of tacit knowledge discussed in Chapter Four. The connection between the idea of method in my second sense as an institutionalization of a problem and the concept of tacit knowledge is that "method" represents a solution to a major epistemological dilemma encapsulated in the doctrine of tacit knowledge. By postulating only explicit dimensions to knowledge, one cannot account for how the formulation and transmission of knowledge takes place. The problems of interpretation, translation, and judgment discussed previously suggest that on a sheerly explicit level we are bereft of a satisfactory theory concerning how our statements "work." The theory of tacit knowledge calls attention to the way in which any statement that we make appears poised on the brink of being overwhelmed by a boundless range of problems that prevent the statement from getting off the ground at all. The restraining protocols summarized by the notion of tacit knowledge that inhibit an inquirer from thoroughly rationalizing the bases of his knowledge claims are transmuted by the idea of method in my second sense into a procedure for stabilizing the identity and boundaries of a statement (in Madison's case, the statement of the problem of factions) through externalizing the statement by continual reenactment. Also, Madison's recourse to method renders the statement's philosophical intractability innocuous—the very source of its pragmatically ordained and achieved solution. It is only because the statement has no philosophical resolution in a narrow substantive sense that it can be resolved in a broader "methodical" sense. The political arrangements of the modern age, characterized by the presence of large institutional structures, can thus be seen from this perspective as a response to certain key dilemmas of skepticism.

Faction and the Public Good

Madison's definition of faction is highly paradoxical. "By a faction," he says, "I understand a number of citizens, whether amounting to a majority or minority of the whole, who are united and actuated by some common impulse of passion, or of interest, adverse to the rights of other citizens, or to the permanent and aggregate interests of the community."[11] This definition is directly antithetical to the commonsense understanding of faction. It is also opposed to the eighteenth-century understanding of the term as codified in *The Shorter Oxford English Dictionary on Historical Principles*, which defines "faction" as "a party in the state or in any community or association." The eighteenth century construed "party" in essentially minority terms. Yet, under Madison's conception not only is the notion of "majority faction" intelligible, but it is the focus of his analysis of faction in Federalist Number Ten. Is Madison using the concept stipulatively to advance a special set of political prescriptions, or can his delineation of faction yet be assimilated to the commonsense understanding of the term?

The case for a special, esoteric meaning of faction is augmented by the phrase that occurs at the end of Madison's definition, "adverse . . . to the permanent and aggregate interests of the community." If interests can be permanent, that would explain how a majority could constitute a faction. Wherever a majority of the population deviated from what a select minority held to be in the paramount interests of the community, its divergence could be branded as a faction. This formulation presupposes that there is an elite group within the community whose delineation of the public interest is more trustworthy and reliable than that of any other group in the population.

A problem with this construal of Madison's argument is that it is in tension with the conception of the public interest that emerges when Madison clarifies how the method of republicanism resolves the central problem of the instability of democratic politics. "Hence, it clearly appears," Madison writes, "that the same advantage which a republic has over a democracy in controlling the effects of faction is enjoyed by a large over a small republic—is enjoyed by the Union over the States composing it. . . . Does it [the advantage] consist in the greater security afforded by a greater variety of parties, against the event of any one party being able to outnumber and oppress the rest? In an equal degree does the increased variety of parties comprised within the Union increase this security. Does it, in fine, consist in the greater obstacles opposed to the concert and accomplishment of the secret wishes of an unjust and interested majority? Here again the extent of the Union gives it the most palpable advantage."[12]

The conception of the public interest emerging from this passage is as the residue when the process of mutual cancellation between antagonistic and partial interests has worked itself out. The public interest is thus the function of the operation of a particular method or process, and does not immediately fall within the province of any elite, however benignly and disinterestedly defined. In response to this one could say that the brakes on the direct translation of majority will into law that the method of republicanism institutionalizes should be interpreted as an elaborate maneuver to ensure the coincidence of legislative enactments with the favored views of Madison's special caste of custodians of "the permanent and aggregate interests of the community." This argument, however, will not work. The justification of republicanism in Federalist Number Ten does not proceed along the lines that this rejoinder suggests. The mutual cancellation and containment process enshrined in republican practice appears as a nominalistic and deflationary onslaught on the concept of the public good or interest—showing how it can be achieved and certified by a thoroughly mundane method divorced from any privileged set of elitist visions. A political epistemology supporting an elite's superintendency of the public interest is lacking in Madison.

The defense of republicanism in Federalist Number Ten evinces a nominalistic design throughout. The concepts of interest, political obligation, and justice residing in the argument are all equally predicated upon a radically simplified "political mechanics." Interests are a kind of "objective correlative" for man's "middling condition" as described by Locke. They develop through a natural progression from Locke's labor theory of property. "From the protection of different and unequal faculties of acquiring property," Madison writes, "the possession of different degrees and kinds of property immediately results; and from the influence of these on the sentiments and views of the respective proprietors ensues a division of the society into different interests and parties."[13] Since human beings invest their energies unequally in the resources available for cultivation around them, they end up with unequal property holdings. The interests that result can never escape the taint of self that is present when the initial investment of unequal amounts and types of labor takes place in objectified nature. Thus, the term "self-interest" invoked to describe what individuals pursue is a pleonasm. There are no inherently benign interests. Even individuals' protestations of idealism mask self-interest. "If the impulse and the opportunity be suffered to coincide," says Madison, "we well know that neither moral nor religious motives can be relied on as an adequate control [against the emergence of factions]. They are not found to be such on the injustice and violence of individuals, and lose their efficacy in proportion to the number combined together, that is, in proportion as their efficacy becomes needful."[14]

A parallel strategy (and ambiguity) is present with regard to the concept of interest as it pervades Madison's resort to the method of republicanism to resolve the problem of the endemic instability of democratic regimes. "Interest" does not get rid of the taint of egotism that haunts all human actions. It simply externalizes and objectifies it—transposes it to a new sphere. Instead of egotism being internal to the individual, a motivating factor affecting all of his actions, egotism is now objectified and reified in specific property holdings. The ambiguity attendant to the method of republicanism is now present here because the process of externalization of egotism that contributes (in the end) to the mitigation of human conflict can be described alternatively as simply the duplication (and reenactment) of a problem in a sphere other than the one in which it originally arose or as fashioning out of the homely materials of the problem approaches toward its solution. Unlike individual manifestations of egotism, the externalized and distanced status of interests permits a reflected image to be cast back to their possessors that enables them to manage their interests much more realistically and humanely than if the objectification process had not taken place.

The stress on "interest" as the theoretical lever making possible the political argument concerning the containment of factions that Federalist Number Ten articulates is suggestive of a particular theory of justice and political obligation. The concept of the public is a residual category in Federalist Number Ten. Egotism gets externalized as interest entirely within the confines of the private sphere. Interests are initially articulated and aggregated outside a governmental setting. Individuals thus evolve their goals and programs in life and determine the means of achieving them in an entirely private capacity. Government is at worst a hindrance and at best a negative regulatory factor in the scheme of the realization of the individual's life-goals. Thus, the theory of political obligation implicit in Federalist Number Ten is that any state which makes it possible for an individual to realize his interests evokes his allegiance and merits his obligation. Political obligation is directly tied to the furtherance and protection of interests.

The theory of justice evoked by Federalist Number Ten can be labeled procedural justice, in contrast to substantive justice. Considerations of justice come into play to mitigate conflicts between opposing interests and to make sure that no one of them aggrandizes itself unduly at the expense of others. Inquiry into questions of justice would proceed on a secondary level once private interests had been advanced. No preliminary inquiry would be legitimated into the justice of particular claims being present, clamoring for attention in the first place. The theory of justice thus focuses on nonviolation of the rules of the game for the acquisition of property and addresses itself only indirectly to questions of distribution. The subordination of the theory of justice to the theory of political obligation is expressed by the fact that once political obligation is tied to the protection of interest (and a centralized governmental apparatus is requisite to this task) then whatever the state does, no matter what equilibria it strikes between opposing interests, is just. As long as the state is preoccupied with reconciling (or balancing) conflicting interests, it is performing the task for which individual citizens have agreed to obey it.

Given the nominalistic and mechanistic approach of Federalist Number Ten to the concepts of private interest, the public interest, justice, and political obligation, to impute to Madison the notion that an elite propertied class (in the Marxist sense) is the proper custodian for "the permanent and aggregate interests of the community" would be radically inconsistent. It would also jar with the known facts of Madison's biography; for example, in the 1790s he sided with Jefferson against Hamilton's centralizing political activities on behalf of burgeoning capitalist interests.[15] It is the restoration of coherence on this point that lends plausibility to Pocock's republican grouping of Madison.[16] Pocock's "tunnel history" of the Atlantic republican tradition[17] renders the concept of "majority faction" intelligible by locating it within the republican system of ideas originating in Renaissance Florence. The dialectic of virtue and corruption—of an ideal projection of social arrangements and its progressive degeneration in the course of getting historically actualized—can get played out by postulating a historically relativized ideal of virtue rooted in the previously dominant intellectual concepts of the age. The custodian for "the permanent and aggregate interests of the community," therefore, according to Madison, is not a transcultural property-holding elite, conforming to the laws of economic determinism, but a thoroughly historically rooted eighteenth-century elite concerned with perpetuating classical ideals of citizenship and civic virtue. To impute to Madison a Marxist reading of historical development resting upon the unfolding of certain "iron laws" of history violates the skeptical political understandings voiced throughout his essay. The emergence and functioning of a political elite in a Marxist fashion would have to be justified in ways that contravene the analysis of interest and the public good incorporated in the bulk of the essay. The virtue of Pocock's interpretation is that it accepts the notion of an elite serving as special custodian of the public interest suggested by Madison's emphasis upon a "majority faction" at the same time that it accommodates the skeptical political epistemology maintained throughout the remainder of Federalist Number Ten. The political elite's defense of the public interest in terms of its historically relativized republican ideals—historically relativized in the dual sense that they harbor no pretensions about unmasking particular class ascendancies throughout history and also that they make the process of historical relativization itself central to their understanding of historical development—is entirely compatible with the skeptical understandings of private interest, public interest, political obligation, and justice expressed in the essay.

The Supersession of Madison's Argument

Madison's focusing on "interest" in his delineation of the fate of democratic politics and his structuring of the interplay of interests so as to engender political stability have been rendered intensely problematic with the passage of time. The crucial role assigned by Madison to the sheer geographic size of the country in keeping interests isolated and unaligned has to a large extent been nullified by the role of modern technology in unifying the country and increasing awareness, contacts, and interaction between both similar and opposed interests. Not only does the geopolitical context in which interests are pursued diverge sharply from Madison's time, but the danger to democracy posed by factions has been correspondingly altered. Horizontal linking of interests across geographical regions is unavoidable but not as menacing to democratic prospects as the inherently dynamic, pyramidal structure of modern business interests that causes businesses to interact most insidiously, with government as their great patron and protector.[18] Federalist Number Ten speaks very little to this distinctively modern phenomenon.

The term "interest" suggests that the goals and programs we pursue are to a large extent a function of rational choice and prudential calculation. This notion, however, has been attacked from two sides. The scope and pervasiveness of modern communications technology has caused many people to question whether what they identify as their interest is truly something they have willed and fashioned. Further, in a post-Marxist and post-Freudian age it has become an open question whether the prudentially characterized interests that form the subject matter of Madison's argument in Federalist Number Ten are as illuminating of human motivation in politics as the darker urges toward domination and gratification identified by Marx and Freud.

The whole frame of reference in which Madison's argument is conducted has been to a large extent superseded by events. A strategy of continual displacement typifies Madison's argument throughout Federalist Number Ten. Passionate egotistic drives are first distanced and objectified into rationally pursued interests[19] and then further distanced and objectified into a multitude of competing interests. The concept of the public interest is displaced from identification with a substantive value or scheme of values onto that shifting set of procedural arrangements that can serve as the optimal accommodation of multiple private interests compatible with the preservation of order. The very conception of the public interest has become privatized in Madison's analysis. Madison's concepts of political obligation and justice also presuppose the primacy of a procedural set of arrangements over the state's espousal of particular substantive values.

The background assumption informing Madison's whole argument thus appears to be one of economic abundance. The very resort to "method" to resolve previously insoluble problems concerning political stability presumes the availability and diffusion of resources to enable the continual-displacement process to take place. The tab is picked up in the end, as it were, by the prospect of economic reward awaiting those average members of society who have patiently endured Madison's series of displacements.

The transmutation of passion into interest, however, is precarious: It is a historically fragile achievement. The problem of political stability can only get endlessly reenacted instead of more enduringly solved if there are enough societal resources to facilitate continual entry of new claimants into the political arena as well as the sustained satisfaction of old claimants. Where prospects of economic growth are drastically curtailed, Madison's "methodical" approach will not work. At that juncture, we face the prospects of a regression, of interests getting converted back into passions and the engendering of uncontrollable political instability.

The status-quo values of order and stability can be shared by everybody, can form the basis of a nation's political culture, precisely because even the presently disadvantaged members or classes of society enjoy a prospect of economic and social mobility that enables them to perceive stability and order as untainted, broadly supportable values. In accordance with either phenomenological conceptualization of Madison's problem and his invocation of "right method" discussed in the first part of this chapter—whether the proliferation of interests is to be seen as constitutive of the problem or its solution—abundance (or at least continued, incremental growth) is presupposed. Perhaps, one last Madisonian recourse remains available to us in order to salvage his apotheosis of method in an age of diminished growth. Perhaps, the adaptation of "right method" appropriate to our postindustrial age is one that stresses the importance of participation itself—conceived as an egalitarian sharing of power and divorced from the prospect of large-scale economic advance—as the new democratic method, the new institutional reenactment of the problem or the fashioning of a solution out of its homely materials, which promotes allegiance to democratic values when they are severed from possibilities of economic growth and thus buttresses political stability.

CHAPTER 6

Leadership, Knowledge, and Truth in Gramsci's Political Thought

I propose to locate the concept of leadership within the broad theoretical context of Gramsci's political philosophy. In doing so, I hope to achieve a double illumination. Leadership is a central category in Gramsci's political thought, and by exploring its patterns of interconnection to other phases of Gramsci's thought I hope to exhibit that centrality. Second, the ways in which leadership emerges as central in Gramsci's thought throw light on current political dilemmas relating to vast power imbalances existing in advanced industrial civilizations—particularly the United States.

The difficulties confronting the expositor of Gramsci are presciently stated by Gramsci himself in describing the difficulties lying in wait for the interpreter of Marx. "One should further bear in mind," Gramsci says, "that the elements of this new mode of conceiving philosophy [introduced by Marx] are contained in aphorisms or in some way dispersed throughout the writings of the founder of the philosophy of praxis [Marx], and that it is necessary precisely to distinguish these elements and develop them coherently."[1] A similar challenge awaits the interpreter of Gramsci. One needs to piece the aphorisms and quasi-independent paragraphs together—striving to discern common philosophical impulses behind the discussion of disparate topics—in order to articulate a coherent philosophy.

Gramsci's considered philosophical position might best be characterized as "dialectical historicism."[2] "Dialectical historicism" is not just a tributary of a relatively isolated and self-contained Western political tradition called Marxism. Gramsci's political philosophy was historically very important for the development of Western European communism in the twentieth century because it deemphasized the role of economic factors in historical causation and placed great stress on ideology, superstructure, and cultural forces generally as significant agencies for social change. In addition, I believe that "dialectical historicism" constitutes a highly intriguing solution to the problem of formulating a non-self-refuting version of skepticism that has haunted Western philosophy from its Platonic origins until the present. I shall try to show in the course of etching in the broad framework of Gramsci's philosophy how dialectical historicism constitutes a resolution to some key dilemmas concerning skepticism.

The dialectical interplay between hegemony and counterhegemony is the mechanism whereby dialectical historicism operates. The concept of hegemony has a rich and varied background in Western intellectual history. I will sketch in this background from Plato through Machiavelli to Hobbes, classical liberal thought, and Marx. I will also analyze some key implications of this dialectic.

Leadership emerges as the pivot of the Gramscian system of ideas because it is the mechanism whereby hegemony and counterhegemony operate.

My order of presentation will follow the outline of the argument just summarized. I will begin with a discussion of the intellectual-historical background of the concept of hegemony and some of its major implications. I will then proceed to try and show how Gramsci's dialectical historicism—his projection of the dialectical interplay between hegemony and counterhegemony—helps to resolve some dominant dilemmas concerning skepticism. I will next examine the role of leadership in "fueling" the dialectic of hegemony versus counterhegemony and consider contemporary applications of the leadership function as envisaged by Gramsci.

Hegemony and Counterhegemony: The Elucidation of the Dialectic and Its Implications

In criticizing Nikolai Bukharin's *Theory of Historical Materialism: A Popular Manual of Marxist Sociology*, Gramsci writes:

> So when the Manual says that the term "immanence" in the philosophy of praxis is used in a metaphorical sense, it is saying nothing. In reality the term immanence has here acquired a special meaning which is not that of the "pantheists" nor any other metaphysical meaning but one which is new and needs to be specified. It has been forgotten that in the case of a very common expression [historical materialism] one should put the accent on the first term—"historical"—and not on the second, which is of metaphysical origin. The philosophy of praxis is absolute "historicism," the absolute secularization and earthliness of thought, an absolute humanism of history. It is along this line that one must trace the thread of the new conception of the world.[3]

According to Gramsci, the central feature of Marx's philosophy of praxis is its historicizing of all elements of man's material and intellectual culture. Whatever social and economic practices and institutions currently prevail in our world, as well as the intellectual and moral categories in whose terms we interpret and evaluate them, have their origins in human self-objectification—an embodiment outward of human energies and exertions. For example, a distinction crucial to twentieth-century analytic philosophy, that between first- and second-order levels of discourse (the plane of language which is concerned to address transactions in the world and that level of discourse which is concerned to legitimize and justify our basic concepts and categories) would be perceived from a Gramscian perspective as misleading and superficial. Both primary and secondary discourse, the vocabulary of description as well as the vocabulary of justification, are grounded in the historical development of man. Man is a thoroughly historicized creature whose visions of the absolute and critical canons are themselves a function of his specific historic location—the result of the evolving interplay between man and his objectifications.

How does dialectical historicism work? What sort of anthropology, or image of man, does it assume? The basic image is the one bequeathed by the moral psychology of classical liberalism. Man is a creature dominated by passion—all of man's reasoning faculties are subordinate to his passions—and his passions define the outer limits of his striving, beyond which he cannot go, as well as what constitutes maximal creativity within those limits. "Only the man who wills something strongly," Gramsci says, "can identify the elements which are necessary to the realization of his will."[4] Passionately appropriated insight and passionately expressed will are fleeting. In order to rescue itself from inconsequence, consciousness must give rise to organization. Some outward structure must be fashioned to correspond to the insight and to embody the will in order to endow them both with a modicum of stability. One can trace the origins of the process of hegemonic formation to these very humble and morally neutral beginnings. Hegemony does not begin as a conspiracy but as an expression of a universal human need to have emotion and will outlast the moment of their direct experience. The concept then expands to include the whole network of economic concentrations of power, religious, ethical, literary, and esthetic institutions and values, and the communications media, which together form a "bloc" of delineations of reality that tends to reinforce the power of the dominant classes. Counterhegemonic forces can range in magnitude from a chance encounter between two people where one persuades the other of the injustice of social arrangements and the need to fashion a more egalitarian distribution of power to such countercultural manifestations as new musical styles or modes of dress that subvert dominant values, new esthetic and literary theories, new religious manifestations, councils where workers participate in the running of their factories, to a full-fledged adversarial political party.[5] The idea of the morally neutral origins of hegemony is expressed in Gramsci's thought by his envisaging the formation of hegemonic and counterhegemonic forces as an unending process, coterminous with human living in time.

When there are enough economic and cultural formations to express the will and to promote the interest of a dominant social class, then hegemony arises in the class-biased, morally perverted sense that justifiably gives rise to counterhegemonic structures. Before exploring the dialectic surrounding hegemony and counterhegemony further, it would be useful to examine hegemony's antecedents and ramifications in Western political thought.

The phenomenological insight that lurks behind the concept of hegemony is that the more fully power is displaced, the more effective it becomes. One can trace the origins of this insight to an intertextual relation that subsists between *The Prince* and the *Republic*. One could say that an implicit intertextual critique voiced by *The Prince* against the *Republic* is that the enervating relationship between the real and the ideal announced by Plato's Theory of Ideas (with the real consisting in a falling-away from or diminution of the ideal) is not something that characterizes the relationship between the earthly realm and some supersensible realm but should properly be located within the earthly realm itself. Power is present in its most convincing form, the burden of the Machiavellian critique implies, when it does not have to be used overtly in order to achieve its intended results. When a reputation for power is sufficient to net a political actor the results he desires, then power is present in its most consummate form. The need actually to resort to power to attain one's ends in politics is symptomatic of the precariousness of one's power. The optimal state that every political actor should strive for is one where the ends of power are achieved—people act in conformity with one's wishes, because they know it is the desire of the particular political actor—without having to mobilize the costly means of power, which always lead to its further erosion.

According to Machiavelli, therefore, power is supremely a function of nonactions, nonevents. It is rooted in a series of counterfactual circumstances. In order to assess the full range of a political actor's power, according to Machiavelli, it is important to take into account what political goals the actor was able to achieve on the basis of a *reputation* for power and what pitfalls he was able to *avoid* because of a strict *economizing* of means in relation to ends that enabled him to husband power for use on future, more dire occasions. It is what takes place beyond the screen of visible action that is a more reliable indicator of the power of statesmen than statesmen's actions taken by themselves.

The stress on a principle of economy throughout Machiavelli's concrete strategic and tactical advice—tailoring means to make them exactly commensurate with the ends desired—reflects the larger insight that power is always in short supply, to the powerful as well as to the powerless. Machiavelli recommends, for example, that the political actor build his relationship with his followers on the basis of fear rather than hatred, which would represent an overshooting of the mark of control and would therefore be counterproductive. The consummate expression of power is its invocation without its direct use. The prescriptive use of civil religion to advance the ends of the state is another example of the same phenomenon in Machiavelli's thought.

One of the things that social-contract theorists learned from Machiavelli is that state-making consists in minimizing overt uses of power. This insight is institutionalized in classical liberal theory in the imagery and argument of the social contract, where the assertion of power is depicted as a *prepolitical, precivil* act. What marks the fashioning of civil society is the containment of power in its unbridled, menacing forms.

The avoidance and sublimation of power are manifested in liberal political theorizing at three other points.

First, on the level of substantive content, Hobbes's delineation of the relationship between reason and the passions—which serves as the enduring moral-psychological model of liberalism—suggests a jettisoning of the concept of power. The idea of power connotes an element of arbitrariness, that things could be other than what they are. We typically employ the idea of power with regard to political matters, for example, because political decision making takes place in a context of at least a partial vacuum of rationality. We can usually adduce rational arguments in support of conflicting sides of political issues, so that the reference to power is meant to indicate that from a sheerly rational perspective the eventual outcome could have been other than what it was. If, however, one regards a particular state of affairs as being purely a matter of conditioning (that no element of choice is present in its formation), then one is unlikely to think or speak in terms of power. This is exactly the case with Hobbes's doctrine of the relationship between reason and the passions. The subordination of reason to the passions—the birth of instrumental, calculating reason—coincides with a societywide emergence out of the dire conditions of the state-of-nature society into the peaceful world of civil society. The passions (i.e., the pleasure–pain apparatus that governs their operation) manage to bring forth out of their own womb in the course of time a calculating mechanism, instrumental reason, which helps to ensure the creation of a more stable context for the realization of the ends that they dictate. But the whole process of the creation and the eventual triumph of instrumental reason is conceived by Hobbes as being a gradual one, the result of the conditioning effects of the pleasure–pain apparatus lodged within each one of us. The unpromising human materials that give rise to the problem of human insecurity—the centrality of the passions—are themselves the source of salvation.[6] The vast conditioning effects of the pleasure–pain apparatus shield from view the human exertion of power until a relatively late stage in social evolution, when the state has already been formed and certain significant intermediate choices, such as that between a monarchy and a parliamentary government, have to be made. Until that point, everything appears to be conditioned by the laws of human nature, the laws of moral psychology.

Second, aside from the specific intellectual content of Hobbes's notion of reason serving as a "scout" for the passions, an additional perspective that might be brought to bear on Hobbes's (and liberalism's) moral-psychological schema is not to analyze what it *says* but what it *does*, its role as a speech act[7]—what it enables Hobbes and later liberal authors and their readers to accomplish. Viewed in this light, what the subordination of reason to the passions facilitates is the masking of the human exercise of power in creating a world characterized by the pursuit of "commodious living." Liberal moral psychology also shields its readers from an awareness of their responsibility for fashioning such a world. The creation of the totally secular, this-worldly mode of existence described in the pages of *Leviathan* is not the result of any deliberate exertion of power at all. It represents the working out of the implications of our being the captives, the playthings, of our passions. We are driven onward by our passions in the creation of a Hobbesian world. We are, in a sense, powerless in its creation.

Finally, in the popular liberal imagination of the eighteenth century, which builds upon the Hobbesian family of notions, popular consent is viewed as an alternative to power. Consider the following almost parenthetical statement by the American Whig pamphleteer Stephen Hopkins: "If the House of Commons did not receive this authority from their constituents, it will be difficult to tell by what means they obtained it except it be vested in them by mere superiority and power."[8] This passage points to a dichotomy between consent and the exercise of power. In this view, consent represents a manifestation of natural necessity, people simply desiring something and moving along on that basis, rather than a fully self-conscious human intervention. Consent in this passage (and in kindred others that I could cite) is viewed as an alternative to power—something purer and more innocent than the raw exercise of power. Consent in classical liberal thought is seen as the political translation of desire, of passion, which involves a bypassing of power.

Marx turns the Machiavellian insights institutionalized in liberal thought and practice into a systematic critique of liberalism. In his theory of ideology, Marx distinguishes between an economic and class structure that defines what the authentic distribution of power within a particular society is and the political and cultural manifestations and products of a society (its superstructural elements) that simultaneously, and in partial tension with each other, mask, reify, and enhance its underlying scheme of power relations. What were the inevitable concomitances of the nature of power in classical liberal theorizing—facilitating a more economical design in the distribution of power—are exposed by Marx as subtle instruments for the enhancement of the dominant class's power.

Gramsci's concept of hegemony stands Marx on his head.[9] Aside from taking over the Marxian notion (which is also, in the different ways I have described, the Machiavellian and classical liberal notion) that a society's political and cultural expressions and artifacts are to be viewed holistically as a manifestation of whatever mobilizations of power are present within that society, Gramsci argues that an opening wedge for revolutionizing power arrangements within society can be obtained by transforming elements of the superstructure as well as by a direct assault on the economic and class structure. "The philosophy of praxis [Gramsci is referring to his version of dialectical historicism] represents a distinct advance and *historically is precisely in opposition to Ideology*."[10] The opposition consists in the fact that taking the Machiavellian notion that all political and cultural expressions and artifacts can be reclassified in terms of power seriously means that levers for social change are much more multifarious than vulgar versions of Marxism allow. Transforming people's awareness and consciousness in a limited social or educational network is as fully a political act as an armed factory insurrection. Power originates in consciousness, in awareness—in perceptions of domination and subordination. To revolutionize these, therefore, constitutes the first expression of the impulse for social and political change.

The sharp demarcation between structure and superstructure in Marx's thought is symptomatic of the possibility of a redistributing of power in the structure and of a dismantling of the superstructure so as to facilitate an apocalyptic reversal, an appropriation of power by the dispossessed. The emphasis on inlets to political renewal and revolution on the superstructural level in Gramsci's thought, by contrast, evokes the notion that restructuring of power relations is an ongoing process. "The philosophy of praxis," Gramsci says, "is consciousness full of contradictions, in which the philosopher himself, understood both individually and as an entire social group, not only grasps the contradictions, *but posits himself as an element of the contradiction* and elevates this element to a principle of knowledge and therefore of action."[11] One of the senses in which the philosopher "posits himself as an element of the contradiction" is that he is coming to dissolve inegalitarian power relations, and yet his superior insight and directly interventionist role create the likelihood that an excess of power will gravitate toward him in the restructuring of power of which he will be a major midwife. Gramsci's emphasis that the philosopher must work toward his own supersession in order for his animating vision of justice and equality to be realized is suggestive of Mao's notion of "permanent revolution," and marks an important deviation from Marxist thought.[12]

All redistributions of power in human communities, according to Gramcsi, are potentially corrupting—as the new inheritors of power evolve oligarchical and hegemonic structures to entrench themselves in power and to exclude a just sharing of power with other, equally legitimate claimants. The most that can be achieved historically, according to Gramsci, are partial redemptions of oppressive configurations of power. The challenge of achieving these redemptions is a continuing one and can be initiated in any sphere of political, cultural, or economic activity.

Gramsci's stress on the partiality of human redemption betrays a strongly Jewish sensibility.[13] In his classic essay "Romantic Religion," Leo Baeck characterizes Christianity as "romantic religion" because it believes in the dispensability of *Mitzvot* (commandments) and makes salvation hinge on a certain state of inner belief. By contrast, Baeck designates Judaism as "classical religion" because redemption is conceived mainly in the plural, as a series of partial redemptions flowing from the performance of individual commandments as they relate to discrete facets of existence. By engaging in these *Mitzvot*, the Jew elevates and transforms different moments of his daily life—from the way he gets up in the morning to the way he treats strangers—and thus achieves that optimal degree of redemption that his life is capable of bearing.[14]

Using Baeck's terminology, one might describe Gramsci's theory of revolution as classical rather than romantic. Revolution for Gramsci never achieves a state of total transformation. "Even the philosophy of praxis," he says, "is an expression of historical contradictions, and indeed their most complete, because most conscious, expression; this means that it too is tied to 'necessity' and not to a 'freedom' which does not yet exist and, historically, cannot yet exist."[15] In historical time, one cannot yet evolve a vocabulary, let alone frame actions, that will facilitate the transcending of contradictions. The most that one can achieve is the partial amelioration of contradictions through an unrelenting interventionism and mass consciousness-raising. Revolution is unceasingly justified, at least as far as the historically trained eye can tell, precisely because redemption is not total.

Another concept employed by a second major twentieth-century interpreter of Jewish tradition—Max Kaddushin's notion of "normal mysticism"—is relevant for an understanding of Gramsci. "Normal mysticism" signified for Kaddushin the theological approach developed by the rabbis whereby the radical otherness of God emphasized by Biblical theology is domesticated and integrated into a complex fabric of daily living. Without sacrificing God's total otherness, his total distinctness from man, the way in which the ordinary Jew relates to it has been normalized. "Through the agency of Halakah [Jewish law]," writes Kaddushin, "prayer becomes the thrice-daily practice of the people as a whole; *Berakot* [blessings] are now the means, on innumerable occasions, of evoking a consciousness of God. . . ; the call to Teshubah, repentance, becomes the function of annually recurring days, indeed, it is embodied in the Daily 'Amidah' [the central portion of the daily prayers]."[16] Analogously, one might say that Gramsci strives for a normalized radicalism. The teachings of political radicalism—the movement of the dialectic of hegemony versus counterhegemony—have to be integrated into the context of everyday life and consciousness. Throughout his career, Gramsci searched for an effective strategy to achieve this. He turned to factory councils (and decentralized, participatory processes of decision making generally) as the most promising vehicles for the attainment of this end. "The socialist state already exists potentially in the institutions of social life characteristic of the exploited labouring class." "The factory council is the model of the proletarian state. All the problems which are inherent in the organization of the proletarian state are inherent in the organization of the councils."[17]

As these latter two quotations indicate, the counterhegemonic force that needs to be brought to bear by the downtrodden classes against the hegemonic ascendancy of the dominant classes is an embryonic counterstructure that encompasses as many phases of the oppressed classes' life as possible, and is not restricted to purely economic or narrowly power-oriented issues. There are striking analogies here with processes of growth and liberation taking place within an individual life, although Gramsci would probably regard these as incomplete outside the context of an effective counterhegemonic offensive mounted together with the fellow members of one's class. What must be counterposed by an estranged individual or class to existing structures are alternate incipient systems and structures, not stray impulses, thoughts, or emotions. Here, as in many other places in his thought, Gramsci is indebted to Machiavelli for the insight that in order to succeed, enemies must learn to use each other's weapons.[18] The ascendant class prevails because its interests have permeated so-called neutral areas of thought and action so that their hegemonic control evokes on many occasions almost reflex responses of obedience from an unsuspecting populace. Aside from all other considerations, power resides merely in system—in the fact that there is a *network* of approved ways of feeling, thinking, and acting buttressing the interests of a particular class. A kind of double economy is achieved through system: the resort to ideational structures instead of merely to economic pressures and coercion to evoke compliance from the multitude relieves the "power drain" on the upper classes. Also, the systematic pattern of relationship subsisting between various components of the superstructure endows the practical and moral precepts flowing from that superstructure with an intrinsic obligatoriness stemming from their location within a larger system. The first task, therefore, of an excluded class in trying to fashion a power base from which to challenge the hegemonic power of an ascendant class is to delegitimize the hegemonic structures of the dominant class by formulating a countervailing hegemonic scheme of its own. The power that accrues from system is immediately fabricated by the articulation of a counterhegemonic structure. As real-world organization begins to correspond to ideational structure, the power of the nascent class becomes compounded.

Hegemonic structures disarm their followers from engaging in protest precisely through the paradoxical fact that consent and involvement in those structures appear voluntary. If I have been given the keys, then the structures that I inhabit cannot possibly be jails. Hegemony orchestrates the energies of the lower classes so that they make the appropriate voluntary moves to maintain themselves and thereby uphold the system. A kind of cognitive dissonance sets in that prevents the lower classes from perceiving how the entire hegemonic structure constitutes the most artful way imaginable for promoting the interests of an adversarial class and depriving the lower classes of a more egalitarian share of power. To forestall the most insidious effects

of this process of cognitive dissonance, it is imperative to form counterhegemonic structures so that the daily actions of the working class
do not reinforce the power positions of the dominant classes.

Another related motive behind the Gramscian counterhegemonic
approach might be to prevent a bond of attachment forming between
persecuted and persecutor. If we become what we do, then people
whose options have been curtailed by their occupying an inferior class
position emotionally identify with what is done to them. To prevent
this process from taking root, Gramsci advocates the formation of
counterhegemonic forces that seek to establish in embryo an alternative scheme of more egalitarian relations that become the model for
societal relations after the revolutionary takeover.

The concept of counterhegemony in Gramsci—and the notion
that counterhegemony must precede the conquest of political power—is also partially rooted in the Machiavellian idea that stresses the
indispensability of conceptual clarity for the achievement of practical
efficacy. Machiavelli, for example, rejects the goal of unconditional
surrender in warfare not so much because it is practically difficult as
because it is conceptually incoherent. In order to know what one
wants (or, stated even more simply, in order to know) one must
continually interact with other like-minded individuals so as to attain a
reliable sense of knowing. Knowledge is rooted in and certified by the
cultivation of a particular praxis. The cultivation of a praxis that will
nurture a secure sense of political and personal knowledge is what the
concept of counterhegemony is in many ways about.

My discussion of the dialectic of hegemony versus counterhegemony suggests the autonomy of the political stance of being-in-the-
world—that it is not assimilable to our conventional categories of
theory and practice. Michael Oakeshott in *Experience and Its Modes*[19]
delineates three modes of experience, three sets of categorical principles under which our experience of the world is organized—history,
science, and practice—and, in his later essay "The Voice of Poetry in
the Conversation of Mankind," he adds a fourth, poetry. In the later
essay, Oakeshott drops the idealist nomenclature of "modes" and
speaks more broadly of "voices." The four voices of practical activity,
poetry, science, and history refer to the methods, vocabularies, and ap-

proaches adopted to study particular subject matters, rather than to the subject matters themselves. The image of a conversation is chosen to capture the appropriate relationship that should subsist between these different voices in the modern world precisely because it suggests reflectiveness, acute self-consciousness, without conclusiveness. In a conversation, Oakeshott says, "different universes of discourse meet, acknowledge each other and enjoy an oblique relationship which neither requires nor forecasts their being assimilated to one another."[20]

A major presupposition of Oakeshott's categorization scheme is that theory (and different forms of theory, and practice) can be kept rigidly separate. Practical endeavors seek directly to change the world. History, science, and poetry seek to theorize the world, but each of them arrests experience at a different point, raising different sorts of questions and betraying varying degrees and types of self-consciousness. Oakeshott defines the voice of philosophy, by contrast, as "the impulse to study the quality and style" of each voice in the conversation; it is therefore parasitic upon the conversation and does not constitute an authentic voice within it. Politics, for Oakeshott, comes under the rubric of the practical voice since it directly endeavors to have an impact on events in the world. From a Gramscian perspective, what Oakeshott overlooks is the unity of theory and practice. In conversing in a political vein, one is focusing on the multitudinous regions in public and private life where power is being exerted by, with, and against the self. The political deserves to be classified as an autonomous voice in the conversation of mankind because it attempts to pierce through the sometimes mythological categories of understanding employed in poetry, science, and history (and in philosophy as well) and through the encrusted patterns of relationship that confront the human actor who is practically motivated to disclose underlying configurations of power that foster or impede change and growth. As my discussion of hegemony and counterhegemony so far has underscored, the concept of the political postulates the interpenetration of theory and practice. The limits and agenda of theorizing are ordinarily set by the social and economic practices prevailing in a particular society at a particular time, and these practices can be most effectively revolutionized by theorizing a whole interconnected pattern of living clustering around alternate concepts and values—that is, by articulating and establishing counterhegemonic structures. To think politically is to develop the intellectual skills to deprive power of any "place to hide."[21]

How do counterhegemonic structures come into being? Who instigates their formation? Who nurtures their development? Here Gramsci's novel conception of the intellectual life comes into play, more specifically his carving out a creative historical role for what he calls "organic" intellectuals in contrast to "traditional" intellectuals. How does one distinguish between "organic" and "traditional" intellectuals? "The traditional intellectuals," Gramsci says, "are detaching themselves from the social grouping to which they have hitherto given the highest and most comprehensive form—hence the most extensive and perfect consciousness of the modern state. In so doing, they are accomplishing an act of incalculable historical significance; they are making and ratifying the crisis of the state in its decisive form."[22] Traditional intellectuals are a severed group of déclassé individuals who deny the legitimacy of the class—usually the middle class—from which they originate and who are unable to give their full allegiance to any currently embodied form of social organization. With regard to "organic" intellectuals, Gramsci says that "one could only have had cultural stability and an organic quality of thought if there had existed the same unity between the intellectuals and the people as there should be between theory and practice. That is, if the intellectuals had been organically the intellectuals of the masses, and if they had worked out and made coherent the principles and the problems raised by the masses in their practical activity, thus constituting a cultural and social bloc."[23] In other passages, Gramsci moves beyond the implications of these sentences by suggesting that "everyone is a philosopher."[24] In still other passages, Gramsci exceeds even these formulations by saying that "just as every man is a philosopher, every man is a man of science"[25] and "one can and therefore one must be 'one's own doctor [psychoanalyst].' "[26]

There are at least two paradoxes in Gramsci's discussion of intellectuals that require elucidation. One is how the selfsame individuals can be both the prime movers in maintaining societal stability and also the dominant instigators of social change. The second paradox has to do with the precise way to comprehend the notion that "everyone is a philosopher." How can a term that was coined to designate elite status of some sort be used to refer to capacities that are in reach of everyone without hopelessly diluting the term and rendering it unintelligible?

To deal with the first paradox first: Drawing on many of the same intellectual-historical sources that animate much of Gramsci's discussion concerning intellectuals, Edward Shils describes the intellectual vocation as follows:

> In every society there are some persons with an unusual sensitivity to the sacred, an uncommon reflectiveness about the nature of their universe and the rules which govern their society. There is in every society a minority of persons who, more than the ordinary run of their fellow men, are inquiring, and desirous of being in frequent communion with symbols which are more general than the immediate concrete situations of everyday life and remote in their reference in both time and space. In this minority there is a need to externalize this quest in oral and written discourse, in poetic or plastic expression, in historical reminiscence or writing, in ritual performance and acts of worship. This interior need to penetrate beyond the screen of immediate experience marks the existence of the intellectuals in every society.[27]

According to Shils, what chiefly characterizes the intellectual is his approaching reality from the perspective of the sacred. What this means, I think, is a refusal to treat any aspect of existence as isolated, but instead to search out the implications and interconnections of whatever discrete aspects of existence lie immediately before one. What defines the divine perspective on reality is precisely that for it there are no anomalous aspects of existence, no loose ends that somehow fail to link up into larger patterns of meaning. Evil and suffering, for example, which constitute the most glaring forms of human anomaly, are seen from the perspective of the sacred as merely abbreviated moments of some larger excellence.

The proclivity of the intellectual to pierce beyond appearance and to pursue the interconnections of things leads to the formation of a special style in written and spoken discourse. The theoretical mode of apprehending and describing reality seems uniquely appropriate to a sensibility bent on subsuming discrete phenomena within larger frameworks of intelligibility and coherence.

The sacralization of existence that the intellectual achieves on the plane of thought by cultivating a theoretical perspective has its counterpart in the sphere of action. Traditions, I believe, form the counterpart in the real world to theories in the realm of thought. Both theories and traditions involve the creation of a fabric of "at-homeness" for human beings in the world. Theories accomplish this by locating isolated, discrete phenomena in some overall pattern of significance. Analogously, traditions are conducive to the same result in the real world by the erection of a network of metaphysical assumptions, ethical imperatives, and approved ways of perceiving and acting within the world that link individual responses to some overall pattern of permanent significance. If the identity of the intellectual is as Shils describes it, then the intellectual needs traditions as desperately as he does theories to accord relevance and value to individual thoughts and actions. For an intellectual, then, it would appear that the matter is usually a question of substitution of traditions; rarely, if ever, is it a question of abandoning traditions altogether. The ideology of the New Left in the 1960s, for example, insinuated the contours of a new tradition, one that was radically at variance with ongoing institutions and structures, but a tradition nonetheless. No important area of life was left outside the pale of New Left ideology. Prescriptions regarding food, sleep, and dress were all incorporated as elements in the new life-style that it advocated.

The intellectual thus emerges in this analysis (Gramsci as filtered through Shils's prism) as the possessor of a dual identity. He is both creator and subverter of traditions. His basic need, apparently, is to fashion ever more accommodating structures of coherence in terms of which to make sense of the manifold phenomena within and around him. Initially, this takes the form of the elaboration of theories, some of which in turn serve as a basis for organizing man's social and political life. When thought is translated into practice, the real world inevitably gives rise to anomalies and unplanned consequences that seriously call into question the aspirations toward comprehensiveness and co-herence animating the original theory. The intellectual at this point, in the guise of subverter of traditions, seeks again (initially on the plane of thought) to fashion a more accommodating structure of coherence and in turn to translate that into reality. The implication in Shils and in Gramsci is that the constant dialectical tension between tradition and thought seems to be a recurring feature of the intellectual life, destined to endure as long as the time-bound nature of human existence is not totally superseded.

With regard to the second paradox mentioned above—how it is possible for the intellectual life to become accessible to all members of society in the modern world—one can take an approach suggested by the innovative work of Joseph Levenson on the transition between Confucianism and modernity in nineteenth- and twentieth-century China.[28] It is possible to raise the consciousness of men and women generally so that their level of critical reflectiveness approximates to that of officially recognized intellectuals in modern societies because, built into the structure of modernity with its proliferation of traditions in collision and confrontation, is the undermining of the prospect of being a philosophical primitive or naif, such as a pristine follower of tradition might have been a millenium ago. Today, the most that one can aspire to is traditionalism—a self-conscious affirmation of tradi-tion in the face of competing ideological alternatives. The possibilities for consciousness-raising, skepticism, and philosophical sophistica-tion engendered by this radical transformation of the modern cultural climate create the setting for every man becoming his own intellectual.

Part of the strategic importance for Gramsci of cultivating organic intellectuals is that their whole process of socialization will lead them to resist the temptation to solo domination. The problem of overween-ing power asserted against the social group of which one is a part stands its best chance of being resolved by the nurturing of organic intellectuals. "The same distinction can be made," says Gramsci, "be-tween the notion of intellectual elites separated from the masses, and that of intellectuals who are conscious of being linked organically to a national–popular mass. In reality, one has to struggle against the above-mentioned degenerations, the false heroisms and pseudo-aristocracies, and stimulate the formation of homogeneous, compact social blocs, which will give birth to their own intellectuals, their own commandos, their own vanguard—who in turn will react upon those blocs in order to develop them, and not merely so as to perpetuate their gypsy domination."[29]

Just as the formation of organic intellectuals is a goal toward which every emergent social group should strive, so the adoption of a cosmopolitan outlook is a besetting temptation of intellectuals that impedes social progress. "This conception of the function of intellectuals," Gramsci writes, "throws light on the reason, or one of the reasons, for the fall of the mediaeval communes, i.e., of the rule of an economic class which did not prove able to create its own category of intellectuals and thus exercise a hegemony as well as a dictatorship. The Italian intellectuals did not have a national–popular character, but one that was cosmopolitan on the model of the Church; it was a matter of indifference to Leonardo whether he sold the designs for the fortification of Florence to Duke Valentino."[30] The concepts of hegemony and counterhegemony, which attempt to capture the movement of historical events, relate to the rationalization and institutional elaboration of what is one's own. The boundaries of the rational and the real are supplied by adventitious circumstances, and cannot be transcended or extended by fiat. These boundaries are arbitrary in ways that do not interfere with, and in fact promote, the articulation and differentiation of a self and a society. It is the height of intellectual hubris to try and repudiate the category of the given and to place everything in question (to put it all up for grabs, as it were) simultaneously. Only by accommodating the arbitrary at each stage of our intellectual and historical progressions can we hope to overcome the arbitrary.[31]

If every emerging social stratum should strive to generate from its own midst organic intellectuals who will provide both the impetus and the intellectual tools to instigate a counterhegemonic movement, it is also the obligation of intellectuals to provide leadership for social change even where the consciousness of the masses appears aloof and distant from such aspirations. One of the vehicles through which organic intellectuals can lead in circumstances where there is a "consciousness gap" between themselves and the masses is by fomenting what Gramsci calls "passive revolution." Gramsci considers "Gandhism and Tolstoyism" as "naive theorisations of the 'passive revolution' with religious overtones."[32] "If a social group is formed," Gramsci writes, "which is one hundred percent homogeneous on the level of ideology, this means that the premises exist one hundred percent for this revolutionising [of praxis]: that is that the 'rational' is actively and actually 'real.' "[33] When the superstructure is totally homogeneous with the structure—when the tensions between the two have been closed through reflective awareness—the individuals animated by this awareness can function as a revolutionary cadre. If the masses, who have not yet attained this level of insight, can somehow be made to suffer and act on its behalf—as they were under Tolstoy's Christianity and Gandhi's program of militant nonviolence—then this is Gramsci's "passive revolution." Gramsci defines man as "concrete will."[34] Only by moving beyond the self through self and collective transformation is there a self at all. If, as Gramsci says, "to be conscious of something is already to modify it,"[35] the converse is also true for him. To modify something, by being caught up in collective action against the status quo, is already to begin to have a truer consciousness of it.

"Passive revolution" ties in with a central distinction in Gramsci's political thought, that between a war of movement and a war of position. Gramsci's dialectical historicism underplays the role of a war of movement (an open and violent confrontation between antagonists) and emphasizes the importance of a war of position—(covert, subtle, nonviolent struggle) as an engine of social change. Since power is often built up and eroded through a series of displacements— "hegemony" versus "counterhegemony"—that do not always catch the public's attention, a war of movement is usually too blunt a tool to promote one's power ends. Also, given the Machiavellian understanding of both liberty and power that Gramsci shares (if one is not forging ahead increasing his liberty and power then one is ipso facto falling downward, losing his liberty and power) the concept of a war of movement seems too crude a notion to capture the mechanisms whereby power can be increased. The concept of a war of position, by contrast, seems to be responsive to the idea that nothing that we do in life is power neutral—that power balances within and between people and groups and classes are affected by virtually everything that we do or fail to do. "Passive revolution" attempts to harness the power-impregnated silences of human life to active revolutionary purposes by emphasizing the extent to which consciousness is a function of social location *and* action. Even if the motives that get us to act appear tainted by what from an orthodox Marxist perspective seems like false consciousness, action polarized along a counterhegemonic axis itself transforms consciousness in a revolutionary direction.

The hegemonic triumph of the liberal bourgeois state is nowhere more apparent than in the eclipse of the state by civil society that became manifest in the nineteenth century.[36] This historical development in the structuring of the liberal state—with the state being very widely viewed as a minor engine of enforcement and redistribution in an otherwise mutually adjusting system of social and economic interactions—was paralleled by the emergence of sociology as a putative successor discipline to political science. "The rise of sociology," Gramsci says, "is related to the decline of the concept of political science and the art of politics which took place in the Nineteenth Century (to be more accurate, in the second half of that century, with the success of evolutionary and positivist theories)."[37] Gramsci seeks to overturn this scheme of historical and intellectual priorities. "Everything that is of real importance in sociology," he emphasizes, "is nothing other than political science."[38] The transvaluation of values that occurred in the nineteenth century concerning the relative positions of civil society and the state also helped to convert society into a fit methodological subject for the approaches and techniques of the natural sciences. "And, lo and behold," Gramsci writes, "society can now be studied with the methods of the natural sciences! Impoverishment of the concept of the state which ensued from such views."[39]

There is a third element in the nineteenth-century transvaluation of political values that Gramsci seeks to reverse. Responsibility is conceptually and practically linked with participation, with active engagement in political affairs. To the extent that the state is conceived as subordinate to society, obeying its own laws of political mechanics that render it amenable to strict scientific study, the individual member of society both is discouraged from getting involved in political matters and is habituated to the idea that his involvement is a mere adjunct to larger historical and societal forces whose resolution obeys strict laws of scientific development. It is only when what Gramsci calls "the subaltern element" "is no longer a thing but a historical person, a protagonist," that "it feels itself to be responsible because it is no longer resisting but an agent, necessarily active and taking the initiative."[40]

Gramsci hopes to reclaim the integrity and the autonomy of the state on a theoretical level through his concepts of hegemony and counterhegemony and, on a practical level, through his invocations of the roles of participation and participatory leadership. The concept of hegemony demystifies the category of civil society. "Civil society" is not a neutral arena where societal forces in competition with each other get their tensions and conflicts worked out in accordance with impartial, superhistorical principles. The very idea of civil society constitutes a disarming mechanism to get the disadvantaged members of society to perceive and classify the forces working to undermine their position as power neutral rather than as power tainted. The concept of hegemony underscores the connection between displacement and power—the neutralization of power is itself the supreme move in the power game. "Hegemony" is an inherently politicizing concept that can galvanize its adherents into an appropriately political response. The formation of counterhegemonic forces that Gramsci continually advocates constitutes an attempt to create an ideological cadre of members of disadvantaged classes whose ideological constructs and institutions totally reflect and coincide with their deprived position at the power base.

The critique of sociology is theoretically homologous with the critique of civil society. "If it is true that man cannot be conceived of," Gramsci writes, "except as historically determined man—i.e., man who has developed, and who lives, in certain conditions, in a particular social complex or totality of social relations—is it then possible to take sociology as meaning simply the study of these conditions and the laws which regulate their development? Since the will and initiative of men themselves cannot be left out of account, this notion must be false."[41] Political science from Gramsci's perspective becomes a kind of master science, a study on all intellectual and practical fronts of the mobilization of human initiative and will. "Is not science itself," Gramsci asks, " 'political activity' and political thought?"[42]

One can cull from the *Prison Notebooks* a far-reaching, systematic critique of positivist social science.

> But it is absurd to think of a purely "objective" prediction. Anybody who makes a prediction has in fact a "programme" for whose victory he is working, and his prediction is precisely an element contributing to that victory.[43] This does not mean that prediction need always be arbitrary and gratuitous, or simply tendentious. Indeed one might say that only to the extent to which the objective aspect of prediction is linked to a programme does it acquire its objectivity: 1. because strong passions are necessary to sharpen the intellect and help make intuition more penetrating; 2. because reality is a product of the application of human will to the society of things (the machine-operator's to his machine); therefore if one excludes all voluntarist elements, or if it is only other people's wills whose intervention one reckons as an objective element in the general interplay of forces, one mutilates reality itself. Only the man who wills something strongly can identify the elements which are necessary to the realization of his will.
>
> When a particular programme has to be realized, it is only the existence of somebody to "predict" it which will ensure that it deals with what is essential—with those elements which, being "organisable" and susceptible of being directed or deflected, are in reality alone predictable.[44]

Gramsci in these passages engages in a metaphysical analysis of the relationship between participation and objectivity. He reverses the common understanding of the relationship between these two elements. Ordinarily, a participant's interests and goals are taken to be subversive of an objective grasp of a situation. Gramsci argues from a diametrically opposed perspective that what structures an objective world is precisely the participant's interests, needs, and biases. In order to carve out a recognizable reality from the indeterminate flux of experience, we need to be passionately driven creatures whose objects-of-will help to define and organize a world. Without the predominance of passion in the human psyche, there would be no objectivity.

In the second of the two citations, Gramsci is sketching the rudiments of a philosophy of social science that coheres with his overall dialectical-historicist views. He points to the indispensable role of the predictor in securing a pragmatic grip on the field of action. A counterhegemonic offensive against the currently prevailing hegemonic organization of beliefs, institutions, and practices requires the intervention of people capable of providing counterorganizational blueprints of reality that will serve as a goad and a vision for excluded classes. The dialectic of historical movement just describes a rhythm of possibilities that needs to be filled in by the simultaneous intellectual and practical organizational skills of individual historical actors. "In reality," Gramsci says, "one can 'foresee' to the extent that one acts, to the extent that one applies a voluntary effort and therefore contributes concretely to creating the result 'foreseen.' Prediction reveals itself thus not as a scientific act of knowledge, but as the abstract expression of the effort made, the practical way of creating a collective will."[45]

For the reasons just outlined, Gramsci is critical of the use of statistical methods in the social sciences. "It should be observed," he writes, "that political action tends precisely to rouse the masses from passivity, in other words to destroy the law of large numbers."[46] For analogous reasons, Gramsci attacks the use of law-like generalizations in the social sciences. "A fact or a series of facts," he says, "is described according to a mechanical process of abstract generalisations, a relationship of similarity is derived from this and given the title of law and the law is then assumed to have causal value. But what novelty is there in that? The only novelty is the collective name given to a series of petty facts, but names are not an innovation."[47] Lurking behind this "tautologous" approach is the avoidance of the recognition of the extent to which the assertion of human will can upset even the most hallowed regularities of human social life.

A very momentous implication follows from this discussion for the idea of responsibility, the positivist interpretation of which formed a major target of Gramsci's attack on the legacy of nineteenth-century ideas discussed above. If objectivity is created through participation, then there are no independent constraints exerted by the field of knowledge that can relieve us of ethical responsibility. In a very palpable sense, epistemology is subordinated to ethics in Gramsci's philosophy.[48] The ultimate validation for the reality we collectively transform and create must come from its comporting with our moral sense. Our wholeness as human beings is finally attested by the fact that we have nothing but our previous exertions of will to blame for the ethical complexion of the world we inhabit.

Dialectical Historicism as a Culmination of the Western Philosophical Tradition

Gramsci's resilience as thinker is sufficient to encompass the prospects of both historical recalcitrance and reversion—the historical process not yielding to our interventionist efforts—and historical novelty, our efforts bringing about results that we did not foresee.

> But even the philosophy of praxis is an expression of historical contradictions, and indeed their most complete, because most conscious, expression; this means that it too is tied to "necessity" and not to a "freedom" which does not exist and, historically, cannot yet exist. If, therefore, it is demonstrated that contradictions will disappear, it is also demonstrated implicitly that the philosophy of praxis too will disappear, or be superseded. In the reign of "freedom" thought and ideas can no longer be born on the terrain of contradiction and the necessity of struggle. At the present time the philosopher—the philosopher of praxis—can only make this generic affirmation and can go no further; he cannot escape from the present field of contradictions, he cannot affirm, other than generically, a world without contradictions, without immediately creating a utopia.[49]

In other words, Gramsci can only spell out the logic of his position as it evolves in relation to current historical circumstances. Current circumstances are marked by rampant contradictions (inequalities of class power; nascent counterhegemonic thrusts against prevailing hegemonic preponderencies) so Gramsci as revolutionary theorist formulates plans of action that endeavor to overcome these contradictions. But since Gramsci lives in the present world and not in the future world of his political imaginings, he cannot state flatly that in the future all present contradictions will be resolved "without immediately creating a utopia." The pragmatic force of such a prediction would be to unhinge the delicate balance of forces governing Gramsci's current deliberations by either making people less willing to exert themselves to bring about such a future because its result was assured or, countervailingly, to act as if no moral price were too high to usher in the prognosticated future. Acting as if the future were known with certainty gives rise to either a misplaced quietism or a misguided activism; in either case, it surreptitiously relieves one of the burden of living in the present. The focal point of revolutionary consciousness is to release us to the prospect of living in the present, with its moral and existential uncertainties unimpaired, lighting the way to a future we can accept.

Gramsci's agnosticism concerning the future goes hand in hand with an imaginative and detailed vision of certain transformations in Western intellectual life he would like to see accomplished in response to current contradictions. I spoke earlier of two broad intellectual types that Gramsci delineates (the "traditional" intellectual and the "organic" intellectual) and I tried to account through my analysis of Shils for the persistence and coexistence of these two types. Gramsci, however, wants to transform the intellectual landscape to hasten the disappearance of traditional intellectuals and engender the proliferation of organic intellectuals. This transformation is powerfully summarized by Jerome Karabel:

> The disappearance of the intellectual as he had been known in the past would occur only when he had accomplished his mission: the stimulation within the working class of a profound revolutionary consciousness exemplified by the mass emergence of a new historical type—the intellectualized proletarian. The new worker would be characterized by the cultural and theoretical sophistication traditionally reserved for an elite, but his ultimate contribution to knowledge would derive from the transformation of man's social being that resulted from his practical activity, for in changing the social context from which philosophy emerges, the revo-

lutionary worker provides the material basis upon which great theoretical advances in philosophy finally depend. Paradoxically, then, the death of the specialized intellectual heralds the birth of a period of unprecedented intellectual advance, informed for the first time in history by the activity of the masses.[50]

The supersession of the traditional intellectual and the reembodiment of intellectual activity in the masses is not only a sociological phenomenon but results from a crisis inherent in Western philosophy itself. Sociology recapitulates theoretical activity. An intellectual crisis that cannot be resolved on an intellectual level also ends up undermining the structures of social differentiation that nurtured and legitimated traditional intellectual activity.

The intellectual crisis has to do with formulating a consistent version of skepticism. In a notebook entry that forms part of his critique of Bukharin's *Manual*, Gramsci writes as follows:

> An inquiry into a series of facts to discover the relation between them presupposes a "concept" that permits one to distinguish that series from other possible series of facts. How can there take place a choice of facts to be adduced as proof of the truth of one's own assumption if one does not have a pre-existing criterion of choice? But what is this criterion of choice to be, if not something superior to each single fact under enquiry? An intuition, a conception, which must be regarded as having a complex history, a process that is to be connected with the whole process of the development of culture (etc.). This observation may be connected with the other one on the "sociological law" in which one simply repeats the same fact twice, the first time as a fact and the second time as a law, and which is a sophism of the double fact and not a law at all.[51]

The discussion in this passage is reminiscent of Plato's problem in the *Meno*. As we have seen in Chapter Four, Plato argues that the traditional method for resolving perplexity by engaging in the activities of problem formulation and problem solution rests upon a paradox. One either knows what one is looking for or one does not. If one knows what one is looking for, then the statement of the problem is pointless. If one does not know what he is looking for, then a delineation of the problem becomes impossible.

Analogously, in the passage cited, Gramsci points to the infinite regress that results, the pointless duplication that gets nowhere, by postulating a conscious source for the criteria that preselect the facts relevant to the solution of a particular problem. If the solution to one's problem is somehow supposed to reside in the facts, then the determination of the relevance of those facts to the solution of the problem has also to be contained in the facts. But in order for the solution to be convincing, the relevance of the facts selected to illumine the problem must somehow be assumed and cannot be directly inferred from the facts themselves. Otherwise, an infinite regress would emerge (whereby one could continually press the question "Why?") that would prevent one from ever solving a particular problem by recourse to a specific set of facts. Whichever approach one takes, one is bereft of an adequate theory to account for the activity of problem solving through the accumulation and analysis of facts. If one acknowledges the role of assumptions in determining relevance, then the facts are not decisive. And if one somehow claims that the issue of relevance is decided by the facts themselves, then one opens the door to an infinite regress of justification, a door that can never be satisfactorily closed.

Skeptical positions in philosophy founder on a variant of the paradox surrounding the activity of problem solving. "The common-sense objection that one can make against scepticism," Gramsci writes, "is this: that to be consistent with himself the sceptic should do nothing else but live like a vegetable, without involving himself in the business of ordinary life. If the sceptic takes part in the debate, it means that he thinks that he can convince people. That is, he is no longer a sceptic, but represents a specific positive opinion, which is usually bad and can triumph only by convincing the community that other opinions are even worse, because useless."[52] If the paradox confronting the problem solver was that he had already to know what he claimed he didn't know, the paradox confronting the skeptic was (depending on how thoroughgoing his skepticism was) either that he had already to know what he claimed was unknowable or that he had already to know what he claimed was false. There are "agnostic" and "atheistic" varieties of skepticism, but to *argue* in defense of skepticism is to explode both.

A plausible way to read Gramsci is to say that these examples of discourse in extremis—problem-solving discourse and skeptical discourse—illuminate for him the nature of less problematic, more conventional discourse. If one accepts Quine's thesis that all of the statements that one takes to be correct (in a particular language) are to be viewed holistically—that they are never hauled before the bar of experience as isolated statements, but that it is always the totality of statements that one regards as correct that confronts experience—then any slack in that body of statements, such as the logical difficulties surrounding problem-solving and skeptical statements, redefines the character of the whole body of statements and modulates the logical angle at which they confront experience.[53] If one adds to the mix of considerations adduced here Quine's thesis of the interdeterminacy of translation,[54] then the theoretical perplexities surrounding problem-solving discourse and skeptical discourse can be generalized to encompass more ordinary regions of discourse as well, since all linguistic formulations, at whatever low level of generality, can be shown to be equally underdetermined by experience. One might say, therefore, that just as the difficulties encountered in offering a coherent account of the activity of problem solving and in formulating a consistent version of skepticism highlight the extent to which patterns of belief and disbelief among a community of language users might be usefully construed as a function of certain constellations of power that rule out particular statements and sanction others, so too in those language regions where the problem of reflexivity, of being able to justify the critical canons in terms of which a particular statement was made, does not loom as central, it is the slope of power distribution within the community that helps to determine exclusion and legitimacy. The language of language, one might say, is not language—but power. Whatever logical protocols, of whatever provisionally justificatory sort, have been traced to legitimize most forms of problem-solving and skeptical statements might best be interpreted as a function of power configurations existing within society, and the same would be true for whatever analogues exist for these protocols in less problematic regions of discourse.

The skepticism that we have identified in Gramsci's philosophy is manifested in his political judgments as well. He writes that "the demonstration [by the leaders of the counterhegemonic forces of the need to undermine the current hegemonic constellation of power] in the last analysis only succeeds and is 'true' if it becomes a new reality, if the forces of opposition triumph; in the immediate, it is developed in a series of ideological, religious, philosophical, political, and juridical polemics, whose correctness can be estimated by the extent to which they are convincing, and shift the previously existing disposition of social forces."[55] According to Gramsci, there is no set of political or narrowly epistemological principles that can validate revolutionary political insight. What validates it is the achievement of revolutionary political success. There is an interesting analogy here with Hume's theory of revolution. According to Hume, no revolutionary political act can be prospectively justified. There is in nearly all cases a residuum of political obligation due the old order based on the fact that it is able to maintain peace and stability. Political revolution can only be retrospectively justified when the temporary disruption has been fairly easily reassimilated into the ongoing arrangements of society.[56] The extremes, Gramsci's radicalism and Hume's conservatism, thus seem to converge in a concept of *a posteriori* justification for political decisions and judgments. The convergence perhaps is not accidental. It might be grounded in a common skepticism that predisposes the inquirer to look toward pragmatic factors, including real-world outcomes, for resolution of philosophical perplexities.[57]

If, as Gramsci says, "the theoretical–practical principle of hegemony has also epistemological significance,"[58] part of that significance lies in the fact that it conceives of the transposition of philosophical argument into the specific codes of enactment of diverse, nonintellectual social practices. The notion of hegemony might be conceived as predicated upon the breakdown of traditional epistemology; "hegemony" therefore functions on one level as an attempt to reconstitute epistemology through other means. The seamless character of knowledge and action postulated by the concept of hegemony discussed earlier in this chapter suggests the prospect of knowledge being acquired, revised, criticized, transformed, and superseded through a series of moves made in a complexly interrelated network of correspondences with traditional epistemology, which permits the downgrading, and sometimes even the bypassing, of exclusively cognitive modes of argument altogether. "Hegemony" from one perspective captures the sense in which we acquire and revise knowledge through doing.

Given the nature of Gramsci's skepticism that we have been examining, his conceptualizations of hegemony can also in a reflexive sense (not as an explanatory concept but from the perspective of what it enables its propounder and his audience to accomplish) be interpreted pragmatically and instrumentally. If what is binding members of society to the present order is in many ways an overtly uncoercive scheme of cultural relations, then the points of access for social and political change are much more readily available than the masses are originally prone to believe. Part of the compelling power of the concept of hegemony thus stems from its double message. On the one hand, it reminds us of the formidableness of the challenge facing us because of the very ubiquity and givenness of the forces binding us to the present social order. On the other hand, with the same set of verbal cues and signals, it instructs us concerning the ease of the task facing us if only we will mobilize, in a not very extraordinary way, our energies of will.

Gramsci's dialectical historicism offers him a further resource of argument for accommodating skepticism and advancing a viable notion of objectivity:

> Man knows objectively insofar as knowledge is real for the whole human race historically unified in a single unitary cultural system.[59] But this process of historical unification takes place through the disappearance of the internal contradictions which tear apart human society, while these contradictions themselves are the conditions for the formation of groups and for the birth of ideologies which are not completely universal but are immediately rendered transient by the practical origin of their substance. There exists therefore a struggle for objectivity (to free oneself from partial and fallacious ideologies) and this struggle is the same as the struggle for the cultural unification of the human race. What the idealists call "spirit" is not a point of departure but a point of arrival, it is the ensemble of the superstructures moving towards concrete and objectively universal unification and it is not a unitary presupposition.[60]

Objectivity from Gramsci's dialectically historicist perspective is consensual and pragmatic. First there must be a closing of the gap within individual societies between superstructure and structure. The ideological machinery of society must reflect the true inputs of *all* the diverse groups that go to produce the material outputs of society. Hegemonic structures must be transformed from mechanisms of exclusion into mechanisms of inclusion. Then an array of all of these mechanisms of inclusion alongside each other and a distillation of their common elements would yield a dialectically historicist acceptable version of objectivity. Given the anticosmopolitan bent of Gramsci's thought discussed earlier, the evolution of such objective norms constitutes more an ideal limit than a historically actionable goal.

The inspiration for Gramsci's dialectical historicism comes, of course, from Marx's conception of praxis.[61] One might say that the idea of praxis represents the integration of agnosticism[62] as a methodological tool for the analysis of philosophical systems as well as other cultural products. The idea of praxis, conceived in the most charitable sense, does not attempt to render a judgment of correctness or falsity concerning intellectual and cultural products. It merely attempts to locate them in a structural scheme of relations of production and to illustrate how the cultural activities and products at the superstructural level cohere with the productive base of society. A praxis approach to cultural products need render no judgment about the transhistorical validity of a particular set of cultural norms and values, nor need it take a position concerning the indefiniteness of the evolutionary process revealed by the concept of praxis itself. It might be that in the course of time a praxis approach will come to seem less fruitful as an analytic tool of culture than other alternate modes of self-understanding. "Praxis" itself might be superseded as a cultural tool by a societal praxis that makes yet undreamt of approaches seem more compelling.

Another way of reading Gramsci's articulation of the dialectic of hegemony versus counterhegemony is as an exteriorization of the drama of Western epistemology. Gramsci's dialectic of hegemony versus counterhegemony captures the irreducibly ironic rhythms of our lives whereby our human assertions of will generate antihumanist structures and the antihumanist structures, in turn, facilitate and evoke our humanistic counterassertions. Analogously, as Gramsci's discussions of problem-solving discourse and skeptical discourse make clear, the pathos of Western epistemology consists in its second-order, metastatements remaining permanently out of harness with the regions of discourse (e.g., problem-solving statements, material-object statements) they purport to explain and analyze. Second-order philosophical statements trying to account for problem-solving statements fail to make the initial connection with a non-question-begging "problem" for which the problem solver is attempting to offer a solution. With regard to skepticism, second-order philosophical statements that express skepticism also fail to connect with their objects because of the difficulties of formulating a non-self-refuting version of skepticism that undermines the skeptical statements themselves before they can affect the targets of skepticism. This interior lack of permanently catching up between the self and its objects dramatized by the limits of Western epistemology is exteriorized by Gramsci in his depiction of the dialectic of hegemony versus counterhegemony.

Given the skeptical, agnostic understandings that permeate Gramsci's deployment of the dialectic of hegemony versus counterhegemony, it is not surprising that he is critical of the idea of progress. Even the possibility of making meaningful interhistorical comparisons is impugned by Gramsci. In a passage that prefigures Paul Feyerabend's notion of the incommensurability of paradigms,[63] Gramsci writes: "But if man is conceived as the ensemble of social relations, it then appears that every comparison between men, over time, is impossible, because one is dealing with different, if not heterogeneous, objects."[64]

Gramsci is willing to go the distance with his pragmatist theory of knowledge. Mass adherence to an ideology becomes the critical test of rationality.

> Mass adhesion or non-adhesion to an ideology is the real critical test of the rationality and historicity of modes of thinking. Any arbitrary constructions are pretty rapidly eliminated by historical competition, even if sometimes, through a combination of immediately favorable circumstances, they manage to enjoy popularity of a kind; whereas construc-

tions which respond to the demands of a complex organic period of history always impose themselves and prevail in the end, even though they may pass through several intermediary phases during which they manage to affirm themselves only in more or less bizarre and hetero-geneous combinations.[65]

The skepticism manifested at various points in Gramsci's dialectically historicist political philosophy is superior to other twentieth-century attempts to articulate a coherent skeptical position for three reasons.

First, the Marxist notion of praxis upon which Gramsci's dialectical historicism builds postulates the idea that everything changes together—material base as well as ideational and cultural superstructure. Skepticism thus truly emerges as a "self-consuming artifact" that need leave no intellectual traces behind to bedevil the proponent of philosophical consistency. Gramsci's dialectical historicism thus accommodates the problem of formulating a consistent version of skepticism more satisfactorily than Polanyi's tacit knowledge because Gramsci does not have to postulate any constants between different cultural epochs—not even tacit, unconscious constants. "It seems as if the philosophy of praxis," Gramsci writes, "is the only consistent 'immanentist' conception"[66]—that is, the only form of skepticism that is not undermined by self-contradiction.

Second, skepticism can be applied reflexively to Gramsci's central concept of hegemony, and hegemony emerges unscathed from the encounter. "Hegemony" constitutes an attempt to deflate all cultural and intellectual products and to construe them by the ways that they advance or retard the power standings of particular political actors and classes. If one turns this canon of criticism against hegemony itself and raises the question of in what sense is *it* a valid analytical tool and not just a partisan camouflage to advance sectarian power purposes, Gramsci has a strong answer. He can point to the pragmatic, instrumentalist character of hegemony itself. In calling attention to the accessibility and overtly uncoercive character of many of the foci where power is being manifested in society, Gramsci makes possible efforts at transforming those foci in ways that would be most beneficial to excluded classes. "Hegemony" thus betrays a virtuous circularity: The concept that breaks down other people's ideas to the point of being able to illustrate the ways in which they promote specific power ends can itself be broken down in the same way. "Hegemony" not only tolerates but directly invites a pragmatic reading: It is an idea whose truth consists in its usefulness in corroding other ideas.

Finally, Gramsci's agnosticism toward the future, despite his efforts to achieve congruence between participatory democratic counter-hegemonic means and participatory democratic revolutionary ends, means that in a genuine sense Gramsci is skeptical of his own skepticism. Class antagonisms might continue in the postrevolutionary aftermath, which would necessitate resort to counterhegemonic confrontation as a strategy for liberating excluded classes, or a whole new configuration of societal and cultural possibilities might emerge that would supersede entirely a "hegemonic" approach. Skepticism, too, for Gramsci is an intellectual tool and not a refuge of certainty—so that in the end it might be superseded by cultural and historical factors that no one presently can foresee.

Leadership as the Motive Force of "Hegemony Versus Counterhegemony"

The dialectic of hegemony versus counterhegemony, the motive force behind Gramsci's dialectical historicism, works when there is appropriate leadership to foment and head counterhegemonic formations. "The Hegelian 'idea,'" Gramsci says, "has been resolved both in the structure and in the superstructure"[67]—that is to say, the dynamics of social change can be initiated both at the superstructural and structural levels. As my discussion of counterhegemony earlier in this chapter indicated, the counterhegemonic forces must replicate within themselves the democratic, egalitarian features that they seek to extend to society at large. Gramsci again like one of his mentors (Machiavelli) is extremely sensitive to the means–end relationship[68] and wants to ensure that the power relations that develop within the counterhege-

monic forces are continuous with the goals postulated for the redistribution of power after the revolution. While keenly sensitive to
the need to preserve a balance between means and ends, Gramsci is
also aware of the huge gap of consciousness that separates (traditional) intellectuals with their insights into the dynamics of historical
change from the subordinated masses. Gramsci is quite frank in acknowledging that innovation and leadership must initially come from
intellectuals:

> Critical self-consciousness means, historically and politically, the creation
> of an elite[69] of intellectuals. A human mass does not "distinguish" itself,
> does not become independent in its own right without, in the widest
> sense, organising itself, and there is no organisation without intellec-
> tuals, that is without organisers and leaders, in other words, without the
> theoretical aspect of the theory–practice nexus being distinguished con-
> cretely by the existence of a group of people "specialised" in conceptual
> and philosophical elaboration of ideas.[70]

Gramsci as revolutionary theorist is thus faced with the very
delicate problem of how to empower the intellectuals so that they
galvanize the masses, while restricting and modifying the intellectuals' intervention in such ways that they lead the masses democratically. Knowledge and a judgment of the importance of popular feeling, in Gramsci's view, "is acquired by the collective organism through
'active and conscious co-participation,' through 'compassionality,'
through experience of immediate particulars, through a system which
one could call 'living philology.' In this way a close link is formed
between great mass, party and leading group; and the whole complex,
thus articulated, can move together as 'collective-man.' "[71]

Gramsci wants leadership to emerge from within a particular
setting—a participatory one. Its remaining close to that praxis will
have a disciplining and restraining effect, inhibiting leadership from
degenerating into domination.[72] Gramsci's motive for wanting to nurture leadership in a participatory context is a dual one, catering to
short-term and long-term considerations. In the short run, a compassionate involvement through participatory give and take with the
people he is leading will temper the leader's trying to assume authori-

tarian control. From a long-term perspective, most intellectuals in the modern world are rootless—traditional intellectuals. The best hope for cultivating organic intellectuals is by having leadership exercised in an intimate participatory setting, which might raise the consciousness of certain members of the excluded classes sufficiently to equip them to function as organic intellectuals.

One must distinguish therefore in the first instance for Gramsci between egalitarian, participatory leadership and hierarchical leadership. "Every relationship of 'hegemony,'" Gramsci says, "is necessarily an educational relationship."[73] The way that a new "historical bloc . . . i.e., unity between nature and spirit (structure and superstructure), unity of opposites and distincts"[74] between excluded classes and intellectuals will be formed is by conceiving their relationship as mutually educational. In education, "the relationship between teacher and pupil is active and reciprocal so that every teacher is always a pupil and every pupil is a teacher."[75] Gramsci's notion of participatory leadership is admirably fleshed out by Paulo Freire in his book *Pedagogy of the Oppressed*:

> Cultural synthesis (precisely because it is a *synthesis*) does not mean that the objectives of revolutionary action should be limited by the aspirations expressed in the world view of the people. If this were to happen (in the guise of respect for that view), the revolutionary leaders would be passively bound to that vision. Neither invasion by the leaders of the people's world view nor mere adaptation by the leaders to the (often naive) aspirations of the people is acceptable.

> To be concrete: if at a given historical moment the basic aspiration of the people goes no further than a demand for salary increases, the leaders can commit one of two errors. They can limit their action to stimulating this one demand or they can overrule this popular aspiration and substitute something more far-reaching—but something which has not yet come to the forefront of the people's attention. In the first case, the revolutionary leaders follow a line of adaptation to the people's demands. In the second case, by disrespecting the aspirations of the people, they fall into cultural invasion.

> The solution lies in synthesis: the leaders must on the one hand identify with the people's demand for higher salaries, while on the other they

must pose the meaning of that very demand as a problem. By doing this, the leaders pose as a problem a real, concrete, historical situation of which the salary demand is one dimension. It will thereby become clear that salary demands alone cannot comprise a definitive solution. The essence of this solution can be found in the previously cited statement by bishops of the Third World that "if the workers do not somehow come to be owners of their own labor, all structural reforms will be ineffective . . . they [must] be owners, not sellers, of their labor . . . [for] any purchase or sale of labor is a type of slavery."

To achieve critical consciousness of the fact that it is necessary to be the "owner of one's own labor," that labor "constitutes part of the human person," and that "a human being cannot be sold nor can he sell himself" is to go a step beyond the deception of palliative solutions. It is to engage in authentic transformation of reality in order, by humanizing that reality, to humanize men. In the antidialogical theory of action, cultural invasion serves the ends of conquest, and conquest the ends of domination. Cultural synthesis serves the ends of organization; organization serves the ends of liberation.[76]

The participatory leader transforms the consciousness of his participatory cohorts without abusing power. The type of organization he gives rise to might be labeled revolutionary, in contrast to routinized organization that is expressive of hierarchical leadership. Revolutionary organization preserves the tense balance between teachers and students whose identities are never permanently fixed and who continue to learn from each other in the course of building up their counterhegemonic forces. Revolutionary organization manifests participatory patterns of interaction throughout its life span, while routinized organization is structured in accordance with oligarchical principles whose members' identities as teachers or learners are fixed in advance. In order to achieve revolutionary transformation, with power being equally shared among the diverse members of a community, there has already to be revolutionary transformation, the counterhegemonic forces waging war against entrenched hegemonies must already be structured along egalitarian lines. The fluid identities of teacher and pupil shared by leaders and members of nascent counterhegemonic forces ensure that equality determines the means as well as defining the end of revolutionary action.

The prerequisites for political leadership that emerge from my discussion of Gramsci are twofold. The first is that in order for someone to qualify for political leadership he or she must experience the prospect of serving as a leader as an extraordinary burden. Since the counterhegemonic force must never lose its participatory ethos while waging war against entrenched hegemonic power, the leader must experience the pull of that participatory involvement and exert himself or herself against it by asserting a leadership role only at the cost of a certain amount of psychic pain and imbalance. Someone who lunges after political leadership is by that very fact disqualified from exercising it. This is a sentiment that Gramsci shares with Plato, who said that the philosopher had to be coaxed into ruling by the recognition that otherwise he would be ruled by someone inferior to himself.[77] If there is not his grudging acceptance of the burdens of political leadership, then the very legitimacy of philosophers ruling is called into question. A political motive governing Plato's choice of philosophers to rule his ideal state is that they are the people who, temperamentally speaking, are least likely to relish the tasks of rulership.

This notion of aversion to rulership as a prerequisite for exercising political leadership is also expressed in the Bible when Moses complains before God: "Wherefore hast thou done evil unto thy servant? And wherefore have I not found favor in thy eyes, that thou puttest the burden of all this people upon me? Have I conceived all this people? Have I born them, that thou should sayest unto me, carry them in thy bosom, as a nursing father beareth the suckling, unto the land which thou swearest unto their fathers? . . . I am not able to bear all this people alone, because it is too heavy for me. And if thou do thus with me, kill me, I pray thee, out of hand, if I have found favor in thy eyes; and let me not see my evil."[78] The biblical text emphasizes that it is this very renunciation of the pretensions of rulership that is a key source of the legitimacy of Moses as ruler. When, in the next chapter of Numbers, Moses is accused by his brother Aaron and his sister Miriam of marrying a Cushite woman, the Biblical text tersely comments: "Now the man Moses was very meek, above all the men who were upon the face of the earth."[79]

The second prerequisite for political leadership according to Gramsci is that leadership remain an open category, much as Gramsci claims the bourgeoisie historically defined themselves[80]—accessible to all the members of the community. On this point Gramsci sides with the Bible—"Would God that all the people of the Eternal were prophets"[81]—and against the overt Platonic teaching. The "cash value" of the concept of organic intellectual is that leadership roles be open to all of the members of the community. The praxis of the modern world in a more remote and a more immediate sense gives rise to the possibility of every man becoming his own intellectual. The more remote way in which modern praxis generates intellectual activity was discussed earlier in reference to Levenson's notion of traditionalism, whereby the multiple traditions operative in the modern world promote a heightened self-consciousness about the tradition one is concerned to defend. Since multiple traditions impinge upon the consciousness of ordinary men and women, they have the effect of awakening in them the intellectual capacities to articulate and promote their own tradition—whether it be conservative or revolutionary. The more immediate modern praxis that nurtures intellectual activity is the formation and manning of the counterhegemonic force itself—which through doing helps to structure and sharpen thought so that ordinary members of a counterhegemonic force become capable of undertaking its leadership functions.

Gramsci believes that in the modern period the war of position has superseded the war of movement. "The same thing happens in the art of politics as happens in military art," Gramsci writes. "War of movement increasingly becomes war of position, and it can be said that a state will win a war insofar as it prepares for it minutely and technically in peacetime. The massive structures of the modern democracies both as state organizations, and as complexes of associations in civil society, constitute for the art of politics as it were the 'trenches' and the permanent proliferations of the front in the war of position: They render merely 'partial' the element of movement which before would be 'the whole' of war, etc."[82] The primacy of the political war of position over the war of movement in the modern period suggests a further qualification for political leadership: staying power, patience. Triumphing over an opponent in the modern war of position sometimes simply means surviving as a viable political actor longer than one's opponent so that one is able to pick up the chips in more auspicious rounds of confrontation. This provides an additional gloss on Gramsci's notion that everyone can become his own intellectual. If victory is often linked with patience, stamina, and resoluteness, then leadership roles are open to vast numbers of men and women whose experience in life has led them to cultivate precisely these qualities.

Gramsci realizes that the emergence of spontaneous leadership from within the counterhegemonic ranks might be diffused and chaotic, so he emphasizes the role of parties as leadership-recruitment forums: "Parties may be said to have the task of forming capable leaders; they are the mass function which selects, develops, and multiplies the leaders which are necessary if a particular social group (which is a 'fixed' quantity, since it can be established how many members there are of any social group) is to become articulated, and be transformed from turbulent chaos into an organically prepared political army."[83] Parties and party leaders constitute a short-term palliative so that counterhegemonic structures do not lose precious time in their protracted war of position against hegemonic concentrations of power. Also, the parties, too, should strive to recruit and nurture organic intellectuals—that is, the parties should preserve their organic tie with the excluded classes.

From a purely formalistic power perspective, there is an important affinity between the concept of leadership and the concept of hegemony in Gramsci's thought. Just as the Machiavellian idea that power appears in its most consummate form when it is effectively displaced and neutralized helps to explain the appeal and the usefulness of the concept of hegemony in Gramsci's thought, so too is leadership prized for analogous reasons. The leader very often, through rational persuasiveness and the evocation of charismatic identification, is able to get people to do what he wants without having to resort to force. Thus, from the perspective of power, the concept of leadership is as much an "economic necessity" as is the concept of hegemony. From this point of view, democratic participatory leadership is less costly than hierarchical leadership, since it requires less coercion and rests most fully on persuasion and consent.

A central tension in Gramsci's thought which emerges from our discussion is that politically speaking he seeks to democratize the intellectual function, while philosophically speaking his skepticism is so thoroughgoing, and so elegantly formulated, that it appears to withstand reflexive challenge—that it seems to cry out for (if not in some informal sense actually depend upon) an elite group of intellectuals with sufficient daring and imagination to create the plurality of worlds that the rest of us agree to inhabit with varying degrees of acquiescence or relish. Gramsci's politics seem incorrigibly democratic, while his metaphysical predispositions appear incorrigibly elitist.

Perhaps the most coherent reading of Gramsci is to say that at the heart of his vision lies a very daring yoking together of opposites. His extreme voluntarism constantly hovers on the edges of necessity—continually recoiling to adjust means to ends. The counterhegemonic buildup of forces must be democratically structured so as to iron out disparities and tensions between means and ends. As an analyst of power, Gramsci's stress falls on economy, on adjusting means to ends so skillfully and minutely that no excessive gestures or investments of power are mobilized to accomplish results that can be achieved with less. This helps to explain the appeal of the concept of counterhegemony for him as a strategy for waging war against entrenched power concentrations. Counterhegemonic forces deflect and displace recourse to overt power to the fullest possible extent, achieving their triumph (when they succeed) through this very displacement. The circumscribing of freedom of choice by factors of necessity (pointing to their merging and coincidence) appears like a leitmotif in Gramsci's political thought. In the end, one could say that he is seeking a justification in terms of necessity for the various substantive political visions pursued by the different constellations of counterhegemonic forces throughout history. The coincidence of freedom and necessity on this score can only arise if the ordinary men and women peopling the counterhegemonic forces can themselves be shown to be the source of the goals and strategies that motivate their cause.[84] The concept of "organic intellectual" completes Gramsci's thought by lending it symmetry and rigor as a metaphysical system. Only when the masses have become intellectualized can the self-disclosure achieved in the human roots of necessity so totally coalesce with the dictates of necessity being acted upon that the sense of human wholeness that our daily experience of history continually fragments is restored.

Participatory Leadership: A Contradiction in Terms?

The contrast between Gramsci's notion of participatory leadership and the hierarchical leadership prevailing in liberal society could not be more striking. The very conceptual schemata employed by such liberal theorists of leadership as James David Barber to analyze its dynamics show how firmly rooted they are in hierarchical understandings of leadership. In his book *The Presidential Character: Predicting Performance in the White House*,[85] Barber employs two variables in analyzing presidential performance. The first is a president's enjoyment level—his attitude toward what he does, whether positive or negative, his self-image. The second variable Barber invokes is a president's activity level—whether he is active or passive in the conduct of his office.[86] Part of what makes Barber's paradigm of analysis of presidential leadership so quintessentially liberal is that he has highlighted those characteristics that have historically contributed to successful entrepreneurial performance and has used them to evaluate presidential performance in the public realm. Barber's analysis assumes that activity matters—that as long as a president is temperamentally predisposed toward being active and has positive emotional affects associated with that activity, contributing to raising his self-esteem—then presidential greatness is virtually assured.

Barber's conception of leadership sees it as a purely interpersonal, public phenomenon, concerned to superintend a multitude of hierarchies whose official aims are to promote economic growth and to preserve international peace. In order for Gramsci's participatory notion of leadership to gain a foothold in our vocabularies, we must first conceive the possibility that leadership is exercised internally, in relation to the self. The participatory leadership that Gramsci advocates can only be practiced in relation to a self that does not experience the leader as an alien intruder (as someone merely trying to manipulate

175

the self) but as someone offering guidance in relation to functions that the self performs in relation to itself. Only if leadership is perceived as an internal "voice" of the self does Gramsci's notion of participatory leadership stand a chance of being effective with its intended audience.

Gramsci conceives of the self as perpetually involved in an activity of structuring—of the exertion of power—in furtherance of the project of retrieving or establishing coherence in relation to the multiplicity of its own actions.

> Reflecting on it, we can see that in putting the question, "what is man?" what we mean is: What can man become? That is, can man dominate his own destiny, can he "make himself," can he create his own life? *We maintain therefore that man is a process, and, more exactly, the process of his actions.* If you think about it, the question itself "What is man?" is not an abstract or "objective" question. It is born of our reflection about ourselves and about others, and we want to know, in relation to what we have thought and seen, what we are and what we can become; whether we really are, and if so to what extent, "makers of our own selves," of our life and of our destiny. And we want to know this "today," in the given conditions of today, the conditions of our daily life, not of any life or any man.[87]

Man is defined by his actions. Yet the very plurality of human actions, leaving so many tantalizing traces for potential self-development, would incapacitate man for future action unless there were constant regrouping of the energies of the self, renewed imposition of (temporary) structures, whose very subordination of particular aspects of self to others on an ongoing basis enabled the self to function. The concept of the political thus emerges in Gramsci's thought as an ontological category—a basic category of human self-understanding.

I think that one can say that the concepts of distance (relating to multiple possibilities of selfhood) and of leadership constitute ontological categories in Gramsci's thought to the same extent (and for analogous reasons) that the political is regarded as an ontological category. One might say that leadership manifests itself initially as an intrapersonal psychic phenomenon—the result of that internal conversation that never ceases as long as we live. When one part of ourselves addresses other parts of ourselves, strategies of leadership are already being mobilized. In the course of fashioning a coherent self poised on the brink of action, leadership is being exercised. Since the possibilities and opportunities available to a self are constantly in flux (and need to be continually reassessed and reappropriated) internal leadership functions never lapse, but form an integral part of a viable concept of self. In contrast to the category of the political, which calls attention to the exertion of power by one component of self against others, the notion of leadership highlights such other modes of relating as persuading, cajoling, and compromising that can subsist between the various aspects of a self in the course of assuming and constantly reassuming a normal human identity capable of making decisions and acting upon them.[88]

Man, for Gramsci, is political in a dual sense: He not only exercises power internally in relation to the self, but over his social and natural environments. By changing these, he gains reliable insight into the nature of his evolving self.

> I mean that one must conceive of man as a series of active relationships (a process) in which individuality, though perhaps the most important, is not, however, the only element to be taken into account. The humanity which is reflected in each individuality is composed of various elements: 1. the individual; 2. other men; 3. the natural world. But the latter two elements are not as simple as they might appear. The individual does not enter into relations with other men by juxtaposition, but organically, inasmuch, that is, as he belongs to organic entities which range from the simplest to the most complex. Thus man does not enter into relations with the natural world just by being himself part of the natural world, but actively, by means of work and technique. Further: These relations are not mechanical. They are active and conscious. They correspond to the greater or lesser degree of understanding that each man has of them. So one could say that each one of us changes himself, modifies himself to the extent that he changes and modifies the complex relations of which he is the hub. In this sense the real philosopher is, and cannot be other than, the politician, the active man who modifies the environment, understanding by environment the ensemble of relations which each of us enters to take part in. If one's own individuality is the ensemble of these

relations, to create one's personality means to acquire consciousness of them and to modify one's own personality means to modify the ensemble of these relations.[89]

Political leadership thus presupposes a self already involved in a participatory manner with its multiple components and possibilities, asserting leadership from moment to moment so as to become capable of effective action. Only participatory leadership, which approximates from the start to the goal it is trying to achieve, can obviate the formation of new classes that stand in an adversarial relation to previous thrusts of counterhegemonic power. The externally motivated hierarchical mode of leadership prevailing in liberal societies can only generate new forms of oppression, new classes: "The source of liberalism's weakness then becomes apparent: it is the bureaucracy—i.e., the crystallization of the leading personnel—which exercises coercive power, and at a certain point it becomes a caste."[90]

Hierarchical leadership, as exemplified by Barber's conception of presidential leadership, presupposes an environment in which a relatively isolated, highly motivated individual can realize his goals without unduly interfering with—or involving—his fellows. In a context of relative abundance, where vast numbers of people have access to goods and status, leadership is usually perceived not as a mode of relationship having natural roots in individual psychology, but as something artificial, an exclusively social phenomenon, having to do with the superintending of conflict over and between large groups. Hierarchical leadership is inhospitable to three contexts that have become increasingly prominent in the modern world: a society experiencing resource scarcities, a modernizing society, and a society grown more self-conscious about the class divisions prevailing within it. All three environments are characterized by a sense of the shrinkage of space and the curtailment of opportunities.

The concept of participatory leadership that views it as an intrapersonal, psychic phenomenon gains plausibility to the extent that it illuminates the sense in which "leadership" will still be going on in an environment marked by resource scarcities that will not respond to activist initiatives alone. Where limits on the sorts of lives people might lead become severe, they especially need participatory leaders who aid in the restructuring of the self in order to fashion viable concepts of personal identity (and viable projects in life) in a dramatically transformed economic and social environment.

Leadership in a modernizing context duplicates to some extent conditions of leadership in a context of resource scarcities. Both involve the fashioning of a satisfactory sense of personal identity in an environment where one has to make do with little. One has to become that sort of self that can maximize the opportunities of a resource-deficient environment. The leader in a modernizing context, as well as in a context of scarcity, constitutes a more literal extension of self than is true in the sort of political environment that Barber is talking about. The political leader in a modernizing context (and in a context of resource scarcities) through precept and example helps in the restructuring process whereby human personality is enabled to adapt to the stringencies of an oppressive environment.

In a society marked by self-consciousness about class inequalities, participatory leadership facilitates the closing of the gap between means and ends, so that the transformed society does not generate hierarchies and inequalities of its own leading to an unending revolutionary spiral. Gramsci's strategy was to attempt to unify the masses along participatory democratic lines as a countervailing approach to fascism, which sought to divide and conquer the masses. Peter Bachrach's approach, within the contemporary American political setting, of trying to form alliances between working-class groups and middle-class groups follows in the footsteps of Gramsci's theorizing a counterhegemonic assault on hegemonic structures. The concept of hegemony calls attention to the interdependence of economic power and modes of cultural organization and expression and to a mutually reinforcing pattern of relationship between these and all other forms of organized power within the community. To undo the interdependence suggested by the notion of "hegemony" requires the forging of as many class and cultural alliances as possible in a common deconstructive endeavor. This is a further instantiation of the Machiavellian teaching that in order to succeed in battle against each other, enemies must learn to use each other's weapons.

Gramsci's chief animating drive, of course, was the transformation of societies characterized by rampant class inequalities into more egalitarian societies. In words that ring prophetic of Reagan's and Bush's America, with its fostering of class polarization, Gramsci wrote: "If the ruling class has lost its consensus, i.e., is no longer 'leading' but only 'dominant,' exercising coercive force alone, this means precisely that the great masses have become detached from their traditional ideologies, and no longer believe what they used to believe previously, etc. The crisis consists precisely in the fact that the old is dying and the new cannot be born."[91] The moral vision behind dialectical historicism involves the historicizing of all "givens"—including, most crucially, the "given" of unequal class relationships. The moral, epistemological, and metaphysical impulses of dialectical historicism converge in the following assessment by Gramsci: "It will be said that what each individual can change is very little, considering his strength. This is true up to a point. But when the individual can associate himself with all the other individuals who want the same changes, and if the changes wanted are rational, the individual can be multiplied an impressive number of times and obtain a change which is far more radical than at first sight ever seemed possible."[92]

CHAPTER 7

Nietzsche, Foucault, and the Prospects of Postmodern Political Philosophy

I wish to suggest that the resources of Nietzsche's thought are such that they are sufficient to resolve the problem of reflexivity. Nietzsche in his epistemology and moral theory appears as an uncompromising skeptic and relativist. These positions, as we have seen, appear to be problematic because a consistent skepticism and relativism seem to compel one to be skeptical of one's own skepticism and to be relativistic about one's own relativism, which means that the extremeness of the original positions has to be modified in the light of the requirements of consistency. Postmodernist thought, with its suspicion of "metanarrativity," appears to offer us a very attractive way out of this dilemma by banishing altogether the need to justify skepticism. Jean-François Lyotard defines the "modern" as "any science that legitimates itself with reference to a metadiscourse of this kind [i.e., "a discourse of legitimation with respect to its own status, a discourse called philosophy"] making an explicit appeal to some grand narrative, such as the dialectics of the Spirit, the hermeneutics of meaning, the emancipation of the rational or working subject, or the creation of wealth."[1] Lyotard defines "postmodern" as "incredulity toward metanarratives."[2] The postmodern is thus characterized by its affirmation of an anarchic condition of autonomous, presuppositionless realms of discourse.[3] The advocates of postmodernism, with their willingness "to drop the opposition between 'true consensus' and 'false consensus,' or between 'validity' and 'power,' "[4] have generally taken Nietzsche, in whom the vocabulary of power proliferates and discussions of validity are kept to a bare minimum, to be an important forerunner of their position. I wish to argue against Lyotard that metanarrativity does not always have to reflexively collapse and that it is possible to construct out of the materials of Nietzsche's arguments a sustainable skeptical and relativist metanarrative.

I shall proceed by first marshaling some pronouncedly skeptical and relativist passages in some of Nietzsche's key works and indicating the problematic to which they give rise. Next, I argue against Gilles Deleuze's postmodernist construal of the dominant tensions in Nietzsche's work. I then go on to try and show how recurring patterns of argument in Nietzsche's work (as well as some of his most famous metaphors) can be mobilized to restore consistency on the issues of skepticism and relativism. After that, and much more tentatively, I propose a conservative reading of Nietzsche's moral theory in keeping with my conservative reading of his epistemology. Next, I try to illustrate some major tensions in Foucault's thought, which undermine the viability of his postmodernism.

Deconstruction and Reflexivity

In *On the Advantage and Disadvantage of History for Life*,[5] Nietzsche not only levels a moral indictment against those engaged in a disinterested pursuit of the past, he advances an epistemological critique as well: "The past always speaks as an oracle: only as master builders of the future who know the present will you understand it."[6] The implicit epistemological critique of this passage can be filled in from a number of different directions: We always only confront tokens from the past in our present as historical investigators, so that their status as artifacts stemming from the past can be called into question by the radical skeptic; the meaning of these tokens is subject to varying interpretations by new generations of interpreters, so that what the tokens signify can never by established with certainty; and so on. Historical knowledge statements that claim to disclose the past can therefore more correctly be viewed as disguised action statements that enable their adherents to do certain things in the present. Historical statements that officially describe what occurred in the past are to be assessed by their capacity to release energies that will transform the present.

Nietzsche's antihistoricism, his skepticism about historical knowledge, gives rise to a problem of consistency. To be consistently skeptical concerning historical knowledge, does not Nietzsche have to be skeptical of his own skepticism, which would disbar him from formulating the epistemological critique that I have summarized in the previous paragraph?

The problem of reflexivity crops up at the beginning of the first essay in *On the Genealogy of Morals*:

> The lordly right of giving names extends so far that one should allow oneself to conceive the origin of language itself as an expression of power on the part of the rulers: they say "this *is* this and this," they seal every thing and event with a sound and, as it were, take possession of it.[7]

This passage immediately evokes Hobbes's nominalistic conception of truth formulated at the beginning of *Leviathan*. "There is nothing in the world universal but names; for the things named are every one of them individual and singular. . . . Truth consisteth in the right ordering of names in our affirmations."[8] What are the reflexive credentials for Nietzsche's and Hobbes's statements? If everything is just a function of naming, then isn't this analysis itself just a piece of naming and therefore entirely arbitrary and unilluminating? Nietzsche, more systematically and explicitly than Hobbes, pursues the political implications of nominalism. Nominalism in Nietzsche's hands becomes a critical tool for the genealogical deconstruction of existing configurations of power. But the issue of reflexivity seems poised to undermine the genealogical enterprise.

In making his case for the irresistibleness of strength or power as the dominant descriptive/normative category of the moral life, Nietzsche attacks the validity of the subject:

> To demand of strength that it should *not* express itself as strength, that it should *not* be a desire to overcome, a desire to throw down, a desire to become master, a thirst for enemies and resistances and triumphs, is just as absurd as to demand of weakness that it should express itself as strength. A quantum of force is equivalent to a quantum of drive, will, effect—more, it is nothing other than precisely this very driving, willing, effecting, and only owing to the seduction of language (and of the fundamental errors of reason that are petrified in it) which conceives and misconceives all effects as conditioned by something that causes effects, by a "subject," can it appear otherwise. For just as the popular mind separates the lightning from its flash and takes the latter for an *action*, for the operation of a subject called lightning, so popular morality also separates strength from expressions of strength, as if there were a neutral substratum behind the strong man, which was *free* to express strength or not to do so. But there is no such substratum; there is no "being" behind doing, effecting, becoming; "the doer" is merely a fiction added to the deed—the deed is everything. The popular mind in fact doubles the deed; when it sees the lightning flash, it is the deed of a deed: it posits the same event first as cause and then a second time as its effect. Scientists do no better when they say "force moves," "force causes," and the like—all its coolness, its freedom from emotion notwithstanding, our entire science still lies under the misleading influence of language and has not disposed of that little changeling, the "subject" (the atom, for example, is such a changeling, as is the Kantian "thing-in-itself"); no wonder if the submerged, darkly glowering emotions of vengefulness and hatred exploit this belief for their own ends and in fact maintain no belief more ardently than the belief that *the strong man is free* to be weak and the bird of prey to be a lamb—for thus they gain the right to make the bird of prey *accountable* for being a bird of prey.[9]

This remarkable central passage in the *Genealogy* evokes the issue of reflexivity at at least two points. According to Nietzsche, the impulse toward power governs both our moral behavior and our moral judgments. The strong are driven by their strength to engage in those actions whose immediate effects might include the inhibition and intimidation of the weak. To the strong the very irresistibleness of their impulses certifies to their being "good." The weak are primarily motivated to hold the strong at bay—to prevent them from giving free rein to their surging strength. A primary mechanism at the disposal of the weak to hold the strong in check are the various moral codes of civilization, with their central category of moral agency which posits that human beings are free to engage in or to refrain from the actions that they undertake. Morality from Nietzsche's perspective becomes a kind of conspiracy mobilized by the weak to prevent the strong from becoming fully cognizant of their powers and to restrain them once they gain this recognition. "It is not the strongest but the weakest who spell disaster for the strong."[10]

The first issue of reflexivity to arise concerning this passage relates to Nietzsche's rooting of moral action and moral judgment in the imperatives of the emotional life, divorced from any consideration of what other moral philosophers have taken to be rational factors. The organizing category for grouping moral behavior and judgment thus becomes "tradition," in the sense that it highlights the centrality of arational elements in the conduct and the deliberations of the moral life. If, according to Nietzsche, the concrete expressions of affirmation by the strong and ressentiment by the weak in particular societies constitute nothing more immutable than tradition, then why should Nietzsche's critique of morality also not be construed as the unfolding of a critical tradition? What elevates Nietzsche's critique of morality to truth when what he is attacking can aspire to no higher status than tradition? How can one formulate a consistent version of relativism that does not engulf and overpower one's own position as well?

The second issue of reflexivity relates to the proto-Wittgensteinian accents in which the argument of this paragraph is framed. Nietzsche speaks about the seductions of language that lead us to posit a doer, a subject, beyond the deeds that are performed. Nietzsche wants to get rid of the idea of a subject (and, concomitantly, of the idea of a free subject) from his moral ontology. He argues that the concept of freedom is a reification superimposed upon a reification. Once the idea of a subject is exposed as a reification, the reification of "freedom" falls by the wayside. If there are no subjects, then the question of freedom originates in a linguistic blunder. At this juncture, however, the issue of reflexivity arises. How accurately is Nietzsche's activity as a theorist encompassed by his own theorizing? Does not Nietzsche have to be enough of a coherent subject to be able to make his generalization about the lack of coherent subjects? Does he not have to transcend his material to be able to describe it in the manner that he does?

The problem of reflexivity again emerges in a famous passage in the second essay of the *Genealogy* where Nietzsche elucidates the origin of "bad conscience":

> All instincts that do not discharge themselves outwardly *turn inward*—this is what I call the *internalization* of man: thus it was that man first developed what was later called his "soul." The entire inner world, originally as thin as if it were stretched between two membranes, expanded and extended itself, acquired depth, breadth, and height, in the same measure as outward discharge was *inhibited*. Those fearful bulwarks with which the political organization protected itself against the old instincts of freedom—punishments belong among these bulwarks—brought about that all those instincts of wild, free, prowling man turned backward *against man himself*. Hostility, cruelty, joy in persecuting, in attacking, in change, in destruction—all this turned against the possessors of such instincts: *that* is the origin of the "bad conscience."[11]

This passage brings into sharp relief the solipsistic bias of Nietzsche's theorizing. Even when man suffers, he does it to himself. His suffering is a function of misdirected aggression, force, and power. As the appropriate outlets for these get thwarted in the course of transition to civil society, man turns his aggressive energy inward against himself. Nietzsche's theory of the bad conscience consists of Hobbesian political assumptions plus the total expulsion of the other with whom a social contract can be negotiated. The emphasis on power in Nietzsche's theorizing constitutes a translation into a political idiom of his solipsistic moral epistemology. The stress on power can be viewed as an implicit declaration on Nietzsche's part of the impossibility of establishing mutually satisfying contact with other people. The concentration on power reflects the severed, individually centered focus of Nietzsche's theorizing.

Solipsism, however, is philosophically untenable. It is inconsistent in the sense that on the meta–meta level (solipsism itself is formulated on the meta level as a theory about the nature of the self), to which solipsism has to be regressed[12] if its meaning and significance are to be understood, there has to be a mapping of the rejection of solipsism's traditional philosophical rivals—those theories that acknowledge the existence of multiple others. This in turn means that on the level of philosophical doctrine there has to be more than solipsism.

Nietzsche's strategy for dealing with asceticism is the same as the one he employs for dealing with guilt. In both cases it is the active, life-affirming will that is struggling to assert itself, although its energy is being misdirected.[13] Again, the issue of Nietzsche's solipsism surfaces and gives rise to the problematic discussed above.

Nietzsche's thought thus converges on the notion of the ubiquity of power. "Power" is the category for analyzing the motivational apparatus of the strong at the same time that guilt, asceticism, and other manifestations of the weakness of the weak are conceptualized as misdirected (or destructively internalized) forms of power. Does not Nietzsche's absorption with power, however, give rise to a gigantic tautology? Power, Nietzsche says, is all; it is the universal measure of human action for the weak as well as for the strong. But if all human action is reduced to an assertion of power, then has not the concept of power lost all explanatory force? In order for "power" to retain its explanatory force and for Nietzsche's theoretical delineations to constitute more than tautologies, the theoretical approaches to the phenomena that he is dealing with, which he rejects, must somehow continue to exist even after he has postulated that power is everything. The explanatory force of the latter notion is parasitic upon the continued existence of the contrasting theoretical entities and concepts that the notion of power in Nietzsche was designed to displace.

Nietzsche criticizes German historical scholarship, with its disciplined aversion to interpretation, as a victim of an illusory will to truth:

> That general renunciation of all interpretation (of forcing, adjusting, abbreviating, omitting, padding, inventing, falsifying, and whatever else is of the *essence* of interpreting)—all this expresses, broadly speaking, as

much ascetic virtue as any denial of sensuality (it is at bottom only a particular mode of this denial). That which *constrains* these men, however, this unconditional will to truth, is faith in the ascetic ideal itself, even if as an unconscious imperative—don't be deceived about that—it is the faith in a *metaphysical* value, the absolute value of *truth,* sanctioned and guaranteed by this ideal alone (it stands or falls with this ideal).[14]

The attack on the will to truth (echoed by Foucault in his famous Inaugural Lecture, *The Discourse on Language*)[15] is difficult to sustain reflexively. Imaginative interpretation is being shunned by German scholars faithful to the ideals of historicism in the name of fidelity to truth (true to the original intentions of an author, true to the historical understandings prevailing in a particular cultural milieu, and so on). Nietzsche condemns this pursuit of truth, but in the name of what? A higher (or deeper) truth? The paradox surrounding Nietzsche's calling into question the will to truth revolves around the fact that, given our semantic protocols, "truth" can only be condemned and transcended in relation to itself. One appeals to standards of truth in discrediting and revising earlier formulations of truth.

Nietzsche and Parsimony

Contemporary Nietzsche scholarship, exemplified in the work of Gilles Deleuze,[16] would claim that Nietzsche's purpose was to undermine the very conceptual dichotomies between truth and falsehood, knowledge and skepticism, and so on, in terms of which I have held him to account in the first section of this chapter. In analyzing Nietzsche's sense of how thought is opposed to life, Deleuze writes: "For rational knowledge sets the same limits to life as reasonable life sets to thought; life is subject to knowledge and at the same time thought is subject to life. Reason sometimes dissuades and sometimes forbids us to cross certain limits: because it is useless (knowledge is there to predict), because it would be evil (life is there to be virtuous), because it is impossible (there is nothing to see or think behind the truth).—But does not critique, understood as critique of knowledge itself, express new forces capable of giving thought another sense? A thought that would go to the limit of what life can do, a thought that would lead life to the limit of what it can do? A thought that would affirm life instead of a knowledge that is opposed to life. Life would be the active force of thought, but thought would be the affirmative power of life. Both would go in the same direction, carrying each other along, smashing restrictions, matching each other step for step, in a burst of unparalleled creativity. Thinking would then mean *discovering, inventing, new possibilities of life.*"[17]

While I am largely in sympathy with Deleuze's reading of Nietzsche, I believe the ontologically extravagant postmodernist position he attributes to him is out of keeping with key tenets of Nietzsche's thought. Deleuze wants to say that Nietzsche is in favor of an anti-foundationalist, anything-goes epistemology that through its story-telling powers of how experience is being assimilated in radical and novel ways helps to map the erosion of such bedrock epistemological distinctions as those between truth and falsehood and knowledge and skepticism. As the citations I have marshaled in the first part of this chapter indicate, I believe that Nietzsche *is* an extreme skeptic and relativist. However, I believe that these positions are defensible within the confines of the traditional distinctions and not merely through their abolition and transcendence. While working within the context of a classical, parsimonious ontology, Nietzsche is able to project imaginatively strategies for salvaging his extreme skepticism and relativism. What is at stake between Deleuze and myself is not how Nietzsche comes out—but how he gets there. I believe that a "postmodernist philosophical agenda" is prefigured in Nietzsche's thought by a radical modernism that strains the resources of the received philosophical tradition to the limit. In order to make my case against Deleuze, I will argue that his pattern of derivation of Nietzsche's thought cannot be correct because Nietzsche is implicitly committed to a principle of parsimony, of economy, in his philosophy that requires him to derive and to justify his extreme skepticism and relativism in accordance with the postulation of the fewest number of philosophical entities and distinctions as possible.

How is the role of a principle of parsimony manifested in Nietzsche's thought? There is a central tension in Nietzsche's essay *On the Advantage and Disadvantage of History for Life* whose intertextual amplification in Nietzsche's later work leads to a new emphasis on a principle of parsimony. Nietzsche's historical epistemology in that essay undercuts his moral theory as reflected in the same essay. If, as we have seen Nietzsche argue, it is "only as master builders of the future who know the present" that we will understand the past,[18] this suggests that there is no stable historical past that the tools of the historian unearth, but only multiple historical pasts responsive to different locations in the present. Given Nietzsche's radically skeptical construal of the historical past, the whole point of his contrast between history and life is undermined. Since there is no objectively recoverable historical past, the only kind of past available to us is one that has been nudged into intellectual focus by the requirements of life. To use a distinction of Michael Oakeshott, there is no such thing as the genuinely historical past, but only different versions of a practical past. With his radically skeptical historical epistemology, Nietzsche is already presupposing what his overarching contrast between history and life is purportedly arguing for. Instead of life serving as a foil for history, Nietzsche conceptualizes historical understanding in such a way that it incorporates the chief elements of what he calls life. His skeptical historical epistemology erodes the whole point of the contrast between history and life.

There is little overt reference to power in Nietzsche's essay on history. The centrality that Nietzsche attaches to power in his later theorizing and the ways in which he delineates the concept can be viewed as an attempt to bring his epistemology and moral theory into more coherent alignment than was true in the early essay on history. The essay on history carves out crucial intellectual space for the category of power but does not elaborate in any great detail about power. In answer to the question of what guides us (or what should guide us) in reviving particular pasts in particular presents, the implicit answer of the essay on history seems to be that whatever conceptions of the past are most empowering in the present are the pasts that get/should get rehabilitated. However, since an explicit vocabulary of power is largely absent from the essay on history, Nietzsche gets caught in the bind that his historical epistemology vitiates his invocation of "history" as a foil for "life." His historical epistemology hinders his formulation of his moral philosophy, which is supposed to grow out of the contrast between history and life, and which stresses the importance of power both in accounting for the moral judgments that we make as spectators and in delineating the moral psychology of an agent. In his later theorizing, by explicitly and systematically invoking the role of power in our judgments and in our actions, Nietzsche is able to achieve a symmetry between his epistemology and his moral philosophy that eluded him in his early essay on history. This symmetry, however, hinges upon the postulation of a principle of parsimony as a crucial subterranean link between his epistemology and his moral theory.

The concept of power in Nietzsche is supposed to galvanize us into suspicion of ideological overlay. The right and the good can only be pursued and affirmed by someone who has demystified his moral vocabulary to the extent of being able to grasp the central animating role performed by the will to power. It is recourse to a pared-down, economical invocation of power that enables us to function optimally as moral spectators and agents. When power comes to be elaborated upon as an official doctrine, the internal warrant for the pride of place assigned to it in Nietzsche's theorizing can, I think, most plausibly be assumed to come from his epistemology. The warrant for the moral preeminence assigned to power might derive from Nietzsche's acceptance of a principle of parsimony in his epistemology. If one postulates the regulative character of parsimony in epistemology (to keep one's concepts, categories, and methods as reduced and simplified as possible), then its extension as a regulative principle of the moral life via the medium of the category of power appears both as isomorphically sound and as compelling in the additional sense that extending a principle of parsimony from one domain of philosophizing to another itself exemplifies a principle of parsimony. After the asymmetry between epistemology and moral philosophy in Nietzsche's early essay on history, harmony between epistemology and moral philosophy gets restored through the explicit and systematic invocation of power under the aegis of the principle of parsimony.

If parsimony is a suppressed but vital premise in Nietzsche's theorizing, then it is incumbent upon us as his interpreters to make sense out of his extreme skepticism and relativism in the light of the sparsest ontological commitments compatible with allegiance to these doctrines—and not to succumb to the ontological extravagance advocated by Deleuze and postmodernists generally.

Nietzsche's inspiration for the implicit justificatory force for a principle of parsimony might come from Machiavelli. A principle of economy leading to the most minimal deployment of violence compatible with the realization of one's ends becomes, as we have seen, the foundational principle of public morality for Machiavelli because its status is secured by the central regulative role economy plays in epistemology. To the question of whether Machiavelli has an epistemology, one could reply that his moral and political theory presupposes centrality being accorded to a principle of parsimony as a buttress to its more narrowly moral and political claims. The internal warrant for Machiavelli's stress on a principle of economy in his moral and political philosophy comes from epistemology. Truth-values are assigned by Machiavelli to particular categories in disparate regions of philosophy on the basis of internal correspondence—that is, coherence.

Tacit Knowledge and the Primacy of Action

The resources of Nietzsche's philosophy provide him with at least two philosophical strategies for resolving the dilemmas I have summarized in the first part of this chapter without having to abandon his commitment to skepticism and to relativism as broad metaphilosophical positions. The first approach involves recognizing the role and scope of tacit knowledge in Nietzsche's thought, which is manifested on a continuing basis from the early *On the Advantage and Disadvantage of History for Life* and *The Birth of Tragedy*[19] to the late *On the Genealogy of Morals*.

On the Advantage and Disadvantage of History for Life mounts a savage attack against German historicism because of its withering effects upon the tacit context in which alone effective action can take place:

> Every living thing needs to be surrounded by an atmosphere, a myste-
> rious circle of mist; if one robs it of this veil, if one condemns a religion, an
> art, a genius to orbit as a star without an atmosphere: then one should not
> wonder about its rapidly becoming withered, hard and barren.[20]

The whole argument of *On the Advantage and Disadvantage of History for Life* constitutes an implicit case for tacit knowledge. Historicism disenchants the present by providing us with scientific knowledge of the past. Our knowledge of the past must remain tacit, submerged, and contextual in order to facilitate heroic, transformative action in the present. The more fully we "know" the past, the more unavailable it becomes for us as a series of actuating cues in the present. Implicit in Nietzsche's argument is a rejection of the possibilities of knowledge in favor of the imperatives of action. Man cannot know with any great degree of reliability. He can only act—where the absence of certainty is not a handicap but a spur.

Nietzsche bemoans the persistence of medieval thought patterns in the modern world despite the vanguard aura of historicism:

> Historical education really is a kind of inborn greyheadedness. . . . Does
> not this paralyzing belief in an already withering mankind rather harbour
> the misunderstanding, inherited from the Middle Ages, of a Christian
> theological conception, the thought that the end of the world is near, of
> the fearfully expected judgment? . . . At an earlier time this "memento
> mori" addressed to mankind as well as the individual, was always a
> torturing thorn and, as it were, the high point of medieval knowledge and
> conscience. The counter dictum of a more recent time: "memento vivere"
> frankly still sounds quite timid, lacks full-throated power and almost has
> something dishonest about it. For mankind is still tied to the memento
> mori and betrays it in its universal historical need: despite the most
> powerful beat of its wings knowledge has been unable to tear itself loose
> and attain freedom, a deep feeling of hopelessness has remained and has
> taken on that historical colouration by which all higher education and
> culture is now surrounded in melancholy darkness.[21]

In this passage, Nietzsche laments the fact that modernity still has to be born. The *memento mori* of the middle ages still lingers into (and predominates in) the middle to late nineteenth century. For modernity to be born—and to prevail—the mysterious mist of tacit knowledge, the submerged background factors surrounding our sentiments and actions, must not be disturbed. As we have seen earlier in Plato's discussion of Pericles' relation to the metaphysician Anaxagoras, metanarrativity itself might be construed as an important element in that mysterious background mist that constitutes a necessary precondition for the articulation of the strong thoughts and deeds that Nietzsche cherishes. There has to be a "something" and not a blank in the background—something that is susceptible of rational reconstruction and conceptualization—that facilitates maximal unleashing of human creative energies in the present. It is the flow and the rhythm between the known and the unknown, the crystallized and the yet unformed— *not* the unknowable and the unformable, that establishes the ideal environment for the achievement of heroic action. It is the dialectic between what we can explicitly formulate and what we have not yet gathered into consciousness but is potentially formulable that defines the ideal context for the realization of the human good.

In a certain sense (and Nietzsche himself to some extent seems to be aware of this)[22] the argument of *The Birth of Tragedy* appears isomorphic with the argument of *On the Advantage and Disadvantage of History for Life*. In both essays Nietzsche argues for the inevitable futility of the typically modernist tendency to rationalize human existence through the proliferation of historical understanding or the generation of Apollinian modes of discourse that enable us to label and to transpose to sequential discourse vast regions of unconscious experience. To sever our Dionysian roots, as the advocates of historicism and the disseminators of Socratic sensibility in different ways attempt to do, will both not work and will deprive us of a cardinal source of empowerment in the pursuit of whatever projects motivate us in life. Historicism and Socratism for Nietzsche are ways of mummifying human existence, deadening us to the vital energies awaiting cultivation in our immediate surroundings by stylizing and ritualizing our lives around scientifically ordained images of the past and engendering a premature sense of belatedness through the eager invocation of multiple rational patterns to encase and render intelligible the flow of experience.

Historicism and Socratism will not work because the possibilities that they circumnavigate and suppress—more imaginative readings of the past and more flexible construals of the present—return to haunt and eventually to undermine the painstaking rationalist structures historicism and Socratism have established. Exploding historicism and Socratism enables us to appreciate the extent to which our visions of the past and avenues of deliberation and judgment and delineation of possibilities for action are not rationally coerced, but are available for us to fashion. This can issue forth in a tremendous sense of empowerment as we seek to relate our Dionysian energies in a less mediated fashion to the prospects and possibilities of our present.

The critique of science and the centrality of the concept of power in the *Genealogy* and *Ecce Homo* also betray a tacit-knowledge emphasis. "Strictly speaking," Nietzsche writes, "there is no such thing as science 'without any presuppositions'; this thought does not bear thinking through, it is paralogical: a philosophy, a 'faith,' must always be there first of all, so that science can acquire from it a direction, a meaning, a limit, a method, a right to exist. (Whoever has the opposite notion, whoever tries, for example, to place philosophy 'on a strictly scientific basis,' first needs to stand not only philosophy but truth itself *on its head*—the grossest violation of decency possible in relation to two such venerable females!)"[23] The affinities between this passage and Plato's discussion of how the movement from problem to solution works and Polanyi's statement that "you cannot formalize the act of commitment"[24] should be immediately apparent.

The structure of Nietzsche's argument concerning power also follows the pattern of tacit knowledge. The identification of the role of power in human affairs constitutes a culmination to the inquiry originally sketched in *On the Advantage and Disadvantage of History for Life*. There, as we have seen, Nietzsche is concerned to identify and practice a form of intellectual inquiry that in contrast to historical study will promote life. Such a form of inquiry will trace the tacit factors at work in the background to our words and deeds in such a way that their mystery, their hiddenness, is not violated.

The concept of power in Nietzsche's thought achieves this result from a dual perspective. On the one hand, "power" functions as a quasi-reductionist, quasi-deterministic category. Through stripping away ideologically tainted explanatory categories and emphasizing the role of basic power drives, the individual actor comes to recognize the extent to which his engagement in action is inevitable. For a person deliberating about whether to act, the reference to power as an explanatory concept fosters a sense of belatedness. If his power drives are depicted in such a way that they situate him in an action-oriented direction, then the anxieties attendant upon action, upon change, are diminished. If power as an explanatory category points to the urgency of action, then the burden of action is eased. One is released into a capacity for action by virtue of having plotted its cogency and, in a certain sense, its inevitability. One no longer has to decide to act (the power-explanatory schema points to one's belatedness on the scene of action) and therefore one becomes capable of heroic, transformative action. Tom Paine in *Common Sense* makes extensive use of this strategy for goading the American colonists into full-scale rebellion against Great Britain by pointing to the many ways in which such historical factors as geographical isolation and manifest destiny have already predetermined their involvement and their success. Their belatedness on the scene of action serves as a goad to their supreme involvement. From the perspective that I have just outlined, "power" in Nietzsche's hands is not decoded—its mysteriousness remains inviolate. It is just operationalized into a spur for action.

From a complementary perspective, Nietzsche's deployment of the concept of power can be viewed as integral to a larger strategy manifested in his metaphysics, epistemology, and ethical theory that might be termed the abolition of interiority. In his philosophy of history, for example, as we have seen, Nietzsche shows that the idea of the genuine historical past is a notion devoid of any inner content. The historical past, according to Nietzsche, is a species of the practical past. We know the past only to the extent that it releases energy for human action in the present. Only to the extent that you can do something with the past do you know the past.

In his ethical theory, Nietzsche overcomes overcoming by making "power" the central category in moral deliberation and judgment.

Power is not efficacious until it issues forth in some kind of action that transforms one's present. In considering and discussing moral factors, the agent and the spectator focus on action.

The abolition of interiority represents a colossal displacement of monotheistic doctrine. No qualities or characteristics can be literally applied to the monotheistic God of Judaism, Christianity, and Islam because by definition he is stipulated as being utterly transcendent and wholly other from our human conceptualizations of him. All the qualities that we ascribe to him, any kind of interior essence, get continually deferred and displaced. Their literal content becomes totally purged. God is known (to the extent that the phrase itself is not an oxymoron) through what he does, not by what he is. Nietzsche deciphers man after the manner of the monotheistic conception of God. The concept of power in Nietzsche's thought points to the continually receding essence of man, which is only disclosed, and disclosable, through action. The idea of power in Nietzsche captures the paradox that it is only through what is ordinarily taken to be a contrastive category to knowledge—action—that we can attain whatever reliable knowledge is vouchsafed to us about man.

When Nietzsche proclaims that God is dead,[25] part of what the statement signifies is the dual sense in which the concept of power that I have summarized serves as a surrogate notion for God. In the first sense, power as a kind of ultimate explanatory concept serves as a guarantor of our belatedness: We are plotted as poised—driven—toward action; we are thereby released into action. In this way, the secular concept of power usurps the role of God, who as an ultimate explanatory concept lying in the background to human action, present but unknowable, frees us to the possibilities of human action. The quasi-reductionist, quasi-deterministic concept of power replaces God as the ultimate guarantor of our belatedness, and therefore also as the liberator of human action.

The second sense in which I analyzed Nietzsche's deployment of "power" above—as furthering Nietzsche's larger project aimed toward the abolition of interiority—also suggests a sense in which the phrase "God is dead" can be understood. God is dead because the secret of his perpetual displacement has been thoroughly internalized and turned to human uses. This is also true for the first sense in which the concept of power serves as a surrogate for God. Once we become conscious of the central role of belatedness as a facilitator of human action, we can devise our own explanatory schema (such as power) to achieve this result, and the symbol of God becomes dispensable. The paradox of both senses of power serving as a surrogate for God is that the moment of highest rejection, in Nietzsche's "God is dead" formulation, is also the moment of the most rampant internalization, in Nietzsche's usage of power. Displacement is manifested in the very act which declares that displacement itself is over.

One of Nietzsche's most important precursors in the pursuit of the abolition of interiority and its relationship to monotheistic theology is Hobbes. One of the most illuminating ways to explicate the relationship between the austerely monotheistic discussion of God in the second half of *Leviathan* and the putatively utilitarian analyses of human nature in the first half of *Leviathan* is to notice the extent to which Hobbes comprehends man in the image of the monotheistic construal of God. An important consequence of Hobbes's purging of the concept of God of paganistic Christian overlays as to recapture a more authentically Old Testament conception of him as wholly other is to make available for purposes of analyses of human phenomena a set of explanatory categories that highlight "endless displacement" as the key to unraveling human nature. Hobbes's concept of power manifests this endless displacement. In the famous passage where Hobbes puts "for a general inclination of all mankind, a perpetual and restless desire of power after power, that ceaseth only in death,"[26] displacement itself is almost explicitly linked with power. Power signifies for Hobbes a continual and insatiable urge for objectifications—as if the appropriation of artifacts were secondary to the doing, the exteriorizing, the assertion of power. A God who is only known through his actions is displaced by Hobbes onto a conception of man whose actions are unknown and unknowable. The appropriate complement to mystery on both the divine and human levels is ceaseless activity that seeks to reclaim through endless new beginnings a meaning that cannot be consummated through any single action.

The erosion of interiority in Hobbes's moral psychology is also evinced by the centrality he assigns to a pleasure–pain apparatus in his diagnosis of human nature. "Pleasure" and "pain" as they are deployed in Hobbes's writings are very often little more than tautologous explanatory categories. When a person does something, to say that he does it because he experiences pleasure is in most instances just a redescription of the action. Analogously, when a person refrains from doing something, to say that his nonaction stems from an avoidance of pain constitutes little more than a redescription of his nonaction. As explanatory categories, "pleasure" and "pain" reify in the *explanans* what is already implied in the *explanandum*. In this they resemble the concept of power, which also functions quasi-tautologously in Hobbes's argument. "Power" just tells us that we are actuated to do what we in fact do. It does not in any immediately apparent sense tell us why we do it.[27]

Whether Hobbes believed in (the monotheistic) God might be an open question, but what the two halves of Hobbes's argument in *Leviathan* make clear is the extent to which the endlessly deferred and displaced monotheistic God portrayed in the second half of the book also appears in the first half as endlessly exteriorizing and displacing man.

Power in Nietzsche's writings fulfills the promise of the intellectual quest inaugurated in *On the Advantage and Disadvantage of History for Life* by serving as the dominant proximal pole that is disclosed to both ourselves and others in the course of our diverse and multiple distal crystallizations in word and deed. Mystery recedes by one step through Nietzsche's invocation of power, but it is not dissipated.

Tacit knowledge, as we have seen, offers us a most promising solution to the problem of formulating non-self-refuting versions of skepticism and relativism, and thus of resolving the logical conundrums in Nietzsche's thought sketched in the first part of this chapter. If the arguments in favor of skepticism and relativism (such as those adduced earlier in this chapter from Nietzsche) seem convincing, and yet skepticism and relativism cannot be stated without also negating themselves, then the solution lies in our acknowledging that we have reached a limit of thought. This means that skepticism has to be seen as a "proximal" pole that enables us to do certain things in the world, such as Nietzsche qua theorist mapping an intellectual terrain for his contemporaries that enables them to engage in heroic, transformative action. Tacit knowledge "dissolves" skepticism as an issue in philosophy because it places it in a context where our paradigms of knowledge are statements that are more "knowing" than anything they can directly justify. Skepticism and relativism, too, paradoxically, have to be believed before they can be known.

Intuitionist Logic and Reverse Causation

If "tacit knowledge" calls attention to the ways in which explicit and conscious formulations draw their sustenance and derive their meaning from implicit and unconscious understandings, then in the body of Nietzsche's work two central, recurring metaphors, suitably decoded, might help us concerning the most satisfactory way to construe the explicit teaching. The two metaphors that might be viewed as performing this strategic role are Dionysianism and eternal recurrence. The former lends support to a logical mapping of the suspension of the law of excluded middle, the latter to a doctrine of reverse causation.

In *Twilight of the Idols*, Nietzsche describes the "faith of Dionysus" as follows: "He does not negate any more."[28] Dionysus thus symbolizes a transcendence of negation. I suggest that the mapping of a logic that suspends the law of excluded middle (e.g., an intuitionist logic)[29] constitutes a useful background postulate that enables Nietzsche's thought to achieve an enhanced coherence.

Nietzsche defines eternal recurrence as "the doctrine . . . of the unconditional and infinitely repeated circular course of all things."[30] This suggests that the arrow of time[31]—the flow of causality—might move in two directions: from future to past, as well as from past to future; from effect to cause, as well as from cause to effect. The image of eternal recurrence thus conjures up the possibility of reverse causation.

I believe that these two ideas of an intuitionist logic—suspension of the law of excluded middle and reverse causation—taken in conjunction offer us a new avenue for resolving the problem of reflexivity, of being able to formulate skepticism and relativism consistently.

For Nietzsche, one might say the concept of God functions as a symbolic reminder of the ineradicableness of otherness. All of our human intellectual constructs, including our efforts at self-understanding, throw up shadows, contain reflexively unassimilable remainders, which it appears impossible ever thoroughly to eliminate. A negative, critical, skeptical statement has to be able to withstand its critical canons being directed inward against the statement itself. The difficulty of accommodating this demand of reflexivity leads to the postulation of ever new, more comprehensive, metaexplanatory statements (that would reflexively be able to encompass themselves as well as the object statements they were concerned to explain), culminating in the most ambitious explanatory statement of all, which posits God's existence. When Nietzsche proclaims that God is dead, he is signaling to us that he considers the problem of reflexivity to be resolved, that the postulation of the God hypothesis is methodologically redundant. The question then becomes where in his theorizing does Nietzsche consider that he has solved the problem? Aside from the implicit tacit-knowledge theorizing, a promising candidate appears to be Dionysus (intuitionist logic) in conjunction with eternal recurrence (reverse causation).

Intuitionist logic was invented by the Dutch mathematician Jan Brouwer in the early part of this century as a strategy enabling him to work out coherently the implications of a conception of mathematical activity as being purely constructivist in character.[32] According to Brouwer, mathematics constitutes a cultural elaboration of the universal intuition of "twoness," of events or things succeeding one another in the world. Brouwer's metamathematical theory conceives of mathematical entities as the product of human inventiveness and ingenuity spawned by this commonly shared intuition, which theoretically can proceed infinitely. If one takes the notion of infinity literally and seriously, then one has to envisage the prospect that later entities in mathematical series will exhibit characteristics and possess properties that directly contravene those shown by earlier members in the series. In other words, one has to postulate the suspension of the law of excluded middle if one is to grapple successfully with the notion of infinity conjoined to a constructivist approach to the foundations of mathematics.

Adopting a Gadamerian (which, as we have seen, is also a Nietzschean) hermeneutical approach to the nature of texts—that all texts remain essentially incomplete, subject to a continuing dialogical relationship between the text and new generations of readers—then the prospect of infinity is endemic to the process of textual understanding as well. Since "meaning" is a function of the fusion of the horizons of understanding of new generations of readers with the original language of the text, there is no way we can predict that the textual meaning discerned by later generations of readers will not directly contradict the meanings perceived by earlier generations. Textual and historical interpretation generally for Gadamer (as well as for Nietzsche) becomes an endless process whose appropriate logic therefore appears to be intuitionistic. Infinity of interpretation, just like infinity of number sequences, invites the formulation of a logic that is tolerant of the abrogation of the law of excluded middle.

Formulations of skepticism are also texts—statements, or utterances, requiring interpretation. As such, an intuitionist logic suspending the law of excluded middle is the most appropriate logic to apply in relation to them. Therefore, their being both true (in the sense that skepticism is the most defensible philosophical position) and not true (in the sense that skepticism cannot be applied reflexively in relation to itself and still preserve the character of skepticism) can be accommodated.

The symbol of Dionysus within the confines of Nietzsche's argument in *The Birth of Tragedy* functions in the same way that I have just analyzed the overall significance of the Dionysian symbol in Nietzsche's work. The artist (the tragedian in particular) chafes against the limits of linear, sequential rationality that he is compelled to follow in his presentation of the dramatic action. What propels him in his writing are demonic urges that express deep rebellion against the traditional limits and boundaries of human life—finitude, daytime linear rationality and nighttime dreamwork rationality, the distinction between desire and the consequences and objects of desire, self and other, sinfulness and holiness, heteronomy and autonomy, morality and pleasure, thought and passion, self-consciousness and self-forget-fulness, and time and desire. The shadowy underside to Apollinian dramatic form is Dionysian possessedness.

In relation to the Dionysian urges themselves, however, Nietz-sche confronts a dilemma that can most satisfactorily be resolved by recognizing that "Dionysus" is suggestive of a multivalued logic—one that transcends the law of excluded middle. In order for Nietzsche to have the dichotomy that facilitates the formulation of his argument in *The Birth of Tragedy* (that between Apollo and Dionysus) the symbol of Dionysus itself will have had to be rationalized so as to yield a linear–rationalist grasp of the Dionysian collapse of limits and boundaries. The original problem that Nietzsche delineates, which was supposed to define the stance of the dramatic artist—that of stating in Apollinian terms what were at the outset Dionysian drives—reappears on the Nietzschean metatheoretical level as the problem of conceptualizing the Dionysian element itself. It, too, cannot be theorized without vio-lating Dionysian imperatives concerning the abolition of distances. In order to render Nietzsche's theorizing of "Dionysus" more coherent, it seems plausible to attribute to him, in line with his emphasis on the cessation of negation quoted earlier, the notion that Dionysus symbol-izes the invocation of a multivalued logic that facilitates the transcen-dence of the law of excluded middle. Nietzsche's discourse concerning Dionysus both is and is not Dionysian. Its reference is to those various collapses of boundaries and limits that I alluded to above. Its sense, however—so that we recognize and are able to identify a Dionysian element in experience—is crucially dependent on some, at least, of those boundaries and limits. If the symbol of Dionysus is supposed to include suspension of the law of excluded middle, then both the inconsistency *and* its resolution are built into "Dionysus."[33]

Intuitionist logic by itself, however, is not sufficient to salvage skepticism, for the issue of reflexivity can be raised with regard to the basic principle of an intuitionist logic, the suspension of the law of excluded middle. The intuitionist wants to claim a higher status for this suspension than that it too simply might be suspended. On the meta–meta level, against which backdrop the metamathematical prin-ciples of intuitionist logic get formulated, the intuitionist philosopher is rejecting realism in mathematics, which declares that mathematical elements correspond to entities in the real world that exert constraints upon their formulation and serve as the ultimate guarantors that the law of excluded middle will hold, and is affirming his own intuitionist version of the foundations of mathematics. Thus, intuitionism does not reflexively accommodate its own principles.

At this point, intuitionism needs to be supplemented by reverse causation. If we can conceive the arrow of time moving backward—so that what was previously the effect (the metalevel of discourse) becomes the cause (of the meta–meta level of discourse that officially preceded it)—then the issue of reflexivity gets finally resolved. The affirmation of intuitionism and the rejection of realism follow rather than precede the formulation of the suspension of the law of excluded middle. Consistency is achieved through a mapping of a pattern of reverse causation.

Nietzsche, Augustine, and Democratic Theory

There is an epistemological–ethical nexus in Nietzsche's thought that facilitates a much more traditional reading of his moral theory than has ordinarily been given. A tacit-knowledge approach to Nietzsche's texts enables us to see the extent to which power (like "the subject" analyzed earlier) just is the outward expression, the deeds, that flows from it. In this way the mystery of the proximal pole of power is not dispelled or dis-enchanted at the same time that we have a more adequate grasp of the dynamics of mental functioning. This view of Nietzsche to which I have been led by epistemological considerations has a striking ethical analogue that restores Nietzsche to a wholly different intellectual-historical context from that in which he is customarily placed.

St. Augustine in *The City of God* defines the desiderata of a virtuous moral life as follows:

> For this reason there is no perfect peace so long as command is exercised over the vicious propensities, because the battle is fraught with peril while those vices that resist are being reduced to submission, while

those which have been overcome are not yet triumphed over in peaceful security, but are repressed under a rule still troubled by anxieties. Thus we are in the midst of these temptations, about which we find this brief saying amongst the divine oracles: "Is a man's life on earth anything but temptation?"; and who can presume that his life is of such a kind that he has no need to say to God, "Forgive us our debts," unless he is a man of overwhelming conceit, not a truly great man, but one puffed up and swollen with pride, who is with justice resisted by him who gives grace to the humble, as it says in the Scriptures, "God resists the proud, but he gives his favour to the humble." In this life, therefore, justice in each individual exists when God rules and man obeys, when the mind rules the body and reason governs the vices even when they rebel, either by subduing them or by resisting them, while from God himself favour is sought for good deeds and pardon for offences, and thanks are duly offered to him for benefits received. But in that ultimate peace, to which this justice should be related, and for the attainment of which this justice is to be maintained, our nature will be healed by immortality and incorruption and will have no perverted elements, and nothing at all, in ourselves or any other, will be in conflict with any one of us. And so reason will not need to rule the vices, since there will be no vices, but God will hold sway over man, and the soul over the body, and in this state our delight and facility in obeying will be matched by our felicity in living and reigning. There, for each and every one, this state will be eternal, and its eternity will be assured; and for that reason the peace of this blessedness, or the blessedness of this peace, will be the Supreme Good.[34]

Nietzsche's moral vision constitutes in many ways a secularization of Augustinianism, where the gap between willing and doing is closed by a conception of power as irresistible forward movement, proceeding from an internal psychological sphere to an external worldly one. Given this conceptualization of the role of power in Nietzsche's thought, there is nothing intrinsic to that notion to prevent its democratization and diffusion among the broad mass of the people. I wish to advance two arguments that might render this prospect more plausible.

1. Power as Nietzsche's most basic category for the analysis of the self suggests something that is available to everyone to a greater or lesser degree. It is something that everyone can aspire to. In this it more resembles Hobbesian passion than Platonic reason.

2. The kind of power that Nietzsche talks about would be spoiled for the powerful if the weak continued to play the power game in accordance with the old rules. Power for the strong is something spiritual. Tremendous reserves of inner strength are released for the strong when they follow Nietzsche's precepts concerning power. The power that Nietzsche envisages does not conjure up the specter of a zero-sum game, but partakes rather of the nature of a sum-sum game. Nietzsche spurns the manifestations of power associated with zero-sum games as a sign of the weakness of the weak. Power conceived in these terms is bound up with the envy and ressentiment of the weak that Nietzsche loathes. The kind of power desired by the weak is corrupted from within by a conception that sharing signifies losing and diminishing. Nietzsche's theorizing of power as a phenomenon whose presence to a large extent depends upon how it is conceptualized is itself a response to one of the imperatives of power conceived in a traditional Machiavellian sense. According to Machiavelli, the less one is dependent on others and the more one is able to rely upon oneself for the attainment of one's objectives, the more powerful one becomes. To eliminate the other, as it were, through one's scorning of begrudging, thus constitutes a supreme Machiavellian move in the achievement of empowerment.

The power of the strong is one that does not give rise to envy and ressentiment because it is conceived from the outset as a sum-sum game. The more people who participate in the project of cultivating their inner strength, the stronger the strong feel. Not having to begrudge to others the strength they are able to cultivate from within is a source of one's own strength. Power conceived in this way, therefore, requires inclusion of the mass of others as a precondition for the exercise of one's own strength. A democratic reading of Nietzsche's thought is thus conceptually linked with Nietzsche's construal of the power of the strong.

Foucault and Reflexivity

The problem of reflexivity haunts Foucault's work from its inception. The historiographical point of Foucault's keeping references to social and economic developments to a minimum in *The Order of Things*[35]—to project relatively autonomous *epistemes*, with minimal sociological linkages and transitions traced between them—is to underscore that the content of theories, ideas, and concepts is underdetermined by experience. Weaving social and economic factors into his narrative would have established a stable, external reference point, or series of such points, by which to correlate changes in ideas. The banishment of such reference points constitutes an implicit denial that ideas are determined by, or can even be validly correlated with, experience.

If there is a vacuum of rational explanatory factors to account for the development of ideas, how is the gap to be filled in? The implicit answer of *The Order of Things* (which is explicitly elaborated upon in Foucault's later writings) is—power. Ideas are largely a function of an arbitrary assertion of power. As we have seen in our discussion of Nietzsche—and this is one of the many Nietzschean tenets that Foucault takes over—power signifies continual exteriorization, continual movement to leave its imprint on the world. Ideas are just one major form of this exteriorization, and can be most validly analyzed from a power perspective.

The theme of the subordination of ideas to configurations of power is most dramatically elaborated upon in *The Discourse on Language*—Foucault's Inaugural Lecture at the Collège de France, delivered in 1970. "Of the three great systems of exclusion governing discourse," Foucault writes, "prohibited words, the division of madness and the will to truth—I have spoken at greatest length concerning the third. With good reason: for centuries, the former have continually tended toward the latter; because this last has, gradually, been attempting to assimilate the others in order both to modify them and to provide them with a firm foundation. Because, if the two former are continually growing more fragile and less certain to the extent they are now invaded by the will to truth, the latter, in contrast, daily grows in strength, in depth and implacability."[36]

The pursuit of truth is as distorting a perspective as the elaboration of falsehood. There is a truth beyond truth that points to the limitations of truth as ordinarily conceived. This truth is one of power—the plenitude of possibilities theoretically available to a human life—and from its vantage point truth in a conventional sense—

(just like taboo and madness) involves a mechanism of exclusion. To pursue truth in an ordinary sense is already to be biased in favor of a particular structuring of human life that rules out less mediated, less hierarchical orderings of experience. The desire to appropriate truth is not morally praiseworthy or even morally neutral (and cost-free), but involves a commitment to a certain ordering of experience that precludes the fashioning of alternative orderings that are more responsive to human power urges than the will to truth. In short, the division between truth and falsehood is "a historically constituted division."[37] In the reversal that Socrates and Plato accomplish in relation to Homer and his successors in order to establish the claims of philosophy against poetry and myth that Hannah Arendt so eloquently describes in *The Human Condition*,[38] Foucault sides with the poets against the philosophers.

A more remote precursor to Foucault (lying in the background to Nietzsche) is Rousseau, who in the *Second Discourse* argues that the contractarian, game-theoretic rationality accepted as the norm for apolitical, liberal man by Hobbes and Locke constitutes a distortion and derogation from more authentic and satisfying human possibilities. Rousseau considers the earliest phase of the state of nature prior to the emergence of human self-consciousness, where autistic self-involvement is virtually indistinguishable from self-forgetfulness,[39] to have been the happiest in human development. Foucault shares Rousseau's appraisal of the fallen nature of rationality. To be rational, to pursue the moral and epistemological truths of rational man, is already to inhabit the sort of universe that can never generate the degree of happiness that human beings aspire to. Rationality—the will to truth—is predicated upon the establishment of distance within the self (between rational and nonrational elements) and between selves (more rational and less rational human beings). Distance—the emergence of self-consciousness—is, however, the root cause of human unhappiness. Power might be the demystified surrogate in Foucault's thought for Rousseau's conception of the rootedness of human beings in the natural order of things that typifies the early phase of the state of nature. To view human beings *sub specie* power rather than truth means to see them in perpetual motion, in perpetual process of becoming, with none of the bedrock distinctions of ordinary human life (including such a salient one as that between truth and falsehood) harboring any guarantee of ultimate durability. Power for Foucault is a sort of holism on wheels—in perpetual motion—so that in this sense one could say that the stress on the primacy of power in Foucault represents a kind of kinetic version of the Rousseauian early phase of the state of nature.

Foucault's derogation of reason and the pursuit of truth to a secondary role in relation to power finds an important echo (and analogue) in Kuhn's philosophy of science. According to Kuhn, the will to truth manifested in the master paradigms of extraordinary science is generally undermined in the course of the traditional cyclical patterns of development of normal science, which were fashioned to institutionalize and refine the inspiring paradigms. Puzzles leading to anomalies impede the progressive extension and application of the original paradigms and eventually generate a crisis atmosphere that serves as the occasion for a new institutionalization of the will to truth. In Kuhn's depiction of how the enterprise of science works, efforts at theoretical totalization have their arbitrary character exposed by periodic "returns of the repressed," which unmask the aspirations to truth of the great theoretical innovators as colossal assertions of power.[40]

It is possible to extrapolate from Kuhn's depiction of the relationship between normal science and extraordinary science a more general theory of how traditions develop, disintegrate, and re-form. Nonscientific, social, and political traditions can be viewed from a Kuhnian–Foucauldian perspective as a generally unsuccessful attempt to reconnect the energies of thought (of a particular historical expression of the will to truth) with the energies of lived life, of immediate experience. Generally, the idea is to have some theoretical vision serve as the basis for organizing man's social or political life. When the translation of thought into action occurs, the real world inevitably gives rise to anomalies and unplanned consequences that seriously call into question the aspirations toward comprehensiveness and coherence animating the original theory. In the process of concretely applying the theory, the primordial claims of the self to a radical autonomy—to indeterminacy, inconsequence, and even meaninglessness—are continually reasserted and undermine the pretensions of the theory. Pretheoretical, presovereign "selves" wreak havoc with particular configurations of the will to truth.

How can Foucault's resort to power as the central explanatory concept be reflexively justified? If everything that occurs in human psychology and in the social and political realms is a manifestation of power, then is not Foucault's theory about the pervasiveness of power itself a manifestation of power? Has not Foucault deflated his theory to the same level as the objects of his theory, and thereby jeopardized the theoretical status of his formulations? If Foucault is viewed as appropriating from Nietzsche not only the overwhelming absorption with the category of power but also the tacit philosophical background to the emphasis on power as I have interpreted it in earlier sections of this chapter, Foucault's problem of reflexivity would appear to be resolved. Almost—but not quite. Foucault's Nietzschean usage of the category of power to address social and political issues as well as matters pertaining to individual personality involves him in tensions and inconsistencies that my previous defense of Nietzsche will not be adequate to resolve. By expanding his identity as theorist to encompass avowedly social and political realms, Foucault might have been unconsciously exposing the limits of Nietzschean analysis when applied to officially public realms.

In order to make his case for the pervasiveness of power, Foucault relies on the textualist thesis that meaning is underdetermined by text and that therefore, in order to account for which interpretations of particular texts do historically manage to gain prominence, we must have recourse to a power hypothesis.[41] For Foucault, the order of sexuality and schemes of punishment are texts, and he traces the role of power, and the suppression of the other, in even these most minimal and characteristic orderings of personality and social relations.[42] To the extent that Foucault adheres to the thesis of textuality—that meaning is underdetermined by text and that, therefore, the interpretation of all texts is literally endless—he is disbarred from crossing the boundary from an internal reading of the texts of sexuality and punishment (one that allows for the continuing play of signifiers) to an external reading (one that shifts the burden of interpretation and explanation to worldly configurations of power that shape and distort the structurings that we make). The two halves of the textualist thesis are in sharp tension with one another. If texts are permanently unfinished—they can always go on being interpreted, if there is nothing in the text itself that establishes closure of interpretation—then a power hypothesis has nothing to latch on to. If a fixed and determinate text can never be authoritatively secured, there is nothing for a power hypothesis to be about. If the resources of internal interpretive play can never be (theoretically) exhausted, then it would appear that an external approach that connects interpretation with certain configurations of power in the world can be endlessly deferred. The intellectual space for it will have been denied as long as internalist readings that make no reference to the world can go on being played out forever.[43]

Foucault's procedure of analysis presupposes some version of positivism—that particular readings of texts are allowed to remain as they are, are not susceptible to more imaginative readings—in order to create theoretical space for his thesis concerning the ubiquity of power to work. The controversy between Foucault and Jacques Derrida concerning how to interpret the *cogito* passage of Descartes—with Foucault arguing for complicity between Descartes and medical–juridical structures in excluding those that have been denominated mad from reflective consideration concerning how men think, and Derrida pursuing a purely internalist reading arguing that Descartes wants to call our most characteristic rationalistic processes into question on the basis of the universal experience of the dream state[44]—can be translated and extended into Foucault's philosophy as a whole. It seems that one needs to choose between Foucault and Derrida. One cannot be a disciple of both.

The problematic of textuality and power is far less disturbing in relation to Nietzsche than it is in Foucault because Nietzsche's analyses of power are much less riveted in social analyses and social structuring. In Nietzsche, power is most often attendant upon the normal and traditional operations of the self, and the role of social and political institutions as engines of distortion is much less prominent in Nietzsche than it is in Foucault. It is Foucault's special grafting of Marx onto Nietzsche in his search for social analogues and manifestations of expressions and distortions of power that gives rise to the special tension that I have just analyzed in Foucault's writings.

CHAPTER 8

Maimonides and Lyotard: Convergences between the Premodern and the Postmodern

A parallelism exists between Maimonides' articulation and defense of monotheism in *The Guide of the Perplexed*[1] and the structure of Lyotard's skeptical and relativist arguments in *The Postmodernist Condition* that gives rise to analogous logical dilemmas and conundrums. I wish to suggest two approaches for resolving these dilemmas. The first involves what Lyotard would probably consider a version of modernism in extremis: invoking a multivalued (in my case, an intuitionist) logic in order to be able to map the suspension of the law of excluded middle and then having recourse to reverse causation by way of upholding intuitionism. The second approach that I pursue in resolving the dilemmas of consistency attendant to Lyotard's and Maimonides' skeptical and relativist and monotheistic formulations is a postmodernist one that argues for the dispensability of metanarrativity. In conclusion, I argue for a possible convergence between the modernist and postmodernist approaches: how postmodernism might constitute the most consummate expression of the modernist program.

Parallel Structure between Monotheistic, Skeptical, and Relativist Arguments

> The meaning of the qualificative attributions I ascribed to Him and the meaning of the attributions known to us have nothing in common in any respect or in any mode; these attributions have in common only the name and nothing else.
>
> The term "existent" is predicated of Him, may He be exalted, and of everything that is other than He, in a purely equivocal sense. Similarly the terms "knowledge," "power," "will," and "life," as applied to Him, may He be exalted, and to all those possessing knowledge, power, will, and life, are purely equivocal, so that their meaning when they are predicated of Him is in no way like their meaning in other applications.
>
> Accordingly, in view of the fact that the relation between us and Him, may He be exalted, is considered as nonexistent—I mean the relation between Him and that which is other than He—it follows necessarily that likeness between Him and us should also be considered nonexistent.[2]

In denying the possibility of extrapolation from our human vocabularies to descriptions of God, Maimonides says the following: "Now everything that can be ascribed to God, may He be exalted, differs in every respect from our attributes, so that no definition can comprehend the one thing and the other."[3] Yet, according to Maimonides, we can state definitely that these attributes do not apply to *Him*. Here the problem of consistency emerges in all of its sharpness. If this statement is true (that God is denied all humanly characterizable attributes) then it is false (that we can know nothing about God). Maimonides' articulation of monotheism is a doctrine whose formulation implies its own falsity.

In the sentence that immediately follows the one I have just quoted, Maimonides attacks the imputation of "existence" to God: "Similarly, as I shall make clear, the term 'existence' can only be applied equivocally to His existence and to that of things other than He."[4] In order for God to exist, he (logically) must not exist. One of the conundrums to which attributing reality to his existence gives rise is his passing over "from potentiality to actuality," which suggests that there is something anterior to God that enabled him to pass over from potentiality to actuality. As soon as one begins to attribute reality to the notion of God as creator, one ends up with an infinite regress. The infinite regress is resolved by purging the concept of God of both meaning and reference. The notion of God becomes a paradigm of the lack of conceptual self-sufficiency of all of our concepts, which can be seen as being merely rhetorically manipulable but drained of unequivocal meaning and certain reference. "God" becomes the norm of our ontologically unmoored—detached—vocabularies.

Maimonides' and Lyotard's projects seem entirely symmetrical with one another: Maimonides wants to get rid of God as conceived in popular religious consciousness; Lyotard in *The Postmodern Condition* wants to get rid of knowledge and of truth as conventionally understood. In both cases, a central point of the demolition is to achieve a certain catholicity and openness in experience. In Maimonides' case, this means being able to level philosophical and theological discourse to the same metaphysical plane—that God does not represent an intrusive, nonrationalizable presence that prevents assimilation of religious talk to philosophical talk and vice versa. For Lyotard, the elimination of metanarrativity and the privileged status that it secures for particular narratives means that heterogeneous forms of experience, and knowledge statements based upon them, are reducible to the same epistemological level with no possibility of forming hierarchies or applying invidious categories of validation between them.

One could perhaps go even further and say that Maimonides' project of regarding Judaism and philosophy as forming a seamless web of inquiry might be most illuminatingly accommodated under Lyotard's conception of postmodernism as involving the absence of fixed criteria of judgment, with flexible criteria being insinuated and supplied by the intellectual activities one is engaged in. For Maimonides, philosophy and Talmudic scholarship feel good together. The criteria by which they can be fitted together will emerge in relation to a life devoted to their merging. The presupposition behind Maimonides' intellectual project would then be a skeptical denial of the objective rightness of criteria of judgment, ethical or epistemological, that were not strictly immanentist or retrospective in character.

Both Maimonides' and Lyotard's projects are vulnerable in an important sense for an analogous reason. Neither the critique of the popular conception of God nor the rejection of knowledge and of truth as conventionally understood can be formulated consistently. Maimonides says that none of the traditional theological terms applies literally to God—God does not see, hear, or even exist in the way traditional religious understanding projects—yet he wants all of his negative criticisms to apply to *God*: The subject of all of his negative, paring-down work is the traditional (mono)theistic God. In order for Maimonides' critical apparatus to have a viable target, he needs precisely to maintain in some form, to some extent, whatever it is that that apparatus shoots down.

The problem of consistency would not arise in relation to a philosophical attack against unicorns (comparable to Maimonides' attack upon the popular conception of God) because Maimonides would concede that unicorns are stipulated by the literary imagination. The issue of consistency arises, however, with regard to monotheistic theology because Maimonides does not want to say that God is merely stipulated as a philosophical or literary fiction. He is more than a projection.

Lyotard also confronts the problem of how to formulate skepticism consistently, so that while he is skeptical of the knowledge claims proferred by theorists in diverse disciplines and schools of philosophy, his own skepticism remains invulnerable to the skeptical attacks he launches against others. Both Maimonides and Lyotard appear to confront analogous problems of incipient self-refutation, of consistency.

How does Maimonides analyze the emergence, and significance, of the monotheistic principle (God's absolute otherness)? He traces its emergence to the patriarch Abraham, who is depicted in Maimonides' intellectual-biographical sketch of him in his "Laws Concerning Idolatry and the Ordinances of the Heathens" as a proto-Aristotelian philosophical inquirer in search of an indubitable first cause:

> But The Creator of the Universe was known to none, and recognised by none, save a few solitary individuals, such as Enosh, Methuselah, Noah, Shem and Eber. The world moved on in this fashion, till that Pillar of the World, the Patriarch Abraham, was born. After he was weaned, while

still an infant, his mind began to reflect. By day and by night he was thinking and wondering: "How is it possible that this (celestial) sphere should continuously be guiding the world and have no one to guide it and cause it to turn round; for it cannot be that it turns round of itself." He had no teacher, no one to instruct him in aught. He was submerged, in Ur of the Chaldees, among silly idolaters. His father and mother and the entire population worshipped idols, and he worshipped with them. But his mind was busily working and reflecting till he had attained the way of truth, apprehended the correct line of thought and knew that there is One God, that He guides the celestial Sphere and created everything, and that among all that exist, there is no god beside Him. He realised that the whole world was in error, and that what had occasioned their error was that they worshipped the stars and the images, so that the truth perished from their minds. Abraham was forty years old when he recognised his Creator. Having attained this knowledge, he began to refute the inhabitants of Ur of the Chaldees, arguing with them and saying to them, "The course you are following is not the way of truth." He broke the images and commenced to instruct the people that it was not right to serve any one but the God of the Universe, to Whom alone it was proper to bow down, offer up sacrifices and make libations, so that all human creatures might, in the future, know Him; and that it was proper to destroy and shatter all the images, so that the people might not err like these who thought that there was no god but these images. When he had prevailed over them with his arguments, the king (of the country) sought to slay him. He was miraculously saved, and emigrated to Haran. He then began to proclaim to the whole world with great power and to instruct the people that the entire Universe had but one Creator and that Him it was right to worship. He went from city to city and from kingdom to kingdom, calling and gathering together the inhabitants till he arrived in the land of Canaan. There too, he proclaimed his message, as it is said "And he called there on the name of the Lord, God of the Universe" (Gen. 21:33). When the people flocked to him and questioned him regarding his assertions, he would instruct each one according to his capacity till he had brought him to the way of truth, and thus thousands and tens of thousands joined him. These were the persons referred to in the phrase, "men in the house of Abraham. . . ."

The essential principle in the precepts concerning idolatry is that we are not to worship any thing created—neither angel, sphere, star, none of the four elements, nor whatever has been formed from them.[5]

What motivates Maimonides' formulation of the monotheistic principle—God's absolute otherness—is a desire to bring the philosophical/scientific quest to a halt. As long as the stuff to which the *explanans* makes reference is in any way continuous with the material to which the *explanandum* refers, the search for reasons and for causes can proceed indefinitely without any letup in the search for a more primary explanation. The only way that the philosophical/scientific quest can be brought to a satisfactory arrest, and philosophical repose achieved, is by postulating (arriving at) an *explanans* which invokes an entity that is totally unassimilable to human conceptual schemata. For Maimonides, the origin of the monotheistic God who is depicted as being wholly other from man arises out of the need to achieve release from philosophical anxiety by postulating an entity as first cause that embodies absolute difference.

One might say that the understanding that Abraham advances in opposition to the animistic outlook of the rest of the world is the centrality of dialectical tension itself for a proper construal of man's situation in the world. The rest of the world are monistic reductionists, inveterate naturalizers of the phenomena within and around them. They want all aspects of their existence to have a qualitative sameness. They want the created and the Creator to be composed of the same stuff, to be reducible to the same material. What Abraham's compatriots sought to do was to annul the metaphysical "distances" (in Nietzsche's sense) of human life. Abraham is an advocate of the reality, the permanence, the ineradicableness of those distances.

Since Maimonides acknowledges that the central themes of the *Guide* are an elucidation of *Ma'aseh Bereshith* (the Work of the Beginning) and *Ma'aseh Merkabah* (the Work of the Chariot),[6] which heretofore had constituted the staples of Jewish esotericism and mysticism, the recourse to writing of the *Guide* itself constitutes a momentous metaphysical act that can most plausibly be interpreted in the light of our discussion concerning the significance of monotheism. As Derrida has emphasized, writing betokens a "metaphysics of absence," in contrast to speech, which presupposes a "metaphysics of presence."[7] A good deal of the content of the *Guide* relates to the nature of God. The choice of a written medium of communication over an oral one figures the endless series of displacements that the Jewish monotheistic conception of God requires and facilitates. Monotheism points in the direction of a metaphysics of absence that assigns primacy to writing above speech.

Resolving the Dilemmas of Skepticism, Relativism, and Monotheism: A Modernist Approach

A first approach toward resolving the dilemmas of formulating consistent versions of skepticism and relativism and monotheism consists in extending the modernist program to encompass sustainable skeptical and relativist metanarratives and thus obviating the job of work of postmodernism, which seeks to restore coherence to skepticism and relativism by rejecting the need for systematic justification altogether.[8] One example of an extended modernist metanarrative would consist of two stages: adumbrating the role of intuitionism as an example of a multivalued logic in formulating consistent versions of skepticism and relativism and monotheism; and sketching out the role of reverse causation in completing the agenda of restoring consistency to these three doctrines.

In pursuing this approach, it is important to note that Lyotard's argument against metanarrativity that was quoted in Chapter Seven would appear to rest on a logical confusion. If such grand metanarratives as those involving the dialectics of the spirit and the emancipation of the working subject are losing their appeal in the last third of the twentieth century, this does not in any way impugn the logical requirement of invoking a local metanarrative in order to fix the meaning and reference of any narrative (scientific or otherwise) we are engaged in deciphering. In Quine's terminology, "We are finding no clear difference between *specifying* a universe of discourse—the range of the variables of quantification—and *reducing* that universe to some other."[9] Quine claims that regression does not involve an infinite regress since it is always necessarily a *partial* exercise. "To question the reference of all the terms of our all-inclusive theory," he says, "becomes meaningless simply for want of further terms relative to which to ask or answer the question."[10]

Once recourse to local metanarratives is acknowledged, a need to resort to intuitionist logic—or some other version of a multivalued logic—is also simultaneously, if tacitly, being invoked, because in nearly all of the interesting, critical cases of regression, one is privileging the background theory in relation to the object theory. For example, when one invokes a skeptical background theory to make sense out of our conceptualization of material things (object theory), the skeptical metanarrative will not have been directed against the theory of skepticism itself. A plausible way to remedy this inconsistency is to have recourse to an intuitionistic (or some other version of a multivalued) logic that maps the suspension of the law of excluded middle, so that skeptical metanarratives can be at once skeptical and not skeptical. Intuitionistic logic itself, as we have seen, is not reflexively sustainable unless one invokes reverse causation.

In order to make his case for severed, totally immanentist narratives,[11] Lyotard has to have recourse to local metanarratives if only for the sake of contrast and rejection. His immanentist position forces him simultaneously to affirm and to deny the existence of these metanarratives. In other words, Lyotard himself in making his argument against metanarrativity is having implicit recourse to a multivalued logic.

Postmodernism in a sense picks up where W. V. Quine and Donald Davidson leave off. Quine wants to get rid of some of the classic answers to some of the standard philosophical questions by banishing analyticity, meaning, and reference from our philosophical ontologies,[12] and Davidson wants to banish the dualism of intellectual scheme and reality.[13] Postmodernism wants to dispose of the traditional questions themselves, which revolve largely around issues of skepticism and relativism. A crucial question to raise concerning postmodernism is whether one can get rid of the questions without simultaneously presupposing the (continuing validity of the) questions.

In addition, and more importantly, modernism (the adherence to metanarrativity) is not viable unless one introduces a concept of tacit knowledge or an intuitionist (or some other version of a multivalued) logic and reverse causation. Once one has these premises in place, one does not need postmodernism—it is ontologically redundant. There is no epistemological job of work for postmodernism to do that is not already being accomplished by modernism. Postmodernism as I have described it is already implicit in the modernist program.

If there is some logical compulsion in the choice of modernism over postmodernism—if one can show that the modernist claim that there are justifiable skeptical and relativist metanarratives is correct and that the postmodernist claim that one can dispense with metanarratives altogether founders on self-contradiction—then one has cleared epistemological space for making the strongest possible rhetorical case for political participation. The equation would go like this: Skepticism–Equality–Participation. If skepticism in its different guises argues that none of us is in a position to affirm the rational superiority of his views or values over those of his fellows, then the appropriate political response is to have as many members of society as possible participate in the numerous collective decisions affecting their lives. Skepticism delegitimizes the formation of any permanent hierarchies in society and provides a continually renewing impetus for the expansion of political participation.

What might hang in the political balance in the debates between modernists and postmodernists is the fate of a radical participatory politics. Without the justificatory leverage afforded by rationally defensible metanarratives, postmodernism appears to leave everything as it is. Foucault's theorizing, as we have seen, yields a plurality of historically articulated and existentially unformed possibilities, with no intellectual tools available for fashioning priorities between them. Modernism, by contrast, holds out the hope of rationally informed, radical political action.[14]

The cardinal exemplification of the suspension of the law of excluded middle in Maimonides' thought comes from his formulation of monotheistic doctrine itself. If God's essence cannot be grasped—if there are no analogues on the literal level to any of the attributes we impute to God—then everything is, logically speaking, possible. So that with regard to the most fundamental question of all in Judaism, God does not exist (in the way the masses conceive his existence, with a literal attribution of qualities) and yet he does exist in an indefinable sense (in prayer as an object of worship, as the ultimate guarantor of the moral universe through the application of rewards and punishments, and as an object of intellectual contemplation).

This pattern of absolute affirmation on two contradictory levels, the divine and the human, replicates itself with regard to the issue of free will versus determinism, where God's total knowledge (in a sense unavailable to us) coexists with unlimited human freedom and responsibility for actions taken:

> Perchance you will say, "Does not the Almighty know everything that will be before it happens"? He either knows that this person will be righteous or wicked, or He does not know. If He knows that he will be righteous, it is impossible that he should not be righteous; and if you say that He knows that he will be righteous and yet it is possible for him to be wicked, then He does not know the matter clearly. As to the solution of this problem, understand that "the measure thereof is longer than the earth and wider than the sea" (Job 11:9), and many important principles of the highest sublimity are connected with it. You, however, need only to know and comprehend what I am about to say. In the Second Chapter of the laws relating to the fundamental principles of the Torah, we have already explained that God does not know with a knowledge external to Himself, like human beings whose knowledge and self are separate entities, but He, blessed be His Name, and His knowledge are One. This, the human intellect cannot clearly apprehend. And just as it is not in human power to apprehend or discover the Creator's Real Essence, as it is said, "for there shall no man see Me and live" (Ex. 33:20), so it is not in human power to apprehend or discover the Creator's knowledge. So the prophet said, "For My thoughts are not your thoughts, neither are your ways My ways" (Is. 55:8). This being the case, we lack the capacity to know how God knows all creatures and their activities. Yet we do know beyond doubt that a human being's activities are in his own hands and the Almighty neither draws him on, nor decrees that he should act thus or not act thus. It is not religious tradition alone by which this is known. It is also supported by clear proofs furnished by science. Hence, it is said in the Prophetic writings that a man will be judged for all his deeds, according to his deeds, whether they be good or evil. And this is the principle on which all the words of Prophecy depend.[15]

What thus seems to be hermeneutically encoded in the doctrine of austere monotheism and its corollary affirmation of complete human free will and responsibility in the face of divine omniscience is a suspension of the law of excluded middle.

As we have seen, the suspension of the law of excluded middle cannot be formulated consistently without invoking a doctrine of reverse causation. The idea of reverse causation is approximated in Maimonides' thought in his radically man-centered formulation of the messianic age, which harbors the suggestion of a determined, human, backward-moving thrust to recapture a lost, more perfect past. Maimonides' conceptualizing both the advent and the prevailing conditions during the messianic age in fully naturalistic terms suggests the morally and spiritually degenerative effects of previous actions becoming the cause, as it were, of their own formerly regarded causes in an effort to reappropriate a more whole, lost past. The humanistically and historically described dynamics of the messianic age figure a metaphysical doctrine of reverse causation, whereby the future, the effects, determines the past, the cause(s).

Maimonides draws a sharp line of distinction between *Olam Habah* (The World to Come) and *Yemot Hamashiach* (The Days of the Messiah). *Olam Habah*, according to Maimonides, is not an earthly realm—a continuation of human history with Israel victorious—but a sheerly transcendental realm of disembodied souls that coexists with our current world and would presumably continue to coexist with it even after the arrival of *Melech Hamashiach* (King Messiah) and that serves as *the* ultimate reward for the righteous. In Maimonides' phrase in *Hilchot Teshuvah* ("The Laws of Repentance"), "The ultimate and perfect reward, the final bliss which will suffer neither interruption nor diminution is the life of the world to come."[16] In contrast to this, Maimonides immediately goes on to add: "The Messianic era, on the other hand, will be realized in this world; which will continue its normal course except that independent sovereignty will be restored to Israel. The ancient sages already said, 'The only difference between the present and the Messianic era is that political oppression will then cease.' "[17]

The locus classicus for Maimonides' formulation of *Yemot Hamashi-*

223

ach is in his *Code, Hilchot Melachim U'Milchamotahem* (Laws of Kings and Their Wars"), chapters eleven and twelve:

> King Messiah will arise and restore the kingdom of David to its former state and original sovereignty. He will rebuild the sanctuary and gather the dispersed of Israel. All the ancient laws will be reinstituted in his days; sacrifices will again be offered; the Sabbatical and Jubilee years will again be observed in accordance with the commandments set forth in the Law.

> Do not think that King Messiah will have to perform signs and wonders, bring anything new into being, revive the dead, or do similar things. It is not so. Rabbi Akiba was a great sage, a teacher of the Mishnah, yet he was also the armor-bearer of Ben Koziba. He affirmed that the latter was King Messiah; he and all the wise men of his generation shared this belief until Ben Koziba was slain in (his) iniquity. Since he was killed it became known to them that he was not (the Messiah). Yet the Rabbis had not asked him for a sign or token.

> If there arise a king from the House of David who meditates on the Torah, occupies himself with the commandments, as did his ancestor David, observes the precepts prescribed in the Written and the Oral Law, prevails upon Israel to walk in the way of the Torah and to repair its breaches, and fights the battles of the Lord, it may be assumed that he is the Messiah. If he does these things and succeeds, rebuilds the sanctuary on its site, and gathers the dispersed of Israel, he is beyond all doubt the Messiah. . . .

> Let no one think that in the days of the Messiah any of the laws of nature will be set aside, or any innovation be introduced into creation. The world will follow its normal course. The words of Isaiah: And the wolf shall dwell with the lamb, and the leopard shall lie down with the kid (Isa. 11:6) are to be understood figuratively, meaning that Israel will live securely among the wicked of the heathens who are likened to wolves and leopards, as it is written: A wolf of the deserts doth spoil them, a leopard watcheth over their cities (Jer. 5:6). They will all accept the true religion, and will neither plunder nor destroy, and together with Israel earn a comfortable living in a legitimate way, as it is written: And the lion shall eat straw like the ox (Isa. 11:7). All similar expressions used in connection with the Messianic age are metaphorical. In the days of King

Messiah the full meaning of those metaphors and their allusions will become clear to all.

As for the third eschatological term, *Techiyat Hamatim* (the Resurrection of the Dead), the clearest formulation of Maimonides' position comes, I think, from *Mamar B'Techiyat Hamatim* (*Essay on the Resurrection of the Dead*). This essay was written to refute those who claimed that Maimonides rejected the notion of resurrection of the dead in his commentary on the Mishnah and in his *Code*. This is the way Maimonides describes his position: "God will resurrect the dead in accordance with His desire and will when He will want and whom He will want, either during the Messianic age or before it or after it."[18] Maimonides emphasizes throughout this essay that resurrection of the dead encompasses resurrection of the body as well as the soul. *Techiyat Hamatim* involves a total resurrection of the person, such that since it defies reason we follow the principle of *ein leche bo elah chidusho*: We restrict our elucidation of the notion to what its sense conveys when literally conceived, consigning to the realm of faith all questions of empirical application. For Maimonides it is with *Techiyat Hamatim* as it is with the very concept of God itself. We only know that it exists, but not what it signifies.

Resolving the Dilemmas of Skepticism, Relativism, and Monotheism: A Postmodernist Approach

There is a second approach for formulating consistent versions of skepticism and relativism and monotheism that affirms postmodernism rather than pointing to the intellectual self-sufficiency of modernism. The need for a postmodernist construal of consistency, at least in relation to monotheism, is suggested by a grave incoherence in Maimonides' systematization of monotheistic teaching. Since the central point of Maimonides' argument is to emphasize God's otherness, his total difference from man, this is accomplished just as much by endowing him with humanly comprehensible attributes as by denying him those attributes. God, who is essentially totally other than man, endowed with (or manifesting) such attributes as omnipotence, omniscience, and benevolence, is as fundamentally unfathomable by us as God deprived of these humanly compassable attributes. The incomprehensibility, the otherness, is preserved either way. Why the staunch stand against the attribution of qualities?

It thus appears that God is not truly wholly other in Maimonides' conception, because otherwise he could possess the panoply of human attributes to their fullest extent and still be God. What nullifies this possibility for Maimonides is his steadfast adherence to God as first cause, necessarily existent, as a strategy for bringing the philosophical quest to a satisfactory halt. It is this holding of God answerable to a human intellectual need that forecloses the acceptance of the wholly other, monotheistic God with a full range of the highest human attributes.

There is a schizophrenic split in Maimonides' argument for deriving and conceptualizing God. With regard to the emotions, the affections, Maimonides formulates his famous denial of attributes. God's goodness, compassion, anger, power, and so forth, are not to be construed literally, but are merely figures of speech conforming to ordinary human conceptions of divinity that in no way refer to or capture God's essence. Only a rigorous process of denial of the literal relevance of these attributes can help us to see God's nature clearly. With regard to the human intellect, however, Maimonides' theorizing points to the reverse conclusion. God is the necessarily existent (whose existence coincides with his essence) because otherwise there would be no satisfactory arrest in the search for reasons and causes. The philosophical/scientific quest, the continual search for the causes and/or reasons for phenomena, can only come to a satisfactory conclusion in the postulation of God as necessarily existent or first cause. God's character as necessarily existent thus makes him answerable to the explorations and conundrums of the human intellect. While Maimonides vehemently denies any point of contact or resemblance between man's emotions and God's, there is an urgently compelling link between man's intellectual ruminations and God. If Maimonides were more thoroughly consistent and denied that intellectually there was any point of contact between our intellectual probings and God, then he could have rehabilitated the conventional understanding of God with all of its manifold attributes in their full pristine literalness. If God is not answerable to our intellectual canons and standards of judgment, if he is not conceptualized as the necessarily existent or first cause, then he does not have to be coherent in accordance with our versions of coherence. He can be compassionate and powerful in a sense fully comprehensible to us and still be God. By being consistent in his dissociation of God from human attributes—by severing God from our intellectual exertions and postures as well as from our emotional qualities—Maimonides paradoxically would have been able to salvage the concept of God in its full human literalness. God would simply be a humanly unfathomable entity to whom the traditional array of theological attributes applied. The "sense" of such a formulation would be clear to us, even if the reference remained inscrutable. However, by denying only the affective attributes (and preserving common ground between our intellectual ruminations and God's existence), Maimonides removes from view the possibility of imputing the traditional attributes to God while remaining faithful to the conception of God's total otherness.

Given this inconsistency, a principle of charitableness in interpretation would counsel reading Maimonides in a postmodernist way rather than in the modernist fashion developed in the second section of this chapter. According to my first modernist approach, which integrates Maimonides' monotheistic formulations into a sustainable metanarrative, the difficulty remains as to why he denies the attribution of humanlike qualities to God, since once God is conceived as wholly other (and this is now seen as a logically sustainable formulation) he could just as well share in humanlike attributes as not exhibit them. The suspension of the law of excluded middle and reverse causation enable us to refer meaningfully to a God who is wholly other than man. If this formulation is taken seriously, it remains neutral as between the choice of imputing or not imputing human attributes to God. Why then does Maimonides so vehemently assert (and defend) the thesis of nonattribution? This suggests that a postmodernist reading of the *Guide* might be more cogent than a modernist reading. From a postmodernist perspective, there is no overarching metanarrative in terms of which to place or to locate the argument of the *Guide*. There are only immanentist narratives temporarily spun out to more effectively gauge the import of the specific arguments one is making. If severed and immanentist narratives are adequate and sufficient in an ontologically relativized universe, then Maimonides can coherently argue for a rigorous affirmation of God's otherness as well as for the nonresemblance of any attributes imputed to him to anything displayed by human beings.

Pursuing this postmodernist approach to Maimonides' monotheism, one could say that the utter existential removal of the monotheistic God issues forth in a paradigm of construal of worldly phenomena that is defined by thoroughly rampant "ontological relativity." If God is wholly other, not only does the decision whether to impute human attributes to him become completely arbitrary, but all other theological formulations concerning his relation to the human world become equally arbitrary. Thus, in his rejection of the Aristotelian position concerning the eternity of the world, Maimonides opts for a monotheistic alternative that in effect becomes the functional equivalent of the Aristotelian viewpoint. Maimonides says that the concept of time cannot be literally applied to God because otherwise an infinite regress would open up, since time is a function of motion, and movement would have to be postulated of a force behind, above, or outside God that facilitated his existing in time. Therefore, according to Maimonides, we must say that the universe has an absolute beginning—that God created the world in time, but that the notion of time in relation to God is as devoid of meaning and reference as is the concept of God itself. Time in relation to God has to be construed "monotheistically," just as God himself has to be construed monotheistically. Maimonides then goes on to say that there is nothing theologically offensive about postulating that the world will exist forever. The conjunction of the "monotheistic" construal of God's creating the world in time with the literal construal of the world's subsisting forever yields the Aristotelian doctrine of the eternity of the universe, while registering a formal rejection of it.[19]

Maimonides' oblique, ambivalent affirmation of the eternity of the world contradicts his search for an acceptable first cause, which to a large extent motivates his monotheistic theorizing. One possible strategy for reconciling these conflicting strands of argument is to point to the role of tacit knowledge in the theoretical economy of the *Guide*. Maimonides' indirect affirmation of the eternity of the world in partially "monotheistic" terms dislodges the quest for a first cause from the central position that it occupies in the formulation of monotheistic principles. This is one juncture in which tacit knowledge is being manifested in the argument of the *Guide*. Problems and solutions, as we have seen in our analysis of Plato's *Meno*, are correlative notions. If the prospect of a solution has been foreclosed, a problem remains unformulable. If in a "monotheistic" paraphrase Maimonides gives his allegiance to the doctrine of the eternity of the world, then the search for first causes has been rendered beside the point. On a submerged and implicit level, Maimonides appears to be undercutting the very problematic that seems to provide the motive force of the argument on an explicit level. How does the presence of elements of tacit knowledge in Maimonides' argument relate to a postmodernist reading of the *Guide* that I am presenting?

The central tenet of Lyotard's postmodernism appears to involve a condensation of a philosophy of tacit knowledge. Postmodernism's "incredulity toward metanarratives" might just be a shorthand way of stating that advances in knowledge are predicated upon investigators' being able to see their way clear to where they want to go, not upon any secure bedrock of assumptions or findings that motivate the formulation of hypotheses or questions or problems. Correspondingly, the significance of the modifier "tacit" in the phrase "tacit knowledge" might be to call into question the possibility of fully elaborating a metanarrative that will suitably undergird the statement at hand. It is in terms of what can be done with a hypothesis or problem that an approach is metatheoretically validated, not in relation to the strength or impeccability of its credentials or pedigree. Statements, theories, hypotheses, questions, and problems thus have content to the degree that they can be correlated with other statements, solutions, and so on. To the extent that postmodernism can be interpreted as calling attention to the future-directedness or potential for correlation of the statements that we make, its content overlaps precisely with "tacit knowledge," which construes our knowledge statements as abridgments of a stream of experience that remains unbounded in relation to both past and future.[20]

I have been arguing that God's otherness and denial of attributes are totally severable concepts and that Maimonides' conflation of the two provides indirect support for a postmodernist reading of his thought. Perhaps a more charitable way still of interpreting Maimonides would be to say that he uses the "denial of attributes" as an instrumentality for stating the thesis of God's otherness. Attributes are denied as a way of providing a humanly accessible conceptual handle on the idea of God's otherness. But Maimonides would acknowledge the conceptual dispensability of the "denial of attributes" construed on a fully literal level. The numerous passages where Maimonides vehemently assaults conventional understandings of God that attribute qualities to him on a literal level would then have to be reinterpreted as heuristic devices for providing a point of entry into the notion of God's otherness, but should not be taken literally on their own terms.

Can a case for a postmodernist reading of monotheistic teaching be made that is independent of Maimonides' supposed conflation between "God's otherness" and "denial of attributes"? Aside from the theoretical impact of Maimonides' ambivalent affirmation of the principle of the eternity of the world discussed above, one can point to a more striking affinity between Maimonides' formulation of monotheistic doctrine and postmodernism. What postmodernism advocates can be seen as an extension of the ontological relativity implicit in a radical affirmation of God's otherness to encompass whatever immanentist narratives we temporarily expand upon in advancing the sorts of arguments that we are concerned to make. All of these immanentist narratives—including skeptical and relativist ones—are relative to the points we wish to make; they have no validity or permanence beyond them. The premodernist Maimonidean monotheistic universe and the postmodernist ontologically relativist universe converge in their shaping of a world in which the ultimate props of argument are relocated from extrahuman theological and metaphysical levels to an unabashedly human realm where human exigencies and needs prevail.[21]

The unity between Maimonides' *Guide* and his pathbreaking multivolume, comprehensive *Code*, embracing all aspects of Jewish law, can be predicated along the postmodernist lines I am developing. Maimonides' metaphysical leveling of religious and philosophical discourse through his pursuit of negative theorizing (God isn't this, he isn't that, etc.) manifested in the *Guide* can be interpreted as releasing his audience into the prospects of a postmodernist universe where multiple and contradictory affirmations can occur. As a result of Maimonides' negative theorizing of God in the *Guide*, Judaism emerges as a series of peripheries in search of an ever-receding center. God's total otherness is suggestive of a human mode of being-in-the-world marked by removal and belatedness—where human meaning and purpose are supplied by our unceasing mobilization of the energies of the will to structure and restructure the field of action. The stress on *Maase Mitzvah* (the Performance of Commandments) in Maimonides' *Code* stems from the insufficiency of human reason plotted in the *Guide*, and is not a function of the plenitude or comprehensiveness of human reason. The periphery of human action must largely contribute toward continually structuring and fashioning a center: There is no center outside that. Given the preeminence assigned to the field of human action that flows from the argument of the *Guide*, Maimonides' *Code* traces and summarizes the rabinically ordained conceptualizations of the multiple subspheres (public and private) where human action realizes itself.

An additional support for postmodernism in Maimonides' philosophy thus comes from the implicit conceptualization of the relationship between God's otherness and the scene of human action that emerges from juxtaposing Maimonides' *Code* to his *Guide*. That scene is projected as one in which ultimate explanatory factors and ultimate logical connectedness and philosophical coherence are unavailable to us and where all we have to work with are the incipient justificatory models present in our mobilization of energies of will themselves. We do things, Maimonides appears to be telling us, and since we are creatures with concrete images of the past and particular visions of the future, we feel continually inclined to supply justificatory frameworks that will link individual actions to past and future and will contribute toward the generation and maintenance of a sense of personal identity. But lacking a secure and permanent intellectually relatable center (a humanly intelligible concept of God), it is the periphery of our perpetual and contradictory encounters with experience that yields the continually shifting and restructured foci of our lives, rather than a center that is outside the sphere of our human exertions and involvements.

The endless doing—the endless immanentizing—that becomes the legatee of the displacement of the literalistic God in Judaism betrays a strongly postmodernist motif. God, as it were, in Maimonideanly inspired Judaism, exists after the fact: after we have established a world in which he exists as a meaningful object of worship and contemplation. The articulation of the concept of God conforms to Maimonides' unraveling of the dilemma of divine omniscience and human free will and his envisioning of the messianic age described above. In all three cases, God, human free will and responsibility, and the messianic age emerge ex post facto. After we have spun out the immanentist narratives embedded in our actions that make room for all four concepts, we can cheerfully and confidently say that they exist. These four concepts are hermeneutically pried from the interstices of various Jewishly grasped scenes of human action.[22]

If my postmodernist construal of monotheism is at all correct, then what Richard Rorty says about it in a recent review in the *New Leader* needs to be turned on its head. Rorty says that "the idea that there is some such thing [that has "shaped every aspect of Western experience"] seems to me just the typical philosophical hope that all the things that one dislikes most will turn out to have a single root, so that one can then cut them away with a single dialectical stroke. I agree that 'Western experience' owes quite a bit to the traditional philosophical attempt to produce a secularized version of monotheism by hypostatizing certain human abilities under the name of 'reason.' But I think that Mill, Nietzsche and Dewey have already shown us what was wrong with that hypostatization."[23] If my second reading of Maimonides is correct, then one of the key codifiers of monotheistic doctrine itself had already grappled systematically with the implications of foreclosing the route of hypostatization and had presented a vision of human life in his *Guide* and in his *Code* where the ontological primacy of action over theoretical "hypostatization" is elaborated and defended.

Confronting again the question of the cogency of postmodernism, one might sharpen the case for postmodernism by saying that consistency, at least with regard to skepticism and relativism, is most satisfactorily achieved with the renunciation of the global and local metanarrative force of skepticism and relativism and their conversion into merely immanentist narratives. Postmodernism enables us to withdraw instantaneously from our skeptical and relativist affirmations, and thus to be consistently skeptical and relativist.

In keeping with this defense of postmodernism, one would have to distinguish between two construals of postmodernism, a modernist one and a postmodernist one. As I indicated above, postmodernism strives to surmount the problem of reflexivity by scrapping altogether the requirement for justification. But if postmodernism is just another theory for mapping the intellectual terrain of modernity, then it too confronts a problem of reflexivity. If postmodernism is construed postmodernistically, then its remapping of the intellectual landscape in a consistent manner so that the requirement of justification can be dispensed with would have to be applied against postmodernism itself. Its particular negative redrawing would have to be seen as one possible redrawing among multiple others, enjoying no intrinsically compelling force over its competitors. A postmodernist reading of postmodernism would yield a classificatory scheme willing postmodernistically to withdraw in the face of other available and potential intellectual ordering schemes.

In making the case for postmodernism, it might be possible to revise the notion of regression to render it harmonious with postmodernist tenets. Instead of tying the meaning and reference of the terms of an object theory to their intertranslatability with the terms of a background theory, one could say that the grounds for making a statement collapse into the uses to which a statement can be put. This formulation could be regarded as an alternative to Quine's notion of regression, and by its orientation toward the future could be easily fitted into the postmodernist position. Or else one could say that my formulation is merely a paraphrase of the Quinian notion—because the use to which a statement is put is merely an invocation of one of the preexisting theoretical frameworks that can be shown to be inter-translatable with the current statement. The virtue of my paraphrase of Quine's notion of regression might then be that it highlights the postmodernist uses to which that notion can be put. This would be especially true if the preexisting theoretical frameworks compatible with a current statement were not taken to be strictly fixed in number, but were rather a function of the new interpretive possibilities residing in the background theories disclosed by the current statement itself. The new statement would thus be taken as carving out, as it were, its own set of relevant antecedents as well as its own set of relevant implications, with the distinction between antecedent and implication being strictly pragmatic (irredeemably arbitrary) in character.

If, as I have been arguing in this section of the chapter, postmodernism constitutes the most consummate, the most fully consistent expression of skepticism and relativism, then the rhetorical link between skepticism, equality, and participation can be maintained more persuasively under a postmodernist dispensation than under a modernist one. The clinching rhetorical argument in favor of modernism would thus have collapsed.

Notes

CHAPTER 1

1. Plato, *The Republic and Other Works*, trans. Benjamin Jowett (Garden City, N.Y.: Anchor, 1973), 388.

2. W. V. Quine, *The Ways of Paradox and Other Essays* (New York: Random House, 1966), 8.

3. Benson Mates, *Skeptical Essays* (Chicago: University of Chicago Press, 1981), 16.

4. What I argue in Chapter Two might be salvageable from a recognition of the inescapability of the problem of consistency confronting formulations of extreme skepticism is an implicit argument in favor of realism—in contrast to nominalism—in philosophy.

5. Stanley Fish, *Self-Consuming Artifacts: The Experience of Seventeenth-Century Literature* (Berkeley: University of California Press, 1972).

6. Jerome Karabel, "Revolutionary Contradictions: Antonio Gramsci and the Problem of Intellectuals," *Politics and Society* 6 no. 2 (1976):123–72.

7. This section of the Introduction attempts to draw a balance sheet between the different approaches to grappling with skepticism that are developed in the body of the book. The reader might find it advantageous to return to this section after completing the remainder of the book.

8. Fred Dallmayr, "Habermas and Rationality," *Political Theory* 16, no. 4 (1988):553–79.

9. Ibid., 559.

10. Richard J. Bernstein, "Fred Dallmayr's Critique of Habermas," *Political Theory* 16, no. 4 (1988):580–93.

11. Ibid., 583.

12. A working out of the principles of a multivalued logic is found in Michael Dummett, *Elements of Intuitionism* (Oxford: Oxford University Press, 1977).

13. My formulation also remains agnostic on the question of the existence of a concrete world outside our own imaginings and projections.

14. Cf. Mark Warren, "Antifoundationalism, Democracy, and the Self" (Paper presented at the 1989 annual meeting of the Western Political Science Association, Salt Lake City, Utah, March 30–April 1, 1989).

CHAPTER 2

1. Carole Pateman, "Some Reflections on *Participation and Democratic Theory*," in *Organizational Democracy and Political Processes*, ed. C. Crouch and F. Heller (New York: John Wiley, 1983); Aryeh Botwinick and Peter Bachrach, "Democracy and Scarcity: Towards a Theory of Participatory Democracy," *International Political Science Review* 4 (1984), 361–73; Peter Bachrach and Aryeh Botwinick, "An Objective Concept of Democratic Participation" (Paper read at the American Political Science Association convention, Washington, D.C., August 30–September 2, 1984).

2. Thomas Hobbes, *Leviathan*, ed. Michael Oakeshott (Oxford: Basil Blackwell, 1946), 19 and 21.

3. Skepticism and relativism are being bracketed together because they share a common point of logical vulnerability, not because the doctrines are interchangeable.

4. Barry Barnes and David Bloor, "Relativism, Rationalism and the Sociology of Knowledge," in Martin Hollis and Steven Lukes, eds., *Rationality and Relativism* (Cambridge, Mass.: MIT Press, 1982), 26.

5. Hilary Putnam, *Reason, Truth, and History* (Cambridge: Cambridge University Press, 1981), 158, 7.

6. The notion of "epistemological equals" carries implications for the restoration of equality between the sexes as well as between the classes.

7. At some point individual participatory groups might decide to follow the principle of majority rule among themselves as well. Cf. Jane Mansbridge, *Beyond Adversary Democracy* (New York: Basic, 1980).

8. John Rawls, *A Theory of Justice* (Cambridge, Mass.: Harvard University Press, 1971), 263.

9. Michael J. Sandel, *Liberalism and the Limits of Justice* (Cambridge: Cambridge University Press, 1982), 66–77.

10. Rawls, *Theory of Justice*, 179.

11. Robert Nozick, *Anarchy, State, and Utopia* (New York: Basic, 1974), 228.

12. My arguments concerning skepticism should not be construed as prejudging the question of the nature of democratic individuality. One can construe that notion in Rousseau's terms as much as one wishes without vitiating the skepticism.

13. Sandel, *Liberalism*, 172.

14. Benjamin Barber in *Strong Democracy* (Berkeley: University of California Press, 1984) is guilty of a similar misreading of the liberal tradition by making liberalism the foil for the participatory society he would like to see established in the United States.

15. This point was made by Bruce Jennings in personal conversation.

16. Bruce Ackerman, *Social Justice in the Liberal State* (New Haven, Conn.: Yale University Press, 1980), 28.

17. I have argued elsewhere for the relevance of Gadamer's argument concerning the interpretation of texts (such as literary, philosophical, or religious texts) that are anchored in a tradition of discourse for more ordinary linguistic utterances governed by the conventions and traditions of ordinary language. See Aryeh Botwinick, *Wittgenstein and Historical Understanding* (Lanham, Md.: University Press of America, 1980).

18. Hans-Georg Gadamer, *Truth and Method*, ed. and trans. G. Barden and J. Cumming (New York: Seabury, 1975), 146, cited in Richard J. Bernstein, *Beyond Objectivism and Relativism: Science, Hermeneutics, and Praxis* (Philadelphia: University of Pennsylvania Press, 1983), 125.

19. Bernstein, *Beyond Objectivism and Relativism*, 126.

20. Putnam, *Reason, Truth, and History*, 7–8.

21. Ibid., 162–63.

22. Donald Davidson, *Inquiries into Truth and Interpretation* (Oxford: Clarendon Press, 1984), 198, cited in Richard Rorty, *Philosophy and the Mirror of Nature* (Princeton, N.J.: Princeton University Press, 1979), 310.

23. Richard Rorty, *Consequences of Pragmatism* (Minneapolis: University of Minnesota Press, 1982), 168. Emphasis in original.

24. Ibid., 167.

25. W. V. Quine, *From a Logical Point of View* (Cambridge, Mass.: Harvard

University Press, 1953; New York: Harper & Row, Harper Torchbooks, 1961), 42–46.

26. Ibid., 42–43.

27. Rorty, *Consequences of Pragmatism*, 166.

CHAPTER 3

1. Richard Rorty, *Consequences of Pragmatism* (Minneapolis: University of Minnesota Press, 1982), 19–36; James C. Edwards, *Ethics without Philosophy* (Tampa: University Presses of Florida, 1982).

2. Ludwig Wittgenstein, *Philosophical Investigations*, 3d ed., trans. G. E. M. Anscombe (New York: Macmillan, 1969), I, 133. All references to the *Philosophical Investigations* in this chapter will be by section number for part I of the book and by page number for part II.

3. Edwards, *Ethics without Philosophy*, 14.

4. David Pears, *Ludwig Wittgenstein* (New York: Viking, 1970), 70.

5. However, Pears adds: "It is clear that he did not include the propositions of religion and morality among factual propositions, and so his neutrality about the point of origin of the system of factual propositions was certainly not intended to allow for the possibility that some of them might be non-empirical. What proves he was not a positivist is his attitude to the propositions of religion and morality after he excluded them from factual discourse." I will have more to say on this last point later on.

6. Peter Winch, ed., *Studies in the Philosophy of Wittgenstein* (London: Routledge and Kegan Paul, 1969), 12–14.

7. Ibid., 13; Wittgenstein quoted from *Philosophical Investigations* I, 293.

8. G. E. M. Anscombe, "On Brute Facts," *Analysis* 18, no. 3 (1958):69–72.

9. The works dating from the 1930s (even though some were translated and published as late as the 1960s and 1970s) are *Philosophical Remarks*, trans. R. Hargreaves and R. White (Oxford: Basil Blackwell, 1975); *Philosophical Grammar*, trans. A. Kenny (Oxford: Basil Blackwell, 1977); and *The Blue and Brown Books*, ed. Rush Rhees (Oxford: Basil Blackwell, 1958). See also G. E. Moore, "Wittgenstein's Lectures in 1930–33," *Mind* 63 (1954), 64 (1955); and Friedrich Waismann, *Wittgenstein und der Weiner Kreis*, ed. B. F. McGuiness (Oxford: Basil Blackwell, 1967).

10. Aryeh Botwinick, *Wittgenstein and Historical Understanding* (Lanham, Md.: University Press of America, 1980), 7–8.

11. Wittgenstein, *Philosophical Investigations* I, 429.

12. Ibid., 11 (no section number is listed for this passage); cited in Anthony Kenny, *Wittgenstein* (Cambridge, Mass.: Harvard University Press, 1977), 225.

13. Saul Kripke, *Wittgenstein on Rules and Private Language* (Oxford: Basil Blackwell, 1982).

14. Ibid., 7–8.

15. Ibid., 68–69.

16. Ibid., 73.

17. Cited in Edwards, *Ethics without Philosophy*, 11.

18. Ludwig Wittgenstein, *Tractatus Logico-Philosophicus*, trans. D. F. Pears and B. F. McGuinness (London: Routledge and Kegan Paul, 1969), 5.6.

19. Ibid., 4.121. Emphasis in original.

20. Ibid., 4.1212.

21. Ibid., 4.11.

22. Cited in Edwards, *Ethics without Philosophy*, 64.

23. Wittgenstein, *Tractatus*, 6.522.

24. Ibid., 6.54.

25. Ibid., 7.

26. Marcel Proust, *Swann's Way*, trans. C. K. Scott Moncrieff (New York: Random House, 1928), 180; cited in Joseph Levenson, *Revolution and Cosmopolitanism* (Berkeley: University of California Press, 1971), xxix.

27. Pears, *Ludwig Wittgenstein*, 179.

28. Wittgenstein, *Philosophical Investigations* I, 654–55.

29. Ibid., 109.

30. Ibid., 124.

31. Ibid., II, 218.

32. Ibid., I, 201.

33. Ludwig Wittgenstein, *On Certainty*, ed. G. E. M. Anscombe and G. H. von Wright (Oxford: Basil Blackwell, 1969), 521.

34. Ibid., 450.

35. Ibid., 519.

36. Ibid., 457.

37. The relationship between "language regions" and "language games" can be formulated as follows: There are usually a plurality of language games within particular language regions.

38. One cannot defend Wittgenstein at this point by saying that philosophy as a second-order discipline is necessarily parasitic upon other regions of discourse for its exercise, and that this extrapolation therefore does not constitute an illegitimate extension of philosophical method to other domains.

Such other distinctive language regions as the sciences (as analyzed in both the *Tractatus* and the *Investigations*, for example) have features that can be transferred, legitimately or illegitimately, to other regions and have the potential for remaking them in their own image. It is the conceptualization of philosophy as a parasitic, second-order discipline that licenses the spread of philosophical terminology and technique to all other regions of discourse that is at issue in the argument in the text.

CHAPTER 4

1. Michael Oakeshott and Sheldon Wolin have emphasized the role of tacit knowledge in illuminating the vocation of the political theorist and in the construal of particular theoretical texts. See especially Oakeshott's "Rationalism in Politics" and "Political Education," in *Rationalism in Politics and Other Essays* (New York: Basic, 1962), 1–36 and 111–36; Wolin's "Political Theory as a Vocation," in *Machiavelli and the Nature of Political Thought*, ed. Martin Fleisher (New York: Atheneum, 1972), 23–75; and Wolin's *Politics and Vision* (Boston: Little, Brown, 1960), chap. 1, 1–27. Neither Oakeshott nor Wolin, however, has sought systematically to relate the theme of tacit knowledge to a reading of Plato, Machiavelli, and Hobbes and to discerning a pattern of interrelationship between them.

2. Michael Polanyi, *The Tacit Dimension* (Garden City, N.Y.: Doubleday, 1966; Anchor, 1967), 4. Polanyi's other major works concerned with the theme of tacit knowledge are *Personal Knowledge: Towards a Post-Critical Philosophy* (Chicago: University of Chicago Press, 1958); *Knowing and Being*, ed. Marjorie Grene (Chicago: University of Chicago Press, 1959); *The Logic of Liberty: Reflections and Rejoinders* (Chicago: University of Chicago Press, 1951); with Harry Prosch, *Meaning* (Chicago: University of Chicago Press, 1964); *Science, Faith, and Society* (Chicago: University of Chicago Press, 1964); and *Scientific Thought and Social Reality*, ed. Fred Schwartz (New York: International Universities Press, 1974).

3. Polanyi, *Tacit Dimension*, 4.

4. Ibid., 10.

5. Ibid., 13.

6. Ibid.

7. Ibid., 15–16.

8. H. A. Hodges, *Wilhelm Dilthey* (New York: Oxford University Press, 1944). There are important affinities between Dilthey's conception of the ac-

tivity of the intellectual historian and Collingwood's. See R. G. Collingwood, *The Idea of History* (London: Oxford University Press, 1946). For a discussion of the presuppositions and limitations of Collingwood's ideas concerning historical method see Aryeh Botwinick, *Wittgenstein and Historical Understanding* (Lanham, Md.: University Press of America, 1981).

9. Polanyi, *Tacit Dimension*, 25.

10. Plato, *Phaedrus*, trans. W. C. Helmbold and W. G. Rabinowitz (Indianapolis: Library of Liberal Arts, 1956), 69–70.

11. Plato, *The Republic of Plato*, trans. Francis MacDonald Cornford (1941; reprint, New York: Oxford University Press, 1975), 254.

12. Plato, *Phaedrus*, 58.

13. Ibid., 60–61.

14. Ibid., 63–64.

15. Plato, *Meno*, trans. Fulton H. Anderson (Indianapolis: Library of Liberal Arts, 1949), 36.

16. Ibid., 37.

17. Plato, *Republic*, 348–59.

18. Polanyi, *Tacit Dimension*, 23.

19. Ibid.

20. Ibid., 24.

21. Thomas Kuhn, *The Structure of Scientific Revolutions*, 2d ed. (Chicago: University of Chicago Press, 1970), 208. The bias against rationalistic advance implicit in Kuhn's argument has been subject to sharp attack. See Israel Scheffler, *Science and Subjectivity* (Indianapolis, Ind.: Bobbs-Merrill, 1967), and Imre Lakatos and Alan Musgrave, eds., *Criticism and the Growth of Knowledge* (Cambridge: Cambridge University Press, 1970).

22. The relative autonomy of theory in relation to fact is reflected also in the Myth of Er (concerning the immortality of the soul), with which Plato concludes the *Republic* (pp. 348–59) and which depicts man as a creature of nearly total self-determination: "But in none of these lives was there anything to determine the condition of the soul, because the soul must needs change its character accordingly as it chooses one life or another."

23. Polanyi, *Tacit Dimension*, 61.

24. Ibid., 25.

25. Karl Popper, classically, has read the *Republic* as evincing the dominant features of a totalitarian society. See *The Open Society and Its Enemies*, vol. 1 (Princeton, N.J.: Princeton University Press, 1950). Plato has been roundly defended by John Wild, *Plato's Modern Enemies and the Theory of Natural Law* (Chicago: University of Chicago Press, 1953) and by John Hallowell, *The Moral*

Foundation of Democracy (Chicago: University of Chicago Press, 1954), as well as by Ronald B. Levinson, *In Defense of Plato* (Cambridge, Mass.: Harvard University Press, 1953).

26. Plato, *Republic*, 205–20, 256–63.

27. Ibid., 102–11, 119–29.

28. Within the auxiliary class, the spirited elements predominate over the rational elements and the passions, and within the artisan class the passions predominate over the other two elements.

29. The conclusion reached here concerning an antitotalitarian reading of the *Republic* bears certain affinities with the approaches taken by Allan Bloom in the introductory essay to his edition of the *Republic* (New York: Basic, 1968) and by Leo Strauss in *The City and Man* (Chicago: Rand McNally, 1964). Nevertheless, the largely epistemologically grounded arguments invoked in the text to defend this position distinguish my approach from that of Strauss and Bloom.

30. George Santayana, *The Last Puritan* (New York: Charles Scribner's Sons, 1935), 6.

31. Strauss identifies many of the key elements in the economy of Plato's argument that I do, but does not perceive their interrelationship (or draw out their implications) in the same way. In Strauss's view, Plato remains steadfastly loyal to the philosophical vocation and rejects the claims of politics. For a final restatement of Strauss's position, see his posthumously published *Studies in Platonic Philosophy* (Chicago: University of Chicago Press, 1983).

32. Plato, *Phaedrus*, 18.

33. Ibid., 21.

34. Ibid., 33.

35. Ibid., 32.

36. Ibid., 40.

37. Harold Bloom, *The Anxiety of Influence* (New York: Oxford University Press, 1973).

38. Niccolò Machiavelli, *The Prince*, trans. George Bull (Baltimore, Md.: Penguin, 1961), 29.

39. Ibid.

40. Ibid., 124–27.

41. Ibid., 127.

42. This was Oakeshott's phrase in his class on Machiavelli at the London School of Economics.

43. Polanyi, *Tacit Dimension*, 80.

44. Machiavelli, *The Prince*, 49.

45. Ibid., 89–90.

46. Ibid., 73.

47. Ibid., 88.

48. Ibid., 133.

49. Ibid., 123.

50. Ibid., 60.

51. Ibid., 61.

52. Ibid., 130–33.

53. The perspective that I am adopting offers an additional gloss on Machiavelli's statement in his Letter of Dedication in *The Prince* that this work represents "*all* that I, over so many years and with so much affliction and peril, have learned and understood" (emphasis added). If tacit knowledge lies at the core of Machiavelli's political teaching, then whatever discontinuities might appear between the arguments of *The Prince* and *The Discourses* appear minor, indeed.

54. Niccolò Machiavelli, *The Discourses*, trans. Christian E. Detmold (New York: Modern Library College Editions, 1950), 118–24.

55. Ibid., 119.

56. Compare what I say below in my delineation of Madison's argument in Federalist Number Ten.

57. Machiavelli, *The Prince*, 86.

58. Ibid., 95–98.

59. The social contract itself is a kind of Machiavellian memo from the arctic zone reminding people of the moves they must make to be rational and farsighted.

60. Machiavelli, *The Prince*, 91–92.

61. Throughout my discussion of the presuppositions of Machiavelli's argument in *The Prince*, I am arguing for an interpretation of his political theory that highlights important linkages between it and subsequent liberal political theorizing. This is in sharp contrast to J. G. A. Pocock in *The Machiavellian Moment* (Princeton, N.J.: Princeton University Press, 1975), who sees Machiavelli's work as a rebellion against the nascent forces of modernity that seeks to rehabilitate a tradition of republican virtue. Aside from local criticisms that can be leveled against Pocock's approach (see, e.g., Isaac Kramnick, "Republican Revisionism Revisited," *American Historical Review* 87 [1982]), there is also the global factor that Pocock acknowledges by saying that he is doing "tunnel history"—taking one idea and extending it as far as he can, to the relative detriment of different ideas (that might receive more emphasis in other, equally legitimate, historical accounts. See Pocock, "Cambridge Para-

digms and Scottish Philosophers," in *Wealth and Virtue: The Shaping of Political Economy in the Scottish Enlightenment*, ed. Istvan Hont and Michael Ignatieff (Cambridge: Cambridge University Press, 1983). In this section, I have attempted to provide the rudiments of an alternative "tunnel history" by exploring how far the idea of Machiavelli as a major precursor of the liberal tradition might be extended.

62. The practical distinction between procedure and substance becomes blurred quickly. The extent of satisfaction granted particular claims under a proceduralist system will have a very important effect on which substantive claims will be present, clamoring for satisfaction, in the future.

63. Machiavelli, *The Prince*, 92.

64. Wolin, *Politics and Vision*, 224–28.

65. Machiavelli often writes as if the content of private morality were fixed and known—where most of the precepts follow as corollaries from the Golden Rule and include such virtues as kindness, generosity, and truth telling.

66. Stuart Hampshire, ed., *Public and Private Morality* (Cambridge: Cambridge University Press, 1978), 49.

67. Ibid., 50.

68. Machiavelli, *The Prince*, 91. Emphasis added.

69. The approach taken by Wolin and Hampshire (and amplified in the text) of seeing Machiavelli as a great public moralist concerned to delineate the precise import of moral principles in a public decision-making context is in marked contrast to such earlier readings as Ernst Cassirer's in *The Myth of the State* (Garden City, N.Y.: Doubleday Anchor, 1955) and Leonard Olschki's in *Machiavelli the Scientist* (Berkeley, Calif.: Gillick, 1945), which depict Machiavelli as an amoral scientist. Wolin's and Hampshire's interpretations of Machiavelli's political teaching cohere very well with the thematics of tacit knowledge—of modulating judgment in relation to the exigencies of the situation that one confronts—that I have been emphasizing throughout my discussion of Machiavelli.

70. Machiavelli, *The Prince*, 62–63.

71. Ibid., 123.

72. The other scientific model Hobbes follows in his discussion of political questions is the resoluto–composite method derived from the Renaissance Paduan School. On the centrality of this model in Hobbes, see J. W. N. Watkins, *Hobbes's System of Ideas* (London: Hutchinson University Library, 1965), 52–55. The way resoluto–composite method is fused with geometric method in Hobbes's work might be described as follows: The basic elements of

man discovered by application of the resoluto part of the method become the first principles in whose terms human nature is recomposed in pursuance of the composite side of the method.

73. Thomas Hobbes, *Leviathan*, ed. Michael Oakeshott (Oxford: Basil Blackwell, 1946), 6.

74. Ibid., 467.

75. Ibid., 19.

76. Polanyi, *Tacit Dimension*, 60–61.

77. "Justness of actions" implies conformity to the requirements of law; "justness of manners" has a wholly different signification, which I discuss below. The distinction is introduced by Hobbes at p. 97.

78. The reversal is only "on one level" because a notion of "power as rationality" (soon to be elaborated upon in the text) is implicit in those aspects of Plato's philosophy that I have already discussed in this chapter.

79. Aryeh Botwinick, *Epic Political Theorists and the Conceptualizations of the State* (Lanham, Md.: University Press of America, 1982).

80. Oakeshott, *Rationalism in Politics*, 254–55.

81. Hobbes, *Leviathan*, 257.

82. See Chapter Eight below.

83. See Chapter Two above.

84. Hobbes, *Leviathan*, 19 and 21.

85. Ibid., 7.

86. Benjamin Barber's renunciation of epistemological arguments in his recent defense of *Strong Democracy: Participatory Politics for a New Age* (Berkeley: University of California Press, 1984) seems to me to be forsaking the opportunity to achieve a deepened coherence in the justification of a participatory democratic politics that the engagement of epistemological issues affords. The approach of "tacit knowledge" pursued in this chapter constitutes, I think, a suitable epistemological framework in which to locate and justify participatory democratic practices.

87. These terms are taken from David Lewis, *Convention: A Philosophical Study* (Cambridge, Mass.: Harvard University Press, 1969).

88. Oakeshott, *Rationalism in Politics*, 294. The principal adversary to this interpretation is Leo Strauss, who argues in both *The Political Philosophy of Hobbes: Its Basis and Its Genesis* (Chicago: University of Chicago Press, 1965) and *Natural Right and History* (Chicago: University of Chicago Press, 1965) that a kind of homogenizing moral mediocrity characterizes the psychology of Hobbesian men, whose overweening vanity is counterbalanced by an excessive fear that holds their vanity in check. It is ironic that Strauss, who taught us

in *Persecution and the Art of Writing* (Westport, Ct.: Greenwood, 1952, 1973) how to read authors who veiled their intentions because of anxieties attendant to the act of writing, should attribute to Hobbes a relatively monolithic moral psychology that makes few allowances for an aristocratic impulse to found or refound states to express itself.

89. Hobbes, *Leviathan*, 97.

90. Ibid., 92.

91. Cited in Oakeshott, *Rationalism in Politics*, 291.

92. Hobbes, *Leviathan*, 60.

93. Polanyi, *Tacit Dimension*, 4.

CHAPTER 5

1. Alexander Hamilton, James Madison, and John Jay, *The Federalist Papers*, ed. Clinton Rossiter (New York: New American Library, 1961), 77.

2. Thomas Hobbes, *Leviathan*, ed. Michael Oakeshott (Oxford: Basil Blackwell, 1946), chap. 6.

3. Niccolò Machiavelli, *The Prince*, trans. George Bull (Baltimore, Md.: Penguin, 1961), 91.

4. Niccolò Machiavelli, *The Discourses*, trans. Christian E. Detmold (New York: Modern Library College Editions, 1950), 450–54, 300–301, 314.

5. Machiavelli, *The Prince*, 62–63.

6. Ibid., 95–98.

7. Arthur O. Lovejoy, *The Great Chain of Being* (Cambridge, Mass.: Harvard University Press, 1936; New York: Harper & Row, Harper Torchbooks, 1960), 52 and *passim*.

8. Ibid.

9. Hamilton, Madison, and Jay, *Federalist Papers*, 78.

10. Ibid., 84.

11. Ibid., 78.

12. Ibid., 83–84.

13. Ibid., 78.

14. Ibid., 81.

15. Douglas Adair, *Fame and the Founding Fathers* (New York: Norton, 1974), 137.

16. J. G. A. Pocock, *The Machiavellian Moment* (Princeton, N.J.: Princeton University Press, 1975), 15.

17. J. G. A. Pocock, "Cambridge Paradigms and Scottish Philosophers,"

in *Wealth and Virtue: The Shaping of Political Economy in the Scottish Enlightenment,* ed. Istvan Hont and Michael Ignatieff (Cambridge: Cambridge University Press, 1983).

18. Charles E. Lindblom, *Politics and Markets* (New York: Basic, 1977).

19. Albert O. Hirschman, *The Passions and the Interests* (Princeton, N.J.: Princeton University Press, 1977).

CHAPTER 6

1. Antonio Gramsci, *Selections from the Prison Notebooks of Antonio Gramsci,* ed. and trans. Quintin Hoare and Geoffrey Nowell Smith (New York: International, 1971), 464. All references to the *Prison Notebooks* will be to this edition.

2. This is the way the editors categorize Gramsci's thought in their introduction to one of the subsections (Gramsci, *Prison Notebooks,* 380).

3. Ibid., 465.

4. Ibid., 171.

5. Gramsci defines hegemony when he says "that the supremacy of a social group manifests itself in two ways, as 'domination' and as 'intellectual and moral leadership.'" He defines counterhegemony when he says that "a social group can, and indeed must, already exercise 'leadership' before winning governmental power (this indeed is one of the principal conditions for the winning of such power); it subsequently becomes dominant when it exercises power but even if it holds it firmly in its grasp, it must continue to 'lead' as well" (ibid., 57–58).

Cf. Carl Boggs: "Gramsci sometimes referred to the Protestant Reformation and the French Revolution as historical examples of successful counterhegemonic politics. In each case the overthrow of the traditional order did not come as a dramatic event or episode but rather through a long and gradual phase of ideological–cultural ferment set in motion by subversive currents (Protestantism, the Enlightenment) linked to emergent social forces. The transfer of institutional power was but a single moment in a continuous modification of class relations that occurs largely 'underneath the surface' of formal structures, norms, and laws. Socialist transformation in the west was expected to follow this general pattern: working-class ascendancy within civil society would be a necessary prelude to frontal assaults on the bourgeois state." Carl Boggs, *The Two Revolutions: Gramsci and the Dilemmas of Western Marxism* (Boston: South End, 1984), 189.

6. Cf. Aryeh Botwinick, *Wittgenstein and Historical Understanding* (Lanham, Md.: University Press of America, 1980), 29–30.

7. J. L. Austin, *Philosophical Papers* (Oxford: Oxford University Press, 1961), 220–39; John R. Searle, *Speech Acts* (Cambridge: Cambridge University Press, 1970).

8. Quoted in Merrill Jensen, ed., *Tracts of the American Revolution: 1723–1776* (Indianapolis, Ind.: Bobbs-Merrill, 1967), 195.

9. What Hannah Arendt says about Western intellectual history being characterized by an apparently endless series of "reversibility maneuvers" seems especially true of the local history of Marxism. See Hannah Arendt, *The Human Condition* (Chicago: University of Chicago Press, 1958; Garden City, N.Y.: Doubleday Anchor, 1959), 273–77.

10. Gramsci, *Prison Notebooks*, 376. Emphasis added.

11. Ibid., 404–5. Emphasis added.

12. Cf. Jerome Karabel, "Revolutionary Contradictions: Antonio Gramsci and the Problem of Intellectuals," *Politics and Society* 6, no. 2 (1976): 170, n. 156.

13. This sensibility is also manifested in a note written in prison ("A Dialogue"), where he says: "Image of Prometheus who, instead of being attacked by the eagles, is devoured by parasites. The Hebrews produced the image of Job. Only the Greeks could have imagined Prometheus, but the Hebrews were more realistic, more pitiless, and their hero more true to life." Gramsci, *Prison Notebooks*, xciii.

14. Leo Baeck, *Judaism and Christianity—Five Essays* (Philadelphia: Jewish Publication Society, 1958).

15. Gramsci, *Prison Notebooks*, 405.

16. Max Kaddushin, *The Rabbinic Mind* (New York: Bloch, 1972), 301.

17. Quoted in James Joll, *Antonio Gramsci* (New York: Penguin, 1977), 53–54.

18. A supreme manifestation of this in Machiavelli's thought is his advocacy of a principle of economy to contain and defeat a malicious fortune. As the cardinal weapon in the armory of fortune is necessity—the aspect of foreclosing our options and constraining our choices—the best counterstrategy to adopt against her is strictly economizing one's actions, making means exactly commensurate with ends, thereby also embodying a principle of necessity: deploying the most minimal series of gestures and exertions compatible with the achievement of one's ends.

19. Michael Oakeshott, *Experience and Its Modes* (1933; reprint, Cambridge: Cambridge University Press, 1966).

20. Michael Oakeshott, *Rationalism in Politics and Other Essays* (New York: Basic, 1962), 198–99.

21. The phrase is Michael Shapiro's.

22. Gramsci, *Prison Notebooks*, 270.

23. Ibid., 330.

24. Ibid., 323.

25. Ibid., 354.

26. Cited in Joll, *Antonio Gramsci*, 119.

27. Edward Shils, *The Intellectuals and the Powers and Other Essays* (Chicago: University of Chicago Press, 1972), 3.

28. Joseph R. Levenson, *Confucian China and Its Modern Fate*, 3 vols. (Berkeley: University of California Press, 1958–65).

29. Gramsci, *Prison Notebooks*, 204–5.

30. Ibid., 56, footnote.

31. Cf. the discussion in Joseph Levenson, *Revolution and Cosmopolitanism* (Berkeley: University of California Press, 1971).

32. Gramsci, *Prison Notebooks*, 107.

33. Ibid., 336.

34. Ibid., 360.

35. Ibid., 353.

36. Cf. Sheldon Wolin's elaboration of this theme in chaps. 9 and 10 of *Politics and Vision* (Boston: Little, Brown, 1960), for which Gramsci's discussion is an important precursor.

37. Gramsci, *Prison Notebooks*, 243.

38. Ibid.

39. Ibid., 244.

40. Ibid., 337.

41. Ibid., 244.

42. Ibid.

43. Cf. Karl Popper, *The Poverty of Historicism* (London: Routledge and Kegan Paul, 1960).

44. Gramsci, *Prison Notebooks*, 171.

45. Ibid., 438.

46. Ibid., 429.

47. Ibid., 430.

48. Cf. Aryeh Botwinick, *Wittgenstein and Historical Understanding* (Lanham, Md.: University Press of America), 46–47, for a discussion of the ways and the extent to which Plato shares this view.

49. Gramsci, *Prison Notebooks*, 405.

50. Karabel, "Revolutionary Contradictions," 171–72.

51. Gramsci, *Prison Notebooks*, 461–62.

52. Ibid., 374.

53. W. V. Quine, *From a Logical Point of View* (Cambridge, Mass.: Harvard University Press, 1953; New York: Harper & Row, Harper Torchbooks, 1961), 42–46.

54. W. V. Quine, *Word and Object* (Cambridge, Mass.: MIT Press, 1960), chap. 2; Jaakko Hintikka and Donald Davidson, eds., *Words and Objections: Essays on the Work of W. V. Quine* (Dordrecht: Reidel, 1969), especially the essays by Gilbert Harman and Barry Stroud.

55. Gramsci, *Prison Notebooks*, 57. Gramsci voices an analogous judgment concerning philosophy when he says that it creates the grounds for its own acceptance through a resocialization of the masses: "We have established that philosophy is a conception of the world and philosophical activity is not to be conceived solely as the 'individual' elaboration of systematically coherent concepts, but also and above all as a cultural battle to transform the popular 'mentality' and to diffuse the philosophical innovations which will demonstrate themselves to be 'historically true' to the extent they become concretely—i.e. historically and socially—universal." (Ibid., 348.)

56. Aryeh Botwinick, *Ethics, Politics, and Epistemology: A Study in the Unity of Hume's Thought* (Washington, D.C.: University Press of America, 1980), 144.

57. Perhaps Maimonides' conceptualization of the Messianic Age in terms of the worldly political success of the Messianic King has a kindred philosophical source. See Chapter Eight below.

58. Gramsci, *Prison Notebooks*, 365.

59. The historical unification of the human race for Gramsci is something known *a posteriori*, if at all—after class conflicts and tensions have been overcome within individual national societies. It is not a goal to be sought for its own sake in advance. See the argument against cosmopolitanism earlier in this chapter.

60. Gramsci, *Prison Notebooks*, 445–46.

61. Gramsci advances beyond the traditional Marxist notion of praxis by advocating the cultivation of foci of micropraxis in addition to those of macropraxis for the unleashing of social change and by attempting to delineate the factors that lead to the merging of the former into the latter.

62. In contrast to atheistic versions of skepticism discussed above.

63. Paul Feyerabend, *Against Method* (New York: Schocken, 1975). Kuhn is relevant as well, despite all of his disclaimers; see Thomas Kuhn, *The Structure of Scientific Revolutions*, 2d ed. (Chicago: University of Chicago Press, 1970).

64. Gramsci, *Prison Notebooks*, 359.

65. Ibid., 341.

66. Ibid., 371.

67. Ibid., 448.

68. Wolin, *Politics and Vision*, 220–24.

69. According to Hoare and Smith, Gramsci's use of the term "elite" is to be distinguished from that of the post-Pareto theorists of "political elites." "The elite in Gramsci is the revolutionary vanguard of a social class in constant contact with its political and intellectual base." Gramsci, *Prison Notebooks*, 334, n. 18.

70. Ibid., 324.

71. Ibid. 429.

72. Ibid., 12, 104–6.

73. Ibid., 350.

74. Ibid., 137.

75. Ibid., 350. James MacGregor Burns seems to appreciate this Gramscian insight: "That role [of the 'great man'] is all the more legitimate and powerful if top leaders help to make their followers into leaders. Only by standing on *their* shoulders can true greatness in leadership be achieved." James MacGregor Burns, *Leadership* (New York: Harper & Row, 1978), 443. Emphasis in original.

76. Paulo Freire, *Pedagogy of the Oppressed*, trans. Myra Bergman Ramos (New York: Continuum, 1986), 184–95. Emphasis in original.

77. Plato, *The Republic of Plato*, trans. Francis MacDonald Cornford (1941; reprint, New York: Oxford University Press, 1975), 29.

78. Num. 11.11–12, 14–15.

79. Num. 12.3.

80. Gramsci, *Prison Notebooks*, 260.

81. Num. 11.29.

82. Gramsci, *Prison Notebooks*, 243.

83. Ibid., 191.

84. The oppressed and the excluded often suffer from an undercultivated will. They must therefore be initiated into the social practices associated with willing—participation and leadership—as part of their human birthright: "To transform the external world, the general system of relations, is to potentiate oneself and to develop oneself. . . . For this reason one can say that man is essentially 'political,' since it is through the activity of transforming and consciously directing other men that man realizes his 'humanity,' his 'human nature.'" (Ibid., 260.)

85. James David Barber, *The Presidential Character: Predicting Performance in the White House*, 3d ed. (Englewood Cliffs, N.J.: Prentice-Hall, 1985).

86. Ibid., 11–14.

87. Gramsci, *Prison Notebooks*, 251. Emphasis added.

88. One can argue that all leadership functions of the sort described in the text are reducible to the notion of the exercise of power, since there is an aspect of reasonableness present in most positions clamoring for attention within the self so that, in the end, power has to be exerted. To indicate the relationship between leadership and the political in Gramsci (and to justify my designation of both as ontological categories) it might be best to distinguish between descriptive ontological categories and ultimate ontological categories. The former refer to concepts or notions that one cannot avoid in describing a situation. Ultimate ontological categories refer to those that one imparted, however provisionally (under the current hegemonic dispensation), ultimate reality to—not only unavoidable ways of speaking but necessary features of the structure of the world. From this perspective, the concept of leadership would form a descriptive ontological category, since to acknowledge the variety of ways in which different aspects of a self might address each other it would appear to make sense to characterize the multifarious modes of interaction captured by my notion of leadership as being descriptively conclusive. On the other hand, the limitations of reason and the enlarged scope of the irrational captured in Gramsci's concept of the political would appear to warrant its being regarded as an ultimate ontological category.

89. Gramsci, *Prison Notebooks*, 352.

90. Ibid., 246.

91. Ibid., 275–76.

92. Ibid., 353.

CHAPTER 7

1. Jean-François Lyotard, *The Postmodern Condition: A Report on Knowledge*, trans. Geoff Bennington and Brian Massumi (Minneapolis: University of Minnesota Press, 1984), xxiii; cited in Richard J. Bernstein, ed., *Habermas and Modernity* (Cambridge: Polity Press, 1985), 161.

2. Lyotard, *Postmodern Condition*, xxiv.

3. While for Lyotard the distinction between modernism and postmodernism revolves around the question of whether a justificatory narrative is required or dispensable in making the cases that one wants to make, for Habermas the distinction centers on the philosophy of the subject having given way to conundrums and dead ends. Moreover, Habermas has been

carrying on a sustained and prolonged debate with the postmodernists from the perspective of his theory of "communicative competence" and what that presupposes concerning a universe of shared assumptions between members of the same linguistic community.

See the following books by Jürgen Habermas: *Communication and the Evolution of Society*, trans. Thomas McCarthy (Boston: Beacon, 1979); *The Theory of Communicative Action*, vol. 1, *Reason and the Rationalization of Society*, trans. Thomas McCarthy (Boston: Beacon, 1984); *The Theory of Communicative Action*, vol. 2, *Lifeworld and System: A Critique of Functionalist Reason*, trans. Thomas McCarthy (Boston: Beacon, 1985); and *The Philosophical Discourse of Modernity: Twelve Lectures*, trans. Frederick Lawrence (Cambridge, Mass.: MIT Press, 1987). See also Stephen K. White, "Foucault's Challenge to Critical Theory," *American Political Science Review* 80, no. 2 (1986):419–32.

While some of Habermas's argument resonates in the critique of postmodernism that follows, most of it was arrived at independently of Habermas's unique set of commitments and assumptions and pursues more narrowly logical, rather than more broadly linguistic, points.

4. Bernstein, ed., *Habermas and Modernity*, 162.

5. Friedrich Nietzsche, *On the Advantage and Disadvantage of History for Life*, trans. Peter Preuss (Indianapolis, Ind.: Hackett, 1980).

6. Ibid., 38.

7. Friedrich Nietzsche, *On the Genealogy of Morals* and *Ecce Homo*, ed. and trans. Walter Kaufmann (New York: Random House, Vintage, 1967), 26. Emphasis in original.

8. Thomas Hobbes, *Leviathan*, ed. Michael Oakeshott (Oxford: Basil Blackwell, 1946), 19 and 21.

9. Nietzsche, *Genealogy* and *Ecce Homo*, 45. Emphasis in original.

10. Ibid., 121–22.

11. Ibid., 84–85. Emphasis in original.

12. W. V. Quine, *Ontological Relativity and Other Essays* (New York: Columbia University Press, 1969), 49.

13. Nietzsche, *Genealogy* and *Ecce Homo*, 129.

14. Ibid., 151. Emphasis in original.

15. Michel Foucault, *The Discourse on Language*, in *The Archaeology of Knowledge*, trans. A. M. Sheridan Smith (New York: Pantheon, 1972), 215–37.

16. Gilles Deleuze, *Nietzsche and Philosophy*, trans. Hugh Tomlinson (New York: Columbia University Press, 1983).

17. Ibid., 101. Emphasis in original.

18. Nietzsche, *Advantage and Disadvantage*, 38.

19. Friedrich Nietzsche, *The Birth of Tragedy* and *The Case of Wagner*, ed. and trans. Walter Kaufmann (New York: Random House, Vintage, 1967).

20. Nietzsche, *Advantage and Disadvantage*, 40.

21. Ibid., 44.

22. Nietzsche, *Birth of Tragedy* and *Case of Wagner*, 135–36; cf. Friedrich Nietzsche, *The Gay Science* (New York: Random House, Vintage, 1974), 93.

23. Nietzche, *Genealogy* and *Ecce Homo*, 152. Emphasis in original.

24. Michael Polanyi, *The Tacit Dimension* (Garden City, N.Y.: Anchor, 1967), 25.

25. Nietzsche, *The Gay Science*, 181.

26. Hobbes, *Leviathan*, chap. 11.

27. "Power" functions in a quasi- (and not fully) tautologous way in Hobbes's and Nietzsche's thought because I, for example, am discerning a meaning in its usage, which means that the concept is not fully empty. I claim the same quasi-tautologous status for "pleasure" and "pain."

28. Friedrich Nietzsche, *Twilight of the Idols*, in *The Portable Nietzsche* ed. and trans. Walter Kaufmann (New York: Viking, 1968), 554.

29. Intuitionist logic is not the only modern logic that accommodates contradiction. Hans Reichenbach developed a three-valued logic that incorporates the value of indeterminacy suggested by the Bohr–Heisenberg interpretation of quantum mechanics, and this logic also leads to the suspension of the law of excluded middle. See Hans Reichenbach, *Philosophic Foundations of Quantum Mechanics* (Berkeley: University of California Press, 1944), 145.

30. Walter Kaufmann, *Nietzsche: Philosopher, Psychologist, Antichrist*, 3d ed. (New York: Vintage, 1968), 317.

31. Compare Richard Morris, *Time's Arrow* (New York: Simon and Schuster, 1984), 128–30.

32. See Charles Parsons, "Mathematics, Foundations of," in *The Encyclopedia of Philosophy*, ed. Paul Edwards (New York: Macmillan, 1967; reprint, 1972), 5:188–213.

33. Nietzsche confronts a problem analogous to what I have just summarized in relation to Dionysus in delineating the concept of life, in *Advantage and Disadvantage*. Just by virtue of making his case for life as against historicist inquiry, Nietzsche converts life itself into an abstraction. The means, rational articulation of what life (in contrast to historical understanding) signifies, overwhelms the end, the pointing to an unbridgeable gulf between history and life. The strategy for resolving this inconsistency would have to approximate to the one I have described in the text in relation to the Dionysus–Apollo contrast.

34. Augustine, *The City of God*, trans. Henry Bettenson (Baltimore, Md.: Penguin, 1972), 893.

35. Michel Foucault, *The Order of Things: An Archaeology of the Human Sciences* (New York: Pantheon, 1970).

36. Foucault, *Discourse on Language*, 219.

37. Ibid., 218.

38. Hannah Arendt, *The Human Condition* (Garden City, N.Y.: Doubleday Anchor Books, 1958), 265–66.

39. Rousseau's description of the earliest phase of the state of nature is also a source for Nietzsche's declarations concerning self-forgetfulness—the need to abrogate self-consciousness periodically.

40. Thomas Kuhn, *The Structure of Scientific Revolutions*, 2d ed. (Chicago: University of Chicago Press, 1970).

41. Richard Rorty, *Consequences of Pragmatism* (Minneapolis: University of Minnesota Press, 1982), 139–59; Michael Shapiro, "Literary Production as a Politicizing Practice," *Political Theory* 12, no. 3 (1984):387–422; White, "Foucault's Challenge to Critical Theory."

42. Michel Foucault, *Discipline and Punish: The Birth of the Prison*, trans. Alan Sheridan (New York: Random House, 1977); Michel Foucault, *The History of Sexuality*, vol. 1, *An Introduction*, trans. Robert French (New York: Random House, 1980).

43. My analysis here is comparable to my analysis earlier in the chapter where I argued that Nietzsche's textualism foils the contrast he attempts to draw between history and life in his essay on history.

44. Robert D'Amico, "Text and Context: Derrida and Foucault on Descartes," in *The Structural Allegory: Reconstructive Encounters with French Thought*, ed. John Fekete (Minneapolis: University of Minnesota Press, 1984), 164–82.

CHAPTER 8

1. Moses Maimonides, *The Guide of the Perplexed*, trans. Shlomo Pines (Chicago: University of Chicago Press, 1963).

2. Ibid., pt. I, chap. 56, pp. 130–31.

3. Ibid., pt. I, chap. 35, p. 80.

4. Ibid.

5. Moses Maimonides, *Code*, vol. 1, *The Book of Knowledge*, "Laws Concerning Idolatry and the Ordinances of the Heathens," chap. I, pars. 2–3; chap. II, par. 1; trans. Moses Hyamson (New York: Feldheim, 1974), pp. 66a–b, 67a.

6. Maimonides, *Guide*, "Introduction."

7. Jacques Derrida, *Writing and Difference*, trans. Alan Bass (Chicago: University of Chicago Press, 1978).

8. If postmodernism is deemed persuasive in its delegitimation of the justificatory enterprise, than we can describe God as wholly other—we can make this central individual point about the nature of God—without having to be concerned about the impact that denial of attributes has on *knowledge* of a wholly other God. From a postmodernist perspective, we can dissociate the individual point from its background assumptions and implications, and thus denial is severable from our ability to fix the object of denial.

9. W. V. Quine, *Ontological Relativity and Other Essays* (New York: Columbia University Press, 1969), 42. Emphasis in original.

10. Ibid., 54.

11. One can distinguish conceptually a local metanarrative from an immanentist metanarrative by saying that the former is logically prior to the argument being made (that it constitutes, as it were, the conceptual prerequisite for the making of an argument), while the latter can only be reconstructed after the fact of the point or the argument having been made (i.e., that the argument carves out for itself "new rules in the game of reasoning"), thus registering the logical dispensability of background theoretical terms in order to render the current formulations intelligible.

12. W. V. Quine, *From a Logical Point of View* (Cambridge, Mass.: Harvard University Press, 1953; New York: Harper & Row, Harper Torchbooks, 1961), 26–46.

13. Donald Davidson, *Inquiries into Truth and Interpretation* (Oxford: Clarendon Press, 1984), 198.

14. Stephen K. White, "Foucault's Challenge to Critical Theory," *American Political Science Review* 80, no. 2 (1986):419–32.

15. Maimonides, *Code*, 1, "Laws of Repentence," chap. 5, par. 5.

16. Ibid., "Laws of Repentance," chap. 9, par. 2. (Moses Hyamson's translation, with one emendation on my part.)

17. Ibid.

18. Maimonides, *Iggerot Harambam*, trans. Joseph Kapach (Jerusalem: Mosad Harv Kook, 1974), 86. My translation.

19. Maimonides, *Guide*, pt. II, chap. 13, p. 282; pt. II, chap. 28, p. 334.

20. Construed in this light, the theory of tacit knowledge can be formalized to encompass any set of potentially correlatable statements needed to maximize the intelligibility and coherence of a given statement, and need not be restricted or delimited as to content. This would seem to contradict the

analysis in Chapter One, which suggests that a tacit knowledge approach for accommodating formulations of extreme skepticism would limit the scope of participatory restructuring of democratic life in contrast to that advocated by radical postmodernists. The formulation in Chapter One can be maintained in the face of the formalization of tacit knowledge described here because "tacit knowledge" is a term that remains systematically ambiguous. It refers both to a philosophical thesis about the limitations and incompleteness (not fully rationalizable character) of knowledge and to a sociological one about how these limitations and incompletenesses are remedied through sociological and psychological processes that are fostered and nurtured within the confines of "tradition" and "community." It is the philosophical thesis that is affected by the reformulation of tacit knowledge in the present context, and not the sociological one. It is the sociological thesis, by contrast, that militates against an open-ended restructuring of institutional and theoretical givens favored by radical postmodernists.

21. In accordance with the argument advanced in Chapter One, a postmodernist construal of monotheistic teaching does not lead to a denial of God's existence. A consistent interpretation of the tenets of postmodernism withdraws from affirming any direct linkage between our notational universes and the "real" universe, so that a postmodernist reading of the doctrine of the eternity of the world does not yield a denial of God's existence.

22. From the perspective that I outline in the text, Nietzsche's and Hobbes's analyses of human nature discussed in Chapter Seven constitute so many intertextual elaborations on Maimonidean monotheistic texts, which retrospectively cast light on the significance of those texts.

23. Richard Rorty, review of *Derrida*, by Christopher Norris, *New Leader*, October 3–17, 1988, 20–21.

Index

Index

Index

Index

Monotheism, 112, 114, 214, 216, 218, 219, 226, 227, 228; and action, 233; and denial of attributes, 110, 226, 227, 230; and hypostatization, 232–33; and intuitionist logic, 223; and reflexivity, 110–11

Moore, G. E., 56–57

Morality, 184; in Hobbes, 104, 108; in Machiavelli, 91, 98, 99–102, 103; in Nietzsche, 185, 190

Moses, 171

Multivalued logic, 14, 15, 16–17, 18, 20. *See also* Intuitionist logic

Mystiche, das, 53

Myth of the Metals, 75–76

Nagel, Thomas, 21–22

Naming process. *See* Nominalism

Narrative, 181

Natural rights, 23

Necessita, 91, 121

New Left, 149

Nietzsche, Friedrich, 218

Nominalism, 19–25, 42, 111; in Hobbes, 26, 95, 105, 107, 111, 183; in Madison, 127, 129; in Nietzsche, 183; in Putnam, 35; in Wittgenstein, 44–45

Nozick, Robert, 28, 29–30

Oakeshott, Michael, 88, 113, 145, 146, 190

Objectivity, 21, 25, 34, 35, 37, 38, 155–56, 163–64

Obligation, 144, 151; in Hobbes, 107–8; in Hume, 162; in Madison, 128, 131

Opportunita, 91

Organic intellectuals, 147, 151, 158, 169, 172, 174

Paine, Thomas, 196

Passive revolution, 152, 153

Participation, 37, 40–41, 77, 153, 221; in

Ackerman, 33; and equality, 25, 36; in Gramsci, 143, 154; in Hobbes, 31; and leadership, 168–69, 170; and legitimacy, 28; and liberalism, 27–28; and objectivity, 155–56; in Plato, 4, 75–77; and postmodernism, 234; and power, 109; and pragmatism, 16, 22; and reflexivity, 15, 16; and revolution, 167, 170; and Rorty, 39–40

Pears, David, 44

Philosophy, 43–44, 51, 52

Picture theory of propositions, 44, 47, 50, 51, 52–53

Plato, 79, 99, 114, 159, 171, 194, 195, 229; leadership, 71; in recollection, 71; and theory of ideas, 73, 75; and theory of knowledge, 73

Pleasure-pain apparatus, 139, 199

Pocock, J. G. A., 7, 129, 130, 243

Polanyi, Michael, 9, 61, 62, 63, 64, 66, 71, 88, 106, 114, 116, 195; parallel to Kuhn, 72, 73

Political culture, 132

Political time: in Machiavelli, 94–95; in Madison, 119

Positivism, 41, 65, 153, 155, 156, 211

Postmodernism, 18, 23, 181, 182, 215, 219, 220, 233; and metanarrativity, 10, 227; and monotheism, 225, 228; and reflexivity, 233

Power, 10, 27, 35, 108–9, 136, 137, 138, 139, 140, 161, 163, 174, 177, 187, 189, 195; in Foucault, 206–7, 209–10; in Gramsci, 133, 141, 144, 150, 152, 167, 168, 170, 174, 176; in Hobbes, 113, 138; in Machiavelli, 94, 100, 121, 137, 141, 206; in Madison, 123, 124; in Marx, 140, 141; in Plato, 75, 98; in Wittgenstein, 53

Practical past, 190

Pragmatism, 14, 15, 16, 18, 19, 20, 22, 38, 39, 41

262

Index

Praxis, philosophy of, 141, 142, 145, 164, 166

Principle of charitableness, 227

Principle of parsimony, 41, 137, 174, 189; in Gramsci, 174; in Machiavelli, 102–3, 121, 138; in Nietzsche, 190, 191–92

Proust, 52, 53

Proximal pole, 63, 64, 66, 70, 72, 75, 82, 87, 88, 89, 90; God as, 116; in Hobbes, 112, 114, 116; in Nietzsche, 199; in Plato, 68, 71, 78, 79, 81; in *The Prince*, 94

Putnam, Hilary, 26, 35–36

Quine, W. V., 6–7, 38–39, 219, 223, 234; and indeterminacy of radical translation, 34, 161; and postmodernism, 220

Ramsey, F. P., 51

Rawls, John, 28–30, 31, 32, 33

Reagan, Ronald, 180

Realism, 10, 17, 18, 19, 21, 25, 39, 42

Reason: in Deleuze, 188; in Hobbes, 107, 120, 139; in Machiavelli, 94, 95; in Madison, 123

Reflexivity, 7, 10, 11–12, 13, 14, 15, 16, 181, 183, 201; in Gadamer, 34; in Gramsci, 174; and hegemony, 163; in Hobbes, 114, 115; and monotheism, 110–11, 216; in Nietzsche, 183, 184, 186; and nominalism, 20–21; and participation, 15–16; in postmodernism, 233; and pragmatism, 14, 16; in Putnam, 35; and reverse causation, 18

Relativism, 4, 26, 181, 185

Religion: in Hobbes, 109–110, 111, 114; in Machiavelli, 138. *See also* Monotheism

Republicanism, 120, 123, 126, 127; and tacit knowledge, 93

Ressentiment, 185, 206

Reverse, causation, 10, 17–18, 220, 223; and intuitionist logic, 18, 213, 219; and reflexivity, 18; and postmodernism, 18–19

"Revisionary ratio," 84

Revolution, 142, 145, 158, 162, 168, 170; and participation, 167, 170

Rhees, Rush, 45

Rorty, Richard, 37–38, 39–40, 41, 232

Sandel, Michael, 31, 32

Santayana, George, 80

Sapir–Whorf hypothesis, 5

Self-referential argument. *See* Reflexivity

Shils, Edward, 148, 149, 150, 158

Skepticism, 7, 8–9, 23, 24, 26–27, 41, 42

Social contract theory, 96, 97, 112, 113–14, 115, 138, 186

Solipsism, 91, 186, 187

Sophists, 83

Speech act, 139

State of nature, 97, 113, 120, 139, 209

Strauss, Leo, 242, 245–46

"Subaltern element," 154

Subception, 62

Subjectivity, 21, 34, 37

Suspension of law of excluded middle. *See* Intuitionist logic

Tacit knowledge, 9, 62–63, 68, 124, 199, 200; and action, 117; and democratic theory, 23; in Dilthey, 64; and Gramsci, 106; in the *Guide*, 220; and infinite regress, 70; and intuitionist logic, 14, 213; and language, 11, 14; and modernity, 62; in the *Meno*, 70; in Nietzsche, 192, 193; and participation, 12, 74; in the *Phaedrus*, 67–69; and pragmatism, 15; and reflexivity, 11–12, 15; and in the *Tractatus*, 52

263

Index